Definitive
XML
Schema

ISBN 0-13-065567-8

90000

9 780130 655677

⟨!CFG----DXS⟩ The Charles F. Goldfarb Definitive XML Series

Megginson
■ Structuring XML Documents

McGrath
■ XML by Example: Building E-commerce Applications

Floyd
■ Building Web Sites with XML

Morgenthal and la Forge
■ Enterprise Application Integration with XML and Java

McGrath
■ XML Processing with Python

Cleaveland
■ Program Generators with XML and Java

Holman
■ Definitive XSLT and XPath

Walmsley
■ Definitive XML Schema

Garshol
■ Definitive XML Application Development

Goldfarb and Prescod
■ Charles F. Goldfarb's XML Handbook™ Fourth Edition

Titles in this series are produced using XML, SGML, and/or XSL. XSL-FO documents are rendered into PDF by the *XEP Rendering Engine* from RenderX: www.renderx.com

About the Series Author
Charles F. Goldfarb is the father of XML technology. He invented SGML, the Standard Generalized Markup Language on which both XML and HTML are based. You can find him on the Web at: www.xmlbooks.com

About the Series Logo
The rebus is an ancient literary tradition, dating from 16th century Picardy, and is especially appropriate to a series involving fine distinctions between markup and text, metadata and data. The logo is a rebus incorporating the series name within a stylized XML comment declaration.

Definitive
XML
Schema

■ Priscilla Walmsley

Prentice Hall PTR, Upper Saddle River, NJ 07458
www.phptr.com

A Cataloging-in-Publication Data record for this book can be obtained from the Library of Congress.

Editorial/Production Supervisor: *Faye Gemmellaro*
Acquisitions Editor: *Mark L. Taub*
Editorial Assistant: *Sarah Hand*
Marketing Manager: *Bryan Gambrel*
Manufacturing Manager: *Maura Zaldivar*
Cover Design: *Anthony Gemmellaro*
Cover Design Director: *Jerry Votta*
Series Design: *Gail Cocker-Bogusz*

© 2002 Prentice Hall PTR
Prentice-Hall, Inc.
Upper Saddle River, NJ 07458

Prentice Hall books are widely used by corporations and government agencies for training, marketing, and resale.

The publisher offers discounts on this book when ordered in bulk quantities. For more information, contact: Corporate Sales Department, Phone: 800-382-3419; Fax: 201-236-7141; Email: corpsales@prenhall.com; or write: Prentice Hall PTR, Corp. Sales Dept., One Lake Street, Upper Saddle River, NJ 07458.

Printed in the United States of America

10 9 8 7 6 5 4 3 2 1

ISBN 0-13-065567-8

Pearson Education LTD.
Pearson Education Australia PTY, Limited
Pearson Education Singapore, Pte. Ltd.
Pearson Education North Asia Ltd.
Pearson Education Canada, Ltd.
Pearson Educación de Mexico, S.A. de C.V.
Pearson Education—Japan
Pearson Education Malaysia, Pte. Ltd.

To Doug, my SH

Overview

Contents

Acknowledgements

First and foremost, I would like to thank Charles Goldfarb for his invaluable guidance and support. Alina Kirsanova and Dmitry Kirsanov did an excellent job preparing this book for publication. I would also like to thank Mark Taub at Prentice Hall for his hand in the making this work possible.

Of course, this book would not have been possible without the efforts of all of the members of the W3C XML Schema Working Group, with whom I have had the pleasure of working for the past two years. The content of this book was shaped by the questions and comments of the people who contribute to XML-DEV and xmlschema-dev.

Finally, I'd like to thank my Dad for teaching me to "get stuck into it," a skill which allowed me to complete this substantial project.

Priscilla Walmsley
Traverse City, Michigan
October 2001

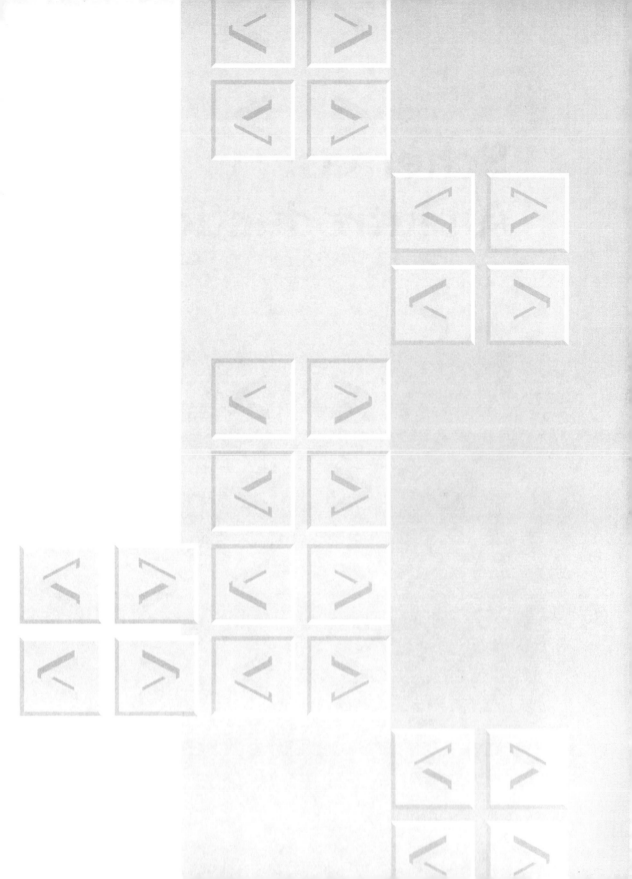

Schemas:
An introduction

T his chapter provides a brief explanation of schemas and why they are important. It also discusses the basic schema design goals, and describes the various existing schema languages.

1.1 | What is an XML schema?

The word *schema* means a diagram, plan, or framework. In XML, it refers to a document that describes an XML document. Suppose you have the XML instance shown in Example 1–1. It consists of a product element that has two children (number and size) and an attribute (effDate).

Example 1–2 shows a schema that describes the instance. It contains element and attribute declarations that assign data types and element-type names to elements and attributes.

Example 1–1. Product instance

```
<product effDate="2001-04-02">
  <number>557</number>
  <size>10</size>
</product>
```

Example 1–2. Product schema

```
<xsd:schema xmlns:xsd="http://www.w3.org/2001/XMLSchema">
  <xsd:element name="product" type="ProductType"/>
  <xsd:complexType name="ProductType">
    <xsd:sequence>
      <xsd:element name="number" type="xsd:integer"/>
      <xsd:element name="size" type="SizeType"/>
    </xsd:sequence>
    <xsd:attribute name="effDate" type="xsd:date"/>
  </xsd:complexType>
  <xsd:simpleType name="SizeType">
    <xsd:restriction base="xsd:integer">
      <xsd:minInclusive value="2"/>
      <xsd:maxInclusive value="18"/>
    </xsd:restriction>
  </xsd:simpleType>
</xsd:schema>
```

1.2 | The purpose of schemas

1.2.1 *Data validation*

One of the most common uses for schemas is to verify that an XML document is valid according to a defined set of rules. A schema can be used to validate:

- The structure of elements and attributes. For example, a `product` must have a `number` and a `size`, and may optionally have an `effDate` (effective date).
- The order of elements. For example, `number` must appear before `size`.

- The data values of attributes and elements, based on ranges, enumerations, and pattern matching. For example, `size` must be an integer between 2 and 18, and `effDate` must be a valid date.
- The uniqueness of values in an instance. For example, all product numbers in an instance must be unique.

1.2.2   A contract with trading partners

Often, XML instances are passed between organizations. A schema may act as a contract with your trading partners. It clearly lays out the rules for document structure and what is required. Since an instance can be validated against a schema, the "contract" can be enforced using available tools.

1.2.3   System documentation

Schemas can provide documentation about the data in an XML instance. Anyone who needs to understand the data can refer to the schema for information about names, structures, and data types of the items. To include further documentation, you can add annotations to any schema component.

1.2.4   Augmentation of data

Schema processing can also add to the instance. It inserts default and fixed values for elements and attributes, and normalizes whitespace according to the data type.

1.2.5   Application information

Schemas provide a way for additional information about the data to be supplied to the application when processing a particular type of document. For example, you could include information on how to map the `product` element instances to a database table, and have the application use this information to automatically update a particular table with the data.

In addition to being available at processing time, this information in schemas can be used to generate code such as:

- User interfaces for editing the information. For example, if you know that `size` is between 2 and 18, you can generate an interface that has a slider bar with these values as the limits.

- Stylesheets to transform the instance data into a reader-friendly representation such as XHTML. For example, if you know that the human-readable name for the content of a `number` element is "Product Number" you can use this as a column header.

- Code to insert or extract the data from a database. For example, if you know that the product number maps to the `PROD_NUM` column on the `PRODUCTS` table, you can generate an efficient routine to insert it into that column.

Tools have only just begun to take advantage of the possibilities of schemas. In the coming years, we will see schemas used in many creative new ways.

1.3 | Schema design

XML Schema is packed with features, and there are often several ways to accurately describe the same thing. The decisions made during schema design can affect its usability, accuracy, and applicability. Therefore, it is important to keep in mind your design objectives when creating a schema. These objectives may vary depending on how you are using XML, but some are common to all use cases.

1.3.1 *Accuracy and precision*

Obviously, a schema should accurately describe an XML instance and allow it to be validated. Schemas should also be precise in describing data. Precision can result in more complete validation as well as better documentation. Precision can be achieved by defining restrictive data types that truly represent valid values.

1.3.2 *Clarity*

Schemas should be very clear, allowing a reader to instantly understand the structure and characteristics of the instance being described. Clarity can be achieved by:

- appropriate choice of names,
- consistency in naming,
- consistency in structure,
- good documentation,
- avoiding unnecessary complexity.

1.3.3 *Broad applicability*

There is a temptation to create schemas that are useful only for a specific application purpose. In some cases, this may be appropriate. However, it is better to create a schema that has broader applicability. For example, a business unit that handles only domestic accounts may not use a `country` element declaration as part of an `address`. They should consider adding it in as an optional element for the purposes of consistency and future usability.

There are two components to a schema's broad applicability: reusability and extensibility. Reusable schema components are modular and well documented, encouraging schema authors to reuse them in other schemas. Extensible components are flexible and open, allowing other schema authors to build on them for future uses. Since reusability and extensibility are important, all of Chapter 21, "Extensibility and reuse," is devoted to them.

1.4 | Schema languages

1.4.1 *Document Type Definitions (DTDs)*

Document Type Definitions (DTDs) are a commonly used method of describing XML documents. They allow you to define the basic structure of an XML instance, including:

- the structure and order of child elements in an element type,
- the attributes of an element type,
- basic data typing for attributes,
- default and fixed values for attributes,
- notations to represent other data formats.

Example 1–3 shows a DTD that is roughly equivalent to our schema in Example 1–2.

Example 1–3. Product DTD

```
<!ELEMENT product (name, size?)>
<!ELEMENT name (#PCDATA)>
<!ELEMENT size (#PCDATA)>
<!ATTLIST product effDate CDATA #IMPLIED>
```

DTDs have many advantages. They are relatively simple, have a compact syntax, and are widely understood by XML implementers. When designed well, they can be extremely modular, flexible, and extensible.

However, DTDs also have some shortcomings. They have their own non-XML syntax, do not support namespaces easily, and provide very limited data typing, for attributes only.

1.4.2   *Enter schemas*

As XML became increasingly popular for data applications such as e-commerce and enterprise application integration (EAI), a more robust schema language was needed. Specifically, XML developers wanted:

- The ability to constrain data based on common data types such as integer and date.
- The ability to define their own data types in order to further constrain data.
- Support for namespaces.
- The ability to specify multiple declarations for the same element-type name in different contexts.
- Object oriented features such as type derivation. The ability to express types as extensions or restrictions of other types allows them to be processed similarly and substituted for each other.
- A schema language that uses XML syntax. This is advantageous because it is extensible, can represent more advanced models and can be processed by many available tools.
- The ability to add structured documentation and application information that is passed to the application during processing.

DTDs are not likely to disappear now that schemas have arrived on the scene. They are supported in many tools, are widely understood, and are currently in use in many applications. In addition, they continue to be useful as a lightweight alternative to schemas.

1.4.3   *W3C XML Schema*

Four schema languages were developed before work began on XML Schema: XDR (XML Data Reduced), DCD, SOX, and DDML. These four languages were considered together as a starting point for XML Schema, and many of their originators were involved in the creation of XML Schema.

The World Wide Web Consortium (W3C) began work on XML Schema in 1998. The first version, upon which this book is based, became an official Recommendation on May 2, 2001. The formal Recommendation is in three parts:

- *XML Schema Part 0: Primer* is a non-normative introduction to XML Schema that provides a lot of examples and explanations. It can be found at `http://www.w3.org/TR/xmlschema-0/`.

- *XML Schema Part 1: Structures* describes most of the components of XML Schema. It can be found at `http://www.w3.org/TR/xmlschema-1/`.

- *XML Schema Part 2: Datatypes* covers simple data types. It explains the built-in data types and the facets that may be used to restrict them. It is a separate document so that other specifications may use it, without including all of XML Schema. It can be found at `http://www.w3.org/TR/xmlschema-2/`.

1.4.4 *Notes on terminology*

1.4.4.1 Schema

"XML Schema" is the official name of the Recommendation and is also sometimes used to refer to conforming schema documents. In order to clearly distinguish between the two, this book uses the term "XML Schema" only to mean the Recommendation itself.

A "schema definition" is the formal expression of a schema.

The initialism "XSDL" (XML Schema Definition Language) is used to refer to the language that is used to create schema definitions in XML. In other words, XSDL is the markup language that uses elements such as `schema` and `complexType`.

The term "schema document" is used to refer to an XML document that is written in XSDL, with a `schema` element as its root. The extension "xsd" is used in the file identifiers of such documents. A schema definition may consist of one or more schema documents, as described in Chapter 4, "Schema composition."

As it is unlikely to cause confusion in this book, for simplicity the word "schema" will be used to refer to both a schema as a concept, and an actual schema definition that conforms to the XML Schema definition language.

1.4.4.2 Type

According to the XML Recommendation, every XML element has an element type. In fact, it is the name of the element type that occurs in the start- and end-tags, as individual elements do not have names (although they may have IDs).

XML Schema, however, uses the word "type" exclusively as a shorthand to refer to simple types and complex types. Perhaps to avoid confusion with this usage, the Recommendation does not use the phrase "element type" in conjunction with schemas. This book follows that same practice and generally doesn't speak of element types per se, although it does refer to "element-type names" where appropriate.

1.4.5 *Additional schema languages*

XML Schema is not the only schema language that is currently in use. While it is very robust, it is not always the most appropriate schema language for all cases. This section describes two other schema languages.

1.4.5.1 RELAX NG

RELAX NG covers some of the same ground as XML Schema. As of this writing, it is currently being developed by an OASIS technical committee. RELAX NG is intended only for validation; the processor does not pass documentation or application information from the schema to the application. RELAX NG does not have built-in data types; it is designed to use other data type libraries (such as that of XML Schema).

RELAX NG has some handy features that are not currently part of XML Schema:

- It includes attributes in the elements' content models. For example, you can specify that a `product` element must either have an `effectiveDate` attribute or a `startDate` attribute. XML Schema does not currently provide a way to do this.

- It allows a content model to depend on the value of an attribute. For example, if the value of the `type` attribute of a `product` element is `shirt`, this `product` element can contain a `size` child. If it is `umbrella`, it cannot. XML Schema provides a similar mechanism through type substitution, but it is less flexible.

- It allows you to specify a content model such as "one `number`, one `size`, and up to three `color` elements, in any order." This is quite cumbersome to express in XML Schema if you do not want to enforce a particular order.

- It does not require content models to be deterministic. This is explained in Section 13.5.6, "Deterministic content models."

However, RELAX NG also has some limitations compared to XML Schema:

- It has no inheritance capabilities. XML Schema's restriction and extension mechanisms allow type substitution and many other benefits, described in Section 14.1, "Why derive types?"

- Because it is only intended for validation, it does not provide application information to the processor. In fact, the RELAX NG processor passes the exact same information that is available from a DTD to the application. This is not a disadvantage if your only objective is validation, but it does not allow you to use the schema to help you understand how to process the instance.

For more information on RELAX NG, see `http://www.oasis-open.org/committees/relax-ng/`.

1.4.5.2 Schematron

Schematron takes a different approach from XML Schema and RELAX NG. XML Schema and RELAX NG are both grammar-based schema languages. They specify what must appear in an instance, and in what order.

By contrast, Schematron is rule-based. It allows you to define a series of rules to which the document must conform. These rules are expressed using XPath. In contrast to grammar-based languages, Schematron considers anything that does not violate a rule to be valid. There is no need to declare every element type or attribute that may appear in the instance.

Like RELAX NG, Schematron is intended only for validation of instances. It has a number of advantages:

- It is very easy to learn and use. It uses XPath, which is familiar to many people already using XML.
- The use of XPath allows it to very flexibly and succinctly express relationships between elements in a way that is not possible with other schema languages.
- The values in an instance can be involved in validation. For example, in XSDL it is not possible to express "If the value of `newCustomer` is `false`, then `customerID` must appear." Schematron allows such co-occurrence constraints.

The limitations of Schematron compared to XML Schema are:

- It does not provide a model of the instance data. A person cannot gain an understanding of what instance data is expected by looking at the schema.

- It is intended only for validation, and it cannot be used to pass any information about the instance, such as data types or default values, to an application.

- Anything is valid unless it is specifically prohibited. This puts a burden to anticipate all possible errors on the schema author.

Because Schematron and XML Schema complement each other, it makes sense to combine the two. An example of embedding a Schematron schema in XSDL is provided in Section 6.3.2, "Schematron for co-occurrence constraints." For more information on Schematron, see `http://www.ascc.net/xml/resource/schematron/schematron.html`.

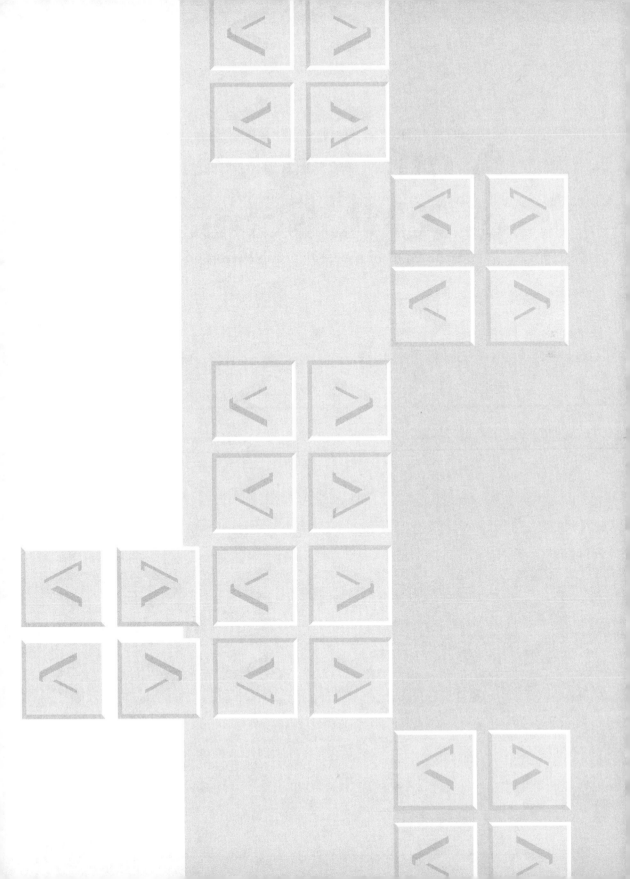

A quick tour
of XML Schema

Chapter

2

This chapter provides a quick tour of the main components of XML Schema. It also introduces a simple example of a schema and a conforming instance that will be used and built upon throughout the book.

2.1 | An example schema

Suppose you have the instance shown in Example 2–1. It consists of a product element that has two children (number and size) and an attribute (effDate).

Example 2–1. Product instance

```
<product effDate="2001-04-02">
  <number>557</number>
  <size>10</size>
</product>
```

Example 2–2 shows a schema that might be used to validate our instance. Its three element declarations and the attribute declaration assign element-type names and corresponding data types to the components they declare.

Example 2–2. Product schema

```
<xsd:schema xmlns:xsd="http://www.w3.org/2001/XMLSchema">
  <xsd:element name="product" type="ProductType"/>
  <xsd:complexType name="ProductType">
    <xsd:sequence>
      <xsd:element name="number" type="xsd:integer"/>
      <xsd:element name="size" type="SizeType"/>
    </xsd:sequence>
    <xsd:attribute name="effDate" type="xsd:date"/>
  </xsd:complexType>
  <xsd:simpleType name="SizeType">
    <xsd:restriction base="xsd:integer">
      <xsd:minInclusive value="2"/>
      <xsd:maxInclusive value="18"/>
    </xsd:restriction>
  </xsd:simpleType>
</xsd:schema>
```

2.2 | The components of XML Schema

Schemas are made up of a number of different kinds of components, listed in Table 2–1. All of the components of XML Schema are discussed in detail in this book, in the chapter indicated in Table 2–1.

2.2.1 *Declarations vs. definitions*

Schemas contain both declarations and definitions. The term *declaration* is used for components that can appear in the instance and be validated by name. This includes elements, attributes, and notations. The term *definition* is used for other components that are internal to the schema, such as data types, model groups, attribute groups, and identity con-

Table 2–1   XML Schema components

Component	Can be named?	Can be unnamed?	Can be global?	Can be local?	Chapter
element	yes	no	yes	yes	8
attribute	yes	no	yes	yes	9
simple type	yes	yes	yes	yes	10–13
complex type	yes	yes	yes	yes	14–15
notation	yes	no	yes	no	7
named model group	yes	no	yes	no	16
attribute group	yes	no	yes	no	16
identity constraint	yes	no	no	yes	18

straints. Throughout this book, you will see the terms "element declaration" and "data type definition," but not "element definition" or "data type declaration."

The order of declarations and definitions in the schema document is insignificant. A declaration can refer to other declarations or definitions that appear before or after it, or even the ones that appear in another schema document.

2.2.2   *Global vs. local components*

Components can be declared (or defined) *globally* or *locally*. Global components appear at the top level of a schema document, and they are always named. Their names must be unique within their component type, within the entire schema. For example, it is not legal to have two global element declarations with the same name in the same schema. However, it is legal to have an element declaration and a complex type definition with the same name.

Local components, on the other hand, are scoped to the definition or declaration that contains them. Element and attribute declarations can be local, which means their scope is the complex type in which they are declared. Simple types and complex types can also be locally defined, in which case they are anonymous and cannot be used by any element or attribute declaration other than the one in which they are defined.

2.3 | Elements and attributes

Elements and attributes are the basic building blocks of XML documents. The instance in Example 2–1 contains three elements (product, number, and size) and one attribute (effDate). As a result, the schema contains three element declarations and one attribute declaration. The product element declaration is global, since it appears at the top level of the schema document. The other two element declarations, as well as the attribute declaration, are local, and their scope is the ProductType type in which they are declared. Elements and attributes are covered in detail in Chapter 7, "Element declarations," and Chapter 8, "Attribute declarations," respectively.

2.3.1 *The tag/type distinction*

Each of the elements and attributes is associated with a *data type*. XML Schema separates the concepts of elements and attributes from their data types. This allows the use of different names for data that is structurally the same. For example, you can write two element declarations, shippingAddress and billingAddress, which have the exact same structure, but different names. You are only required to define one data type, AddressType, and use it in both element declarations. In addition to allowing different names, you can allow the corresponding elements to appear in different places in the document. A shippingAddress element may only be relevant in the shipment information section of a purchase order, while a billingAddress may appear only in the billing section.

You can also have two element declarations with the same name, but different data types, in different contexts. For example, a `size` element can contain an integer when it is a child of `shirt`, or a value "`S`", "`M`", or "`L`" when it is a child of `hat`.

2.4 | Data types

Data types allow for validation of the content of elements and the values of attributes. They can be either *simple types* or *complex types*. The term "data type" or simply "type" is used throughout this book to mean "simple or complex type." The XML Schema Recommendation only uses the word "type" for this purpose. However, because the word "type" is also used in other ways (for example, in "element type"), this book sometimes uses the term "data type" for clarity.

2.4.1 *Simple vs. complex types*

Elements that have been assigned simple types have character data content, but no child elements or attributes. Example 2–3 shows the `size`, `comment`, and `availableSizes` elements that have simple types.

Example 2–3. Elements with simple types

```
<size>10</size>
<comment>Runs large.</comment>
<availableSizes>10 large 2</availableSizes>
```

By contrast, elements that have been assigned complex types may have child elements or attributes. Example 2–4 shows the `size`, `comment`, and `availableSizes` elements with complex types.

Example 2–4. Elements with complex types

```
<size system="US-DRESS">10</size>
<comment>Runs <b>large</b>.</comment>
<availableSizes><size>10</size><size>2</size></availableSizes>
```

Attributes always have simple types, not complex types. This makes sense, because attributes themselves cannot have children, or other attributes. Example 2–5 shows some attributes that have simple types.

Example 2–5. Attributes with simple types

```
system="US-DRESS"
availableSizes="10 large 2"
```

2.4.2 *Named vs. anonymous types*

Data types can be either *named* or *anonymous*. Named types are always defined globally (at the top level of a schema document) and are required to have a unique name. Anonymous types, on the other hand, must not have names. They are always defined entirely within an element or attribute declaration, and may only be used once, by that declaration. The two types in Example 2–2 are both named types. An anonymous type is shown in Example 2–6.

2.4.3 *The type definition hierarchy*

XML Schema allows data types to be *derived* from other data types. In Example 2–2, the simple type `SizeType` is derived from the `integer` simple type. A complex type can also be derived from another type, either simple or complex. It can either restrict or extend the other type. For example, you could define a complex type `UKAddressType` that extends `AddressType` to add more children.

The derivation of types from other types forms a type definition hierarchy. Derived types are related to their ancestors, and inherit

Example 2–6. Anonymous type

```
<xsd:element name="size">
  <xsd:simpleType>
    <xsd:restriction base="xsd:integer">
      <xsd:minInclusive value="2"/>
      <xsd:maxInclusive value="18"/>
    </xsd:restriction>
  </xsd:simpleType>
</xsd:element>
```

qualities from them. They can also be substituted for each other in instances. If the shippingAddress element declaration refers to the data type AddressType, a corresponding element can also have the data type UKAddressType in the instance.

This is very powerful because applications that are designed to process generic AddressType elements can also process UKAddressType elements without caring about the differences. Other processors that do care about the differences between them can distinguish between the different data types.

2.5 | Simple types

2.5.1 *Built-in simple types*

Forty-four simple types are built into the XML Schema Recommendation. These simple types represent common data types such as strings, numbers, date and time values, and also include legacy types for each of the valid attribute types in XML 1.0. The built-in types are summarized in Table 2–2, and discussed in detail in Chapter 12, "Built-in simple types."

Example 2–2 assigned the built-in simple type integer to the number elements, and the built-in simple type date to the effDate attribute.

Table 2–2   Built-in simple type summary

Category	Built-in types
strings and names	`string`, `normalizedString`, `token`, `Name`, `NCName`, `QName`, `language`
numeric	`float`, `double`, `decimal`, `integer`, `long`, `int`, `short`, `byte`, `positiveInteger`, `nonPositiveInteger`, `negativeInteger`, `nonNegativeInteger`, `unsignedLong`, `unsignedInt`, `unsignedShort`, `unsignedByte`
date and time	`duration`, `dateTime`, `date`, `time`, `gYear`, `gYearMonth`, `gMonth`, `gMonthDay`, `gDay`
legacy types	`ID`, `IDREF`, `IDREFS`, `ENTITY`, `ENTITIES`, `NMTOKEN`, `NMTOKENS`, `NOTATION`
other	`boolean`, `hexBinary`, `base64Binary`, `anyURI`

2.5.2   *Restricting simple types*

New simple types may be derived from other simple types by *restricting* them. Example 2–2 showed the definition of a simple type `SizeType` that restricts the built-in type `integer`. We applied the *facets* `minInclusive` and `maxInclusive` to restrict the valid values of the `size` elements to be between 2 and 16. Using the twelve facets that are part of XML Schema, you can specify a valid range of values, constrain the length and precision of values, enumerate a list of valid values, or specify a regular expression that valid values must match. These twelve facets are summarized in Table 2–3. Chapter 9, "Simple types," explains how to derive new simple types.

2.5.3   *List and union types*

Most simple types are *atomic types*, like the ones we have seen so far. They contain values that are indivisible, such as `10`. There are also two other varieties of simple types: list and union types.

Table 2–3 Facets

Category	Facets
bounds	`minInclusive, maxInclusive,` `minExclusive, maxExclusive`
length	`length, minLength, maxLength`
precision	`totalDigits, fractionDigits`
enumerated values	`enumeration`
pattern matching	`pattern`
whitespace processing	`whiteSpace`

List types have values that are whitespace-separated lists of atomic values, such as `<availableSizes>10 large 2</availableSizes>`.

Union types may have values that are either atomic values or list values. What differentiates them is that the set of valid values, or "value space," for the type is the union of the value spaces of two or more other simple types. For example, to represent a dress size, you may define a union type that allows a value to be either an integer from 2 through 18, or one of the string values `small`, `medium`, or `large`.

List and union types are covered in Chapter 11, "Union and list types."

2.6 | Complex types

2.6.1 *Content types*

The "contents" of an element are the character data and child elements that are between its tags. There are four types of content for complex types: *simple, element, mixed,* and *empty*. The content type is independent of attributes; all of these content types allow attributes. Example 2–7 shows the instance elements `size`, `product`, `letter`, and `color` that have complex types. They represent the four different content types.

Example 2–7. Elements with complex types

```
<size system="US-DRESS">10</size>

<product>
  <number>557</number>
  <size>10</size>
</product>

<letter>Dear <custName>Priscilla Walmsley</custName>...</letter>

<color value="blue"/>
```

- The `size` element has simple content, because it contains only character data.
- The `product` element has element-only content, because it has child elements, but no character data content.
- The `letter` element has mixed content, because it has both child elements and character data content.
- The `color` element has empty content, because it does not have any content (just attributes).

2.6.2   *Content models*

The order and structure of the child elements of a complex type are known as its *content model*. Content models are defined using a combination of model groups, element declarations or references, and wildcards. In Example 2–2, the content model of `ProductType` was a single `sequence` model group containing two element declarations. There are three kinds of model groups:

- `sequence` groups require that the child elements appear in the order specified.
- `choice` groups allow any one of several child elements to appear.
- `all` groups require that all the child elements appear 0 or 1 times, in any order.

These groups can be nested, and may occur multiple times, allowing you to create sophisticated content models. Example 2–8 shows a more complex content model for `ProductType`. Instances of this new definition of `ProductType` must have a `number` child, optionally followed by up to three children which may be either `size` or `color` elements, followed by any one element from another namespace.

Example 2–8. More complicated content model

```
<xsd:complexType name="ProductType">
  <xsd:sequence>
    <xsd:element name="number" type="xsd:integer"/>
    <xsd:choice minOccurs="0" maxOccurs="3">
      <xsd:element name="size" type="SizeType"/>
      <xsd:element name="color" type="ColorType"/>
    </xsd:choice>
    <xsd:any namespace="##other"/>
  </xsd:sequence>
  <xsd:attribute name="effDate" type="xsd:date"/>
</xsd:complexType>
```

An `any` element is known as a wildcard, and it allows for open content models. There is an equivalent wildcard for attributes, `anyAttribute`, which allows any attribute to appear in a complex type.

2.6.3 *Deriving complex types*

Complex types may be derived from other types either by restriction or extension.

Restriction, as the name suggests, restricts the valid contents of a type. The values for the new type are a subset of those for the base type. All values of the restricted type are also valid according to the base type.

Extension allows for adding additional child elements and/or attributes to a data type, thus extending the contents of the type. Values of the base type are not necessarily valid for the extended type, since required elements or attributes may be added. Example 2–9 shows the definition of `ShirtType` that is a complex type extension. It adds another element declaration, `color`, and another attribute declaration, `id`, to `Product-Type`. New element declarations or references may only be added to the end of a content model, so instances of `ShirtType` must have the children `number`, `size`, and `color`, in that order.

Example 2–9. Complex type extension

```
<xsd:complexType name="ShirtType">
  <xsd:complexContent>
    <xsd:extension base="ProductType">
      <xsd:sequence>
        <xsd:element name="color" type="ColorType"/>
      </xsd:sequence>
      <xsd:attribute name="id" type="xsd:ID" use="required"/>
    </xsd:extension>
  </xsd:complexContent>
</xsd:complexType>
```

2.7 | Namespaces and XML Schema

Namespaces are an important part of XML Schema, and they are discussed in detail in Chapter 3, "Namespaces." Example 2–10 shows our now-familiar schema, this time with a target namespace declared. Let's take a closer look at the attributes of a `schema` element.

1. The namespace `http://www.w3.org/2001/XMLSchema` is mapped to the `xsd:` prefix. This indicates that the elements used in the schema document itself, such as `schema`, `element`, and `complexType`, are part of the XML Schema Namespace.

2. A target namespace, `http://example.org/prod`, is declared. Any schema document may have a target namespace, which applies to the global (and some local) components that are declared or defined in it. A schema document can only have one target namespace, though schemas can be composed of multiple schema documents with different target namespaces.

3.   The target namespace is mapped to the `prod` prefix.

Example 2–10. Product schema document with target namespace

```
<xsd:schema xmlns:xsd="http://www.w3.org/2001/XMLSchema"
            targetNamespace="http://example.org/prod"
            xmlns:prod="http://example.org/prod">

  <xsd:element name="product" type="prod:ProductType"/>

  <xsd:complexType name="ProductType">
    <xsd:sequence>
      <xsd:element name="number" type="xsd:integer"/>
      <xsd:element name="size" type="prod:SizeType"/>
    </xsd:sequence>
    <xsd:attribute name="effDate" type="xsd:date"/>
  </xsd:complexType>

  <xsd:simpleType name="SizeType">
    <xsd:restriction base="xsd:integer">
      <xsd:minInclusive value="2"/>
      <xsd:maxInclusive value="18"/>
    </xsd:restriction>
  </xsd:simpleType>

</xsd:schema>
```

Example 2–11 shows a new instance, where the namespace is declared. In order for an instance to be valid according to a schema, the namespace declaration in the instance must match the target namespace of the schema document.

In this case, only the `product` element has a prefixed name. This is because the other two elements and the attribute are declared locally. By default, locally declared components do not take on the target namespace. However, this can be overridden by specifying `element-FormDefault` and `attributeFormDefault` for the schema document. This is discussed in detail in Chapter 20, "Naming considerations."

Example 2–11. Instance with namespace

```
<prod:product xmlns:prod="http://example.org/prod"
              effDate="2001-04-02">
  <number>557</number>
  <size>10</size>
</prod:product>
```

2.8 | Schema composition

Schemas can be composed of one or more schema documents. Example 2–2 showed a schema document that was used alone to validate an instance. There was no distinction made between the schema and its document.

However, some schemas are composed of multiple schema documents. One way to compose schemas of multiple documents is through the include and import mechanisms. Include is used when the other schema document has the same target namespace as the "main" schema document. Import is used when the other schema document has a different target namespace. Example 2–12 shows how you might include and import other schema documents.

The include and import mechanisms are not the only way for processors to assemble schema documents into a schema. There is not always a "main" schema document that represents the whole schema. Instead, a processor might join schema documents from various predefined locations, or take multiple hints from the instance. See Chapter 4, "Schema composition," for more information on schema composition.

2.9 | Instances and schemas

A document that conforms to a schema is known as an instance. An instance can be validated against a particular schema, which may be

Example 2–12. Schema composition using `include` and `import`

```
<xsd:schema xmlns:xsd="http://www.w3.org/2001/XMLSchema"
            xmlns="http://example.org/ord"
            targetNamespace="http://example.org/ord">

  <xsd:include schemaLocation="moreOrderInfo.xsd"/>

  <xsd:import namespace="http://example.org/prod"
              schemaLocation="productInfo.xsd"/>
  <!--...-->
</xsd:schema>
```

made up of multiple schema documents. There are a number of different ways for the schema documents to be located for a particular instance. One way is using the `xsi:schemaLocation` attribute. Example 2–13 shows an instance that uses the `xsi:schemaLocation` attribute to map the namespace to a particular schema document.

Example 2–13. Using `xsi:schemaLocation`

```
<prod:product xmlns:prod="http://example.org/prod"
              xmlns:xsi="http://www.w3.org/2001/XMLSchema-instance"
              xsi:schemaLocation="http://example.org/prod prod.xsd"
              effDate="2001-04-02">
  <number>557</number>
  <size>10</size>
</prod:product>
```

Using `xsi:schemaLocation` is not the only way to tell the processor where to find the schema. XML Schema is deliberately flexible on this topic, allowing processors to use different methods for choosing schema documents to validate a particular instance. These methods include built-in schemas, use of internal catalogs, use of the `xsi:schemaLocation` attribute, and dereferencing of namespaces. Chapter 5, "Instances and schemas," covers the validation of instances in detail.

2.10 | Annotations

XML Schema provides many mechanisms for describing the structure of XML documents. However, it cannot express everything there is to know about an instance or the data it contains. For this reason, XML Schema allows annotations to be added to almost any schema component. These annotations can contain human-readable information (under documentation) or application information (under appinfo). Example 2–14 shows an annotation for the product element declaration. Annotations are covered in Chapter 6, "Schema documentation and extension."

Example 2–14. Annotation

```
<xsd:schema xmlns:xsd="http://www.w3.org/2001/XMLSchema"
            xmlns:doc="http://example.org/doc">
  <xsd:element name="product" type="ProductType">
    <xsd:annotation>
      <xsd:documentation xml:lang="en"
        source="http://example.org/prod.html#product">
        <doc:description>These elements represent a product.
        </doc:description>
      </xsd:documentation>
    </xsd:annotation>
  </xsd:element>
</xsd:schema>
```

2.11 | Advanced features

XML Schema also has some more advanced features. These features are available if you need them, but are certainly not an integral part of every schema. Keep in mind that you are not required to use all of XML Schema. You should choose a subset that is appropriate for your needs.

2.11.1 *Reusable groups*

XML Schema provides the ability to define groups of element and attribute declarations that are reusable by many complex types. This facility promotes reuse of schema components and eases maintenance efforts. Named model groups are fragments of content models, and attribute groups are bundles of related attributes that are commonly used together. Chapter 15, "Reusable groups," explains reusable groups.

2.11.2 *Identity constraints*

Identity constraints allow you to uniquely identify nodes in a document and ensure the integrity of references between them. They are similar to the primary and foreign keys in databases. They are described in detail in Chapter 17, "Identity constraints."

2.11.3 *Substitution groups*

Substitution groups are a flexible way to designate certain element declarations as substitutes for other element declarations in content models. If you have a group of related elements that may appear interchangeably in the instances, you can reference the substitution group as a whole in content models. You can easily add new element declarations to the substitution groups, from other schema documents and even other namespaces, without changing the original declarations in any way. Substitution groups are covered in Chapter 16, "Substitution groups."

2.11.4 *Redefinition*

Redefinition allows you to define a new version of a schema component, while keeping the same name. This is useful for extending or creating a subset of an existing schema document. It is also useful for performing minor modifications over time. Redefinition is covered in Chapter 18, "Redefining schema components."

Namespaces

nderstanding namespaces is essential to understanding XML Schema. This chapter introduces namespaces and explains their relationship to schemas.

3.1 | Namespaces in XML

Before we delve into the use of namespaces in schema documents, let's take a minute to learn about namespaces in general. Namespaces are surprisingly simple considering how much confusion and controversy they cause. The purpose of namespaces is to provide containers for the names used in XML. An element-type name, such as `table`, can have several meanings. Its meaning in XHTML is very different from its meaning in FurnitureML. Namespaces provide context for element-type and attribute names in instances. An element-type or attribute name in an instance may be directly associated with, or "in a"[1] namespace.

3.1.1   *Namespace names are URIs*

Namespace names are Uniform Resource Identifiers (URIs). URIs encompass URLs of various schemes (e.g., HTTP, FTP, gopher, telnet), as well as URNs (Uniform Resource Names). Many namespaces are written in the form of an HTTP URL, such as `http://example.org/prod`. It is also legal to use a URN, such as `urn:example:org`.

The main purpose of a namespace is not to point to a location where a resource resides. Instead, it is intended to provide a unique name that can be associated with a particular person or organization, much like Java package names. Therefore, namespace names are not required to be dereferencable. That is, there does not necessarily need to be an HTML page or other resource that can be accessed at `http://example.org/prod`. The namespace URI could point to a schema, an HTML page, a directory of resources, or nothing at all. This is explained further in Section 5.5, "Dereferencing namespaces."

Namespace names are case-sensitive. Two namespaces are considered different if their capitalization is different, even if they have the form of equivalent URLs. For example, `http://example.org/prod` and `http://example.org/proD` represent different namespaces, because the last letters are capitalized differently.

---

1.   The *Namespaces in XML* Recommendation avoids referring to a name as being "in a" namespace. In fact, it does not provide a word to describe a name's relationship to its namespace. This book uses the term "in a" namespace to mean that a name is directly in a namespace, i.e. that it must be qualified to be associated with that namespace. However, this is not official W3C terminology.

Although relative URI references, such as ../prod are legal as URIs, they are not appropriate namespace names. A namespace name should be unique, and it is difficult to ensure the uniqueness of ../prod.

3.1.2 *Namespace declarations and prefixes*

An instance may include one or more namespace declarations that relate elements to namespaces. This happens through a prefix, which serves as a proxy for the namespace.

Namespace are declared using a special attribute that starts with the letters xmlns. Example 3–1 shows an instance whose root element has a namespace declaration. This declaration maps the namespace http://example.org/prod to the prefix prod. All of the element-type names in the document, namely product, number, and size, are prefixed with prod. The system attribute does not have a prefixed name, so it is not "in" the namespace.

Example 3–1. Namespace declaration

```
<prod:product xmlns:prod="http://example.org/prod">
  <prod:number>557</prod:number>
  <prod:size system="US-DRESS">10</prod:size>
</prod:product>
```

Prefixes are convenient because they are generally shorter than namespace names, so they make the document more readable. A more important reason for prefixes, though, is that namespace names may contain characters that are not permitted in XML names. Prefixes are constrained by the rules for XML non-colonized names, as described in Section 3.1.4, "Name terminology." There is no limit to how many characters long a prefix can be, but it is best to keep prefixes short for readability.

Although the instance author may arbitrarily choose prefixes, there are commonly used prefixes for some namespaces. For example, the xsl prefix is usually mapped to the Extensible Stylesheet Language

(XSL) namespace. It is legal to map the prefix `bob` to the XSL namespace and write a stylesheet with every XSL element-type name prefixed with `bob`. However, this is not recommended because it is confusing. For the XML Schema Namespace, the commonly used prefixes are `xsd` and `xs`.

It is not possible to map a prefix to a namespace name that is the empty string. In Example 3–1, it would have been illegal to specify `xmlns:prod=""`.

You can declare more than one namespace in the same instance, as shown in Example 3–2. Two prefixes, `ord` and `prod`, are mapped to the namespaces `http://example.org/ord` and `http://example.org/prod`, respectively. The element-type names in the document are prefixed with either `ord` or `prod`, to relate them to one of the two namespaces.

Example 3–2. Multiple namespace declarations

```
<ord:order xmlns:ord="http://example.org/ord"
           xmlns:prod="http://example.org/prod">
  <ord:number>123ABBCC123</ord:number>
  <ord:items>
    <prod:product>
      <prod:number>557</prod:number>
      <prod:size system="US-DRESS">10</prod:size>
    </prod:product>
  </ord:items>
</ord:order>
```

Note that `number` appears twice, with two different prefixes. This illustrates the usefulness of namespaces, which make it obvious whether it is a product number or an order number. In most cases, the two can be distinguished based on their context in the instance, but not always.

You do not need to declare `xmlns:ord` and `xmlns:prod` as attributes in the `order` element declaration in your schema. In fact, it is illegal to declare them. All schema processors understand that attributes prefixed with `xmlns` and the unprefixed attribute with the name `xmlns` are always permitted.

3.1.3 *Default namespace declarations*

An instance may also include a default namespace declaration that maps
unprefixed element-type names to a namespace. The default namespace
declaration uses the attribute `xmlns`, with no colon or prefix. In
Example 3–3, the start `order` tag contains a default namespace declaration. This declaration relates the namespace `http://exam-
ple.org/ord` to all of the unprefixed element-type names in the doc-
ument, namely `order`, `number`, and `items`.

Example 3–3. Default namespace declaration

```
<order xmlns="http://example.org/ord"
       xmlns:prod="http://example.org/prod">
  <number>123ABBCC123</number>
  <items>
    <prod:product>
      <prod:number>557</prod:number>
      <prod:size system="US-DRESS">10</prod:size>
    </prod:product>
  </items>
</order>
```

Note that the default namespace declaration can be combined with
other namespaces declarations in the same document and even in the
same tag.

Default namespace declarations do not directly apply to attributes.
In this case, the `system` attribute, although its name is not prefixed,
is not in the default namespace `http://example.org/ord`. It is not
directly in any namespace at all. For further explanation of the relationship between attributes and namespaces, see Section 3.1.7, "Attributes
and namespaces."

Unlike other namespace declarations, a default namespace declaration
may also be the empty string (that is, `xmlns=""`). This means that
unprefixed element-type names are not in any namespace.

3.1.4 *Name terminology*

In the context of namespaces, there are a number of different kinds of names. They include:

Qualified names, known as QNames, are names that are qualified with a namespace name. This may happen one of two ways:

1. The name contains a prefix that is mapped to a namespace. In Example 3–3, `prod:product` is a prefixed, qualified name.
2. The name does not contain a prefix, but there is a default namespace declared for that element. In Example 3–3, `items` is an unprefixed, qualified name. This applies only to elements; there is no such thing as an unprefixed, qualified attribute name, as you will see in Section 3.1.7, "Attributes and namespaces."

Unqualified names, on the other hand, are names that are not in any namespace. For element-type names, this means that they are unprefixed and there is no default namespace declaration. For attribute names, this means that they are unprefixed, period.

Prefixed names are names that contain a namespace prefix, such as `prod:product`. Prefixed names are qualified names, assuming there is a namespace declaration for that prefix in scope.

Unprefixed names are names that do not contain a prefix, such as `items`. Unprefixed element-type names can be either qualified or unqualified, depending on whether there is a default namespace declaration.

Local names are the part of a qualified name that is not the prefix. In Example 3–3, local names include `items` and `product`.

Non-colonized names, known as NCNames, are simply XML names that do not contain colons. That means that they are case-sensitive, they may start with a letter or underscore, and contain letters, digits, underscores, dashes, and periods. They cannot start with the letters "XML" either in lower or uppercase. All local names and unprefixed names are NCNames. Prefixes are also NCNames, because they follow these same rules.

3.1.5 *Scope of namespace declarations*

In the previous examples, namespace declarations appeared in the start-tag of the root element. Namespace declarations, including default namespace declarations, can appear in any start-tag in the document. Example 3–4 shows the previous `order` example, but with the namespace declaration for the `http://example.org/prod` namespace moved down to the `product` tag.

Example 3–4. Namespace declarations in multiple tags

```
<order xmlns="http://example.org/ord">
  <number>123ABBCC123</number>
  <items>
    <prod:product xmlns:prod="http://example.org/prod">
      <prod:number>557</prod:number>
      <prod:size system="US-DRESS">10</prod:size>
    </prod:product>
  </items>
</order>
```

The scope of a namespace declaration is the element in whose start-tag it appears, and all of its children, grandchildren, and so on. In Example 3–4, it would be invalid to use the `prod` prefix outside of the `product` element and its children. In Example 3–5, the second `product` element uses the `prod` prefix, which is illegal because the namespace declaration is outside its scope.

Generally, it is preferable to put all your namespace declarations in the root element's start-tag. It allows you to see at a glance what namespaces a document uses, there is no confusion about their scope, and it keeps them from cluttering the rest of the document.

3.1.6 *Overriding namespace declarations*

Namespace declarations can also be overridden. If a namespace declaration appears within the scope of another namespace declaration with the same prefix, it overrides it. Likewise, if a default namespace decla-

Example 3–5. Invalid prefix outside of scope

```
<order xmlns="http://example.org/ord">
  <number>123ABBCC123</number>
  <items>
    <prod:product xmlns:prod="http://example.org/prod">
      <prod:number>557</prod:number>
      <prod:size system="US-DRESS">10</prod:size>
    </prod:product>
    <prod:product>
      <prod:number>559</prod:number>
      <prod:size system="US-DRESS">10</prod:size>
    </prod:product>
  </items>
</order>
```

ration appears within the scope of another default namespace declaration, it overrides it.

Example 3–6 illustrates this. In the `order` tag, the prefix `prod` is mapped to `http://example.org/prod`. In `number`, it is mapped to `http://example.org/prod2`. The second namespace declaration overrides the first within the scope of the `number` element. This includes the `number` element itself.

Example 3–6. Overriding a namespace declaration

```
<order xmlns="http://example.org/ord"
       xmlns:prod="http://example.org/prod">
  <number>123ABBCC123</number>
  <items>
    <prod:product>
      <prod:number xmlns:prod="http://example.org/prod2">
        557</prod:number>
      <prod:size system="US-DRESS">10</prod:size>
    </prod:product>
  </items>
</order>
```

3.1.7 *Attributes and namespaces*

The relationship between attributes and namespaces is slightly simpler than the relationship between elements and namespaces. Prefixed attribute names, as you would expect, are in whichever namespace is mapped to that prefix. Attributes with prefixed names are also known as global attributes. Unprefixed attribute names, however, are never directly[1] in a namespace. This is because they are not affected by default namespace declarations. Example 3–7 shows a `size` element that has two attributes: `app:system` and `system`. `app:system` is associated with the namespace `http://example.org/app` through the `app` prefix. The unprefixed `system` attribute is not in any namespace at all, despite the default namespace declaration.

Example 3–7. Two attributes with the same local name

```
<product xmlns="http://example.org/prod"
         xmlns:app="http://example.org/app">
  <number>557</number>
  <size app:system="R32" system="US-DRESS">10</size>
</product>
```

Although an element cannot have two attributes with the same name, this example is valid because the attribute names are in different namespaces (or rather, one is in a namespace and one is not), and they therefore have different qualified names.

Example 3–8 is also valid, even though the default namespace and the namespace mapped to the `prod` prefix are the same. This is again because the unprefixed `system` attribute is not in any namespace.

---

1. I say *directly* to mean that the attribute must be qualified to be recognized as a part of that namespace. Some people would make the case that an attribute is in the namespace of its element. While it is indirectly associated with that namespace, it is not directly "in" it, using my sense of the word.

Example 3–8. Two more attributes with the same local name

```
<product xmlns="http://example.org/prod"
         xmlns:prod="http://example.org/prod">
  <number>557</number>
  <size system="US-DRESS" prod:system="R32">10</size>
</product>
```

Example 3–9 shows an invalid duplication of attributes. The problem is not that two different prefixes are mapped to the same namespace; this is perfectly acceptable. However, it is not valid for an element to have two attributes with the same name that are in the same namespace, even if they have different prefixes.

Example 3–9. Invalid duplicate attributes

```
<product xmlns:prod="http://example.org/prod"
         xmlns:prod2="http://example.org/prod">
  <number>557</number>
  <size prod:system="US-DRESS" prod2:system="R32">10</size>
</product>
```

3.1.8 *A summary example*

To summarize our discussion of namespaces, Example 3–10 provides a more complex instance that shows various combinations of namespace declarations in different scopes.

Table 3–1 explains which namespace each name is in, and why.

For more detailed information on namespaces, see the W3C Recommendation, *Namespaces in XML*. It is located at http://www.w3.org/TR/REC-xml-names/.

Example 3–10. A summary example

```
<envelope>
  <order xmlns="http://example.org/ord"
         xmlns:prod="http://example.org/prod">
    <number>123ABBCC123</number>
    <items>
      <product xmlns="http://example.org/prod">
        <number prod:id="prod557">557</number>
        <name xmlns="">Short-Sleeved Linen Blouse</name>
        <prod:size system="US-DRESS">10</prod:size>
        <prod:color xmlns:prod="http://example.org/prod2"
                    prod:value="blue"/>
      </product>
    </items>
  </order>
</envelope>
```

3.2 | The relationship between namespaces and schemas

Namespaces and schemas have a many-to-many relationship.

A namespace can be described by zero to many schemas. Namespaces can exist without any schemas to describe them. Other namespaces may be described by many schemas. These schemas may be designed to be used together, or be completely incompatible with each other. They could be different perspectives on the same information, or be designed for different purposes, such as varying levels of validation or system documentation. They could be different versions of each other. There are no rules that prevent several schemas from being defined for the same namespace, with overlapping declarations. As long as the processor does not try to validate an instance against all of them at once, this is completely legal.

A schema can declare names for zero to many namespaces. Some schemas have no namespace at all. Other schemas are comprised of multiple schema documents, each with their own target namespace. This is described in detail in Chapter 4, "Schema composition."

Table 3–1 Explanation of summary example

Element-type name/ attribute name	Namespace (http://example.org/...)	Explanation
envelope	none	no prefix, no default namespace in scope
order	ord	takes default namespace from order (itself)
number (child of order)	ord	takes default namespace from order
product	prod	takes default namespace from product (itself)
number (child of product)	prod	takes default namespace from product
prod:id	prod	prefix ties it to namespace declaration in order
name	none	default namespace set to empty string, which is equivalent to saying that it has no namespace
prod:size	prod	prefix ties it to namespace declaration in order
system	none	unprefixed attribute names are never in a namespace, even if there is a default namespace declaration
prod:color	prod2	prefix ties it to namespace declaration in color (itself)
prod:value	prod2	prefix ties it to namespace declaration in color

3.3 | Using namespaces in XSDL

3.3.1 *Target namespaces*

Each XSDL schema document can declare and define components for one namespace, known as its target namespace. Every component declared or defined by a global declaration (element, attribute, type, group) is associated with that target namespace. Example 3–11 shows a schema document that declares a target namespace of `http://example.org/prod`. Three element declarations are global, and all of them use the namespace `http://example.org/prod`. Local element declarations may or may not use the target namespace of the schema document, as described in Section 20.2, "Qualified vs. unqualified names."

Example 3–11. Declaring a target namespace

```
<xsd:schema xmlns:xsd="http://www.w3.org/2001/XMLSchema"
            xmlns="http://example.org/prod"
            targetNamespace="http://example.org/prod">

  <xsd:element name="product" type="ProductType"/>
  <xsd:element name="number" type="xsd:integer"/>
  <xsd:element name="size" type="SizeType"/>

  <xsd:complexType name="ProductType">
    <xsd:sequence>
      <xsd:element ref="number"/>
      <xsd:element ref="size"/>
    </xsd:sequence>
  </xsd:complexType>
  <!--...-->
</xsd:schema>
```

Example 3–12 shows how the corresponding elements could appear in an instance. Because they are associated with the `http://example.org/prod` namespace, they must be qualified in some way, either through a prefix or by a default namespace declaration.

Example 3–12. Prefixed element-type names in an instance

```
<prod:product xmlns:prod="http://example.org/prod">
  <prod:number>557</prod:number>
  <prod:size>10</prod:size>
</prod:product>
```

A schema document cannot have more than one target namespace. However, you can link together schema documents that have different target namespaces, using the `import` function. This is described in Section 4.4.3, "`import`."

If you do not plan to use namespaces, you are not required to specify a target namespace. In this case, omit the `targetNamespace` attribute entirely.

3.3.2 *The XML Schema Namespace*

Since XSDL documents are XML, namespaces also apply to them. For example, all the elements used in XSDL, such as `schema`, `element`, and `simpleType`, are in the XML Schema Namespace, whose namespace name is `http://www.w3.org/2001/XMLSchema`. In addition, the names of the built-in simple types are in this namespace.

The prefixes most commonly mapped to this namespace are `xsd` or `xs`. It is recommended that you use one of these for clarity, although you could just as easily use any other prefix. Example 3–13 shows a schema document that maps the XML Schema Namespace to `xsd` and prefixes all of the element-type names in the schema document.

Example 3–13. Declaring the XML Schema Namespace

```
<xsd:schema xmlns:xsd="http://www.w3.org/2001/XMLSchema">
  <xsd:element name="number" type="xsd:integer"/>
  <xsd:element name="size" type="SizeType"/>
  <xsd:simpleType name="SizeType">
  <!--...-->
  </xsd:simpleType>
</xsd:schema>
```

It is interesting to note that while all the element-type names are prefixed, all of the attribute names are unprefixed. This is because none of the attributes in the XML Schema Namespace is declared globally. This is explained further in Section 8.4, "Qualified vs. unqualified forms."

The `xsd` prefix is also used when referring to the built-in type `integer`. This is because `integer` is a simple type that is defined in the schema for schemas, whose target namespace is the XML Schema Namespace.

Mapping a prefix such as `xsd` to the XML Schema Namespace is one of the three options for namespace declarations in XSDL documents. See Section 3.3.4, "Namespace declarations in schema documents," for more information.

3.3.3 *The XML Schema Instance Namespace*

The XML Schema Instance Namespace is a separate namespace for the four schema-related attributes that may appear in instances. These attributes, whose names are commonly prefixed with `xsi`, are: `type`, `nil`, `schemaLocation`, and `noNamespaceSchemaLocation`. They are described in Section 5.1, "Using the instance attributes."

3.3.4 *Namespace declarations in schema documents*

Schema documents must contain namespace declarations of both the target namespace and the XML Schema Namespace in order to resolve the references between schema components. There are three ways to set up the namespace declarations in your schema document, each of which is described in this section.

3.3.4.1 Map a prefix to the XML Schema Namespace

You can map the XML Schema Namespace to a prefix such as `xsd` or `xs`, and make the target namespace the default namespace. Example 3–14 shows a schema document that uses this approach. This method is used throughout this book. Its advantage is that it makes it clear which components are defined by XML Schema, especially when it comes to referencing built-in types.

Example 3–14. Prefixing the XML Schema Namespace

```
<xsd:schema xmlns:xsd="http://www.w3.org/2001/XMLSchema"
            xmlns="http://example.org/prod"
            targetNamespace="http://example.org/prod">
  <xsd:element name="number" type="xsd:integer"/>
  <xsd:element name="size" type="SizeType"/>
  <xsd:simpleType name="SizeType">
  <!--...-->
  </xsd:simpleType>
</xsd:schema>
```

If your schema document does not have a target namespace, you must map a prefix to the XML Schema Namespace. Otherwise, you will have no way of referencing other schema components that are defined in your schema document. Example 3–15 shows a schema document that does not have a target namespace, and defaults the XML Schema Namespace. This is invalid, because the declaration of size references the type SizeType. Since the default namespace is the XML Schema Namespace, the processor will look unsuccessfully for a definition of SizeType in the XML Schema Namespace.

Example 3–15. Invalid absence of prefixes

```
<schema xmlns="http://www.w3.org/2001/XMLSchema">
  <element name="number" type="integer"/>
  <element name="size" type="SizeType"/>
  <simpleType name="SizeType">
  <!--...-->
  </simpleType>
</schema>
```

3.3.4.2   Map a prefix to the target namespace

Another alternative is to map a prefix to the target namespace, and make the XML Schema Namespace the default namespace. Example 3–16 shows a schema document that uses this approach. The names in the declarations themselves do not need to be prefixed because they automatically become part of the target namespace. The only place the prefix is used is in references to other components. For example, the declaration of `size` references the type `SizeType` by its qualified name. If it did not prefix the name of the type, the processor would look unsuccessfully for a definition of `SizeType` in the XML Schema Namespace.

Example 3–16. Prefixing the target namespace

```
<schema xmlns="http://www.w3.org/2001/XMLSchema"
        xmlns:prod="http://example.org/prod"
        targetNamespace="http://example.org/prod">
  <element name="number" type="integer"/>
  <element name="size" type="prod:SizeType"/>
  <simpleType name="SizeType">
  <!--...-->
  </simpleType>
</schema>
```

If you plan to use identity constraints, you may be required to map a prefix to the target namespace. See Section 17.9, "Identity constraints and namespaces," for more information.

3.3.4.3   Map a prefix to all namespaces

It is also possible to map prefixes to all the namespaces, as shown in Example 3–17. This has the advantage of clarity, particularly when your schema documents import other namespaces.

Example 3–17. Prefixing all namespaces

```
<xsd:schema xmlns:xsd="http://www.w3.org/2001/XMLSchema"
            xmlns:prod="http://example.org/prod"
            targetNamespace="http://example.org/prod">
  <xsd:element name="number" type="xsd:integer"/>
  <xsd:element name="size" type="prod:SizeType"/>
  <xsd:simpleType name="SizeType">
  <!--...-->
  </xsd:simpleType>
</xsd:schema>
```

Schema
composition

W e tend to think of schemas as individual XML documents. However, in XML Schema terminology, these are actually *schema documents*. Schemas can be composed of one or more schema documents. This chapter explains how schema documents are assembled into a schema through various mechanisms, including mechanisms built into XSDL and processor-specific handling.

4.1 | Modularizing schema documents

Consider a project that involves orders for retail products. The order will contain information from several different domains. It will contain general information that applies to the order itself, such as the order number and date. It may also contain customer information, such as customer name, number, and address. Finally, it may contain product information, such as product number, name, description, and size.

The first decision is how to break up the schema documents. Do you want one big schema document, or three schema documents, one for each of the subject areas (order, customer, and product)? There are a number of advantages to breaking up the schemas into multiple documents:

- *Easier reuse.* If schema documents are small and focused, they are more likely to be reused. For example, a product catalog application might want to reuse the definitions from the product schema. This is much more efficient if the product catalog application is not forced to include everything from the order application.

- *Ease of maintenance.* Smaller schema documents are more readable and manageable.

- *Reduced chance of name collisions.* If different namespaces are used for the different schema documents, name collisions are less likely.

- *Access control.* Security can be managed per schema document, allowing more granular access control.

There are a number of ways to divide your components into schema documents, for instance:

- *Subject area.* If your instance will contain application data, this could mean a schema document per application or per database. If you are using XML for textual documents, you may have a different schema document for each type of document.

- *General/specific.* There may be a base set of components that can be extended for a variety of different purposes. For example, you may create a schema document that contains generic (possibly abstract) definitions for purchase orders and invoices, and separate schema documents for each set of industry-specific extensions.

- *Basic/advanced.* Suppose you have a core set of components that are used in all instances, plus a number of optional components. You may want to define these optional components in a separate schema document. This allows an instance to be validated against just the core set of components, or the enhanced set, depending on the application.

Another issue when you break up schema documents is whether to use the same namespace for all of them, or break them up into separate namespaces. This issue is covered in detail in Section 20.3, "Structuring namespaces."

4.2 | Defining schema documents

A schema document can be a physical XML file whose root element is schema, but this is only one form of schema document. A schema document may also be a fragment of another XML document (that is referenced using a fragment identifier or an XPointer), a DOM tree in memory, or some other physical representation.

Each schema document describes components for at most one namespace, known as its target namespace. Several schema documents can describe components in the same namespace. Some schema documents have no target namespace at all. Figure 4–1 shows several schema documents in different namespaces.

4.2.1 *Defining a schema document in XSDL*

In XSDL, each schema document is represented by a schema element, whose syntax is shown in Table 4–1.

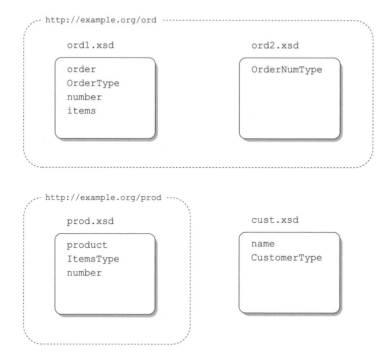

Figure 4–1   Schema documents

4.3 | Schema assembly

4.3.1 *Assembling schemas from multiple documents*

XSDL provides the include and import mechanisms to assemble schema documents into a schema. These mechanisms are described in the next section. However, they are not the only way to assemble schema documents. There is not always a "main" schema document that represents the whole schema. Some other alternatives are:

- The instance author can specify multiple schema locations in the instance.
- The processor can assemble schema documents from predefined locations.

Table 4–1   XSDL syntax: schema document

Name			
schema			

Parents			
none			

Attribute name	*Type*	*Required/default*	*Description*
id	ID		unique ID
version	token		version of the schema document
xml:lang	language		natural language of the schema document
target-Namespace	anyURI		namespace to which all global schema components belong, see Section 3.3.1
attribute-FormDefault	"qualified" | "unqualified"	"unqualified"	whether local attribute declarations should use qualified names, see Section 8.4
elementForm-Default	"qualified" | "unqualified"	"unqualified"	whether local element declarations should use qualified names, see Section 7.5
blockDefault	"#all" | list of ("substitu-tion" | "extension" | "restriction")		whether to block element substitution or type substitution, see Section 14.7

Table 4–1   XSDL syntax: schema document

Attribute name	Type	Required/default	Description
finalDefault	"#all" | list of ("extension" | "restriction" | "list" | "union")		whether to disallow type derivation, see Section 16.6.1 for element declarations, Section 14.7.1 for complex types, Section 9.5 for simple types

Content

```
(include | import | redefine | annotation)*, ((attribute |
attributeGroup | complexType | element | group | notation |
simpleType), annotation*)*
```

- Multiple command line parameters can be used to list the locations of the schema documents.

Which of these methods is used depends on the processor. XML Schema provides several options for the processors, and does not dictate a particular strategy for schema assembly. In Section 5.8, "Using specific schema processors," we look at how four different processors handle schema assembly and validation.

4.3.2 *Uniqueness of qualified names*

The qualified names of globally declared components must be unique in the schema, not just a schema document. When assembling a schema from multiple schema documents, be careful not to introduce duplicate qualified names. Example 4–1 shows two schema documents, both of which contain global element declarations for order.

It is not illegal for two schema documents to exist that have duplicate names, since they may be used at different times in different situations.

Example 4–1. Illegal duplication of element-type names

ord1.xsd:

```
<xsd:schema xmlns:xsd="http://www.w3.org/2001/XMLSchema"
            xmlns="http://example.org/ord"
            targetNamespace="http://example.org/ord">
  <xsd:include schemaLocation="ord2.xsd"/>
  <xsd:element name="order" type="OrderType"/>
</xsd:schema>
```

ord2.xsd:

```
<xsd:schema xmlns:xsd="http://www.w3.org/2001/XMLSchema"
            xmlns="http://example.org/ord"
            targetNamespace="http://example.org/ord">
  <xsd:element name="order" type="OrderType"/>
</xsd:schema>
```

However, since `ord1.xsd` includes `ord2.xsd`, they will both be used together, and this is illegal. Remember, the qualified name includes the namespace name, so this example would be valid if the two schema documents had different target namespaces (and `ord2.xsd` had been imported rather than included).

This rule holds true for all named, global components, including attributes, simple and complex types, named model groups, attribute groups, constraints, and notations. The uniqueness of qualified names is within the type of component. For example, it is illegal to have two element declarations for `order`, but it is legal to have both an element declaration and a simple type definition with that name. However, simple and complex data types cannot share the same qualified name.

4.3.3 Missing components

In some cases, declarations or definitions will refer to components that are outside the schema document. For example, in Example 4–2, the `order` element declaration uses the data type `OrderType` that is not defined in the schema document. This is not illegal unless a processor tries to use that declaration, and cannot find a definition of OrderType.

Example 4–2. Missing component

```
<xsd:schema xmlns:xsd="http://www.w3.org/2001/XMLSchema"
            xmlns="http://example.org/ord"
            targetNamespace="http://example.org/ord">

  <xsd:element name="number" type="xsd:integer"/>
  <xsd:element name="order" type="OrderType"/>
</xsd:schema>
```

In this case, the processor might obtain access to a schema document that contains the OrderType definition, by any of the means of assembly described in Section 4.3.1, "Assembling schemas from multiple documents."

Even if a schema document that contains the definition of Order-Type is never found, the processor will still be able to validate a number element. The fact that there are unresolved references in the schema is only an error if that reference is directly involved in the validation.

4.3.4 *Schema document defaults*

As we saw in Section 4.2.1, "Defining a schema document in XSDL," schema documents can have four defaults specified: attribute-FormDefault, elementFormDefault, blockDefault, and final-Default. As schema documents are assembled into schemas, these defaults are not overridden in any way. The defaults of a schema document still apply to all components defined or declared in that particular schema document. For example, if ord2.xsd has elementForm-Default set to unqualified, all of the local element declarations in ord2.xsd will have unqualified names, even if ord2.xsd is included in another schema document that has elementFormDefault set to qualified.

4.4 | include, redefine, and import

4.4.1 include

An include is used when you want to include other schema documents in a schema document that has the same target namespace. This provides for modularization of schema documents. For example, you may want to break your schema into several documents: two different order schema documents, and a customer schema document. This is depicted in Figure 4–2.

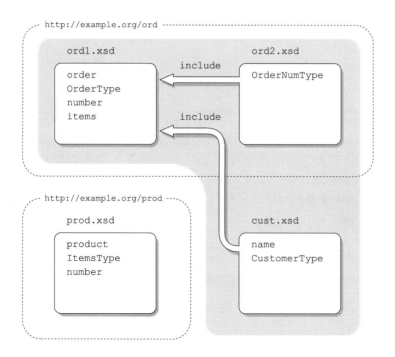

Figure 4–2   Includes

In XSDL, includes are represented by an include element, whose syntax is shown in Table 4–2.

The include elements may only appear at the top level of a schema document, and they must appear at the beginning (along with the import and redefine elements).

Table 4–2   XSDL syntax: include

Name			
include			

Parents			
schema			

Attribute name	Type	Required/default	Description
id	ID		unique ID
schemaLocation	anyURI	required	location of the included schema document

Content			
annotation?			

The schemaLocation attribute indicates where the included schema document is located. This attribute is required, although the location is not required to be resolvable. However, if it is resolvable, it must be a complete schema document.

Example 4–3 shows the use of include in a schema document. The schema author wants to use the data type OrderNumType in the number element declaration. However, OrderNumType is defined in a different schema document. The include statement references the location of the schema document, ord2.xsd, that contains the definition of OrderNumType.

The schema documents ord1.xsd and ord2.xsd have the same target namespace. When you use includes, one of the following must be true:

- Both schema documents have the same target namespace.
- Neither schema document has a target namespace.
- The including schema document has a target namespace, and the included schema document does not have a target namespace.

Example 4–3. Include

ord1.xsd:

```
<xsd:schema xmlns:xsd="http://www.w3.org/2001/XMLSchema"
            xmlns="http://example.org/ord"
            targetNamespace="http://example.org/ord">

  <xsd:include schemaLocation="ord2.xsd"/>

  <xsd:element name="order" type="OrderType"/>
  <xsd:complexType name="OrderType">
    <xsd:sequence>
      <xsd:element name="number" type="OrderNumType"/>
      <!--...-->
    </xsd:sequence>
  </xsd:complexType>

</xsd:schema>
```

ord2.xsd:

```
<xsd:schema xmlns:xsd="http://www.w3.org/2001/XMLSchema"
            xmlns="http://example.org/ord"
            targetNamespace="http://example.org/ord">

  <xsd:simpleType name="OrderNumType">
    <xsd:restriction base="xsd:string"/>
  </xsd:simpleType>
</xsd:schema>
```

In the third case, all components of the included schema document take on the namespace of the including schema document. These components are sometimes called chameleon components, because their namespace changes depending on where they are included. This is shown in Example 4–4.

Note that in cust.xsd, the element declaration of name can reference the type CustNameType without any namespace prefix. Even though these components will take on the target namespace of the ord.xsd schema document, the unprefixed references between components in cust.xsd will be honored.

Example 4–4. Chameleon include

ord1.xsd:

```
<xsd:schema xmlns:xsd="http://www.w3.org/2001/XMLSchema"
            xmlns="http://example.org/ord"
            targetNamespace="http://example.org/ord">

  <xsd:include schemaLocation="cust.xsd"/>

  <xsd:element name="order" type="OrderType"/>
  <xsd:complexType name="OrderType">
    <xsd:sequence>
      <xsd:element name="number" type="OrderNumType"/>
      <xsd:element name="customer" type="CustomerType"/>
      <!--...-->
    </xsd:sequence>
  </xsd:complexType>
</xsd:schema>
```

cust.xsd:

```
<xsd:schema xmlns:xsd="http://www.w3.org/2001/XMLSchema">

  <xsd:complexType name="CustomerType">
    <xsd:sequence>
      <xsd:element name="name" type="CustNameType"/>
      <!--...-->
    </xsd:sequence>
  </xsd:complexType>
  <xsd:simpleType name="CustNameType">
    <xsd:restriction base="xsd:string"/>
  </xsd:simpleType>
</xsd:schema>
```

There can be multiple `include` elements in a schema document. There can also be multiple levels of includes in schema documents. For example, `ord1.xsd` can include `ord2.xsd`, which includes `cust.xsd`, and so on. It is not an error to include the exact same schema document twice. However, this may cause performance problems because the processor will need to verify that they are exactly the same.

4.4.2 `redefine`

A `redefine` is similar to an `include`, with the additional option of specifying new definitions of some or all of the components in the redefined schema document. Only certain types of schema components can be redefined, namely complex types, simple types, named model groups, and attribute groups. This is depicted in Figure 4–3. Like included schema documents, redefined schema documents must have the same target namespace as the redefining schema document, or none at all.

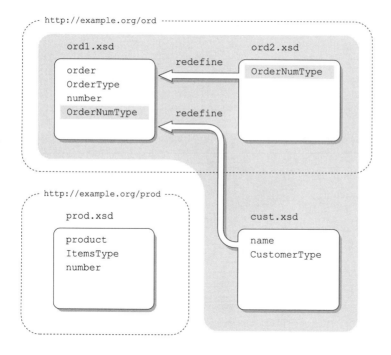

Figure 4–3   Redefine

In XSDL, redefines are represented by a `redefine` element. Because of the complexities of redefinition, all of Chapter 18, "Redefining schema components," is devoted to it.

4.4.3 `import`

An import is used to tell the processor that you will be referring to components from other namespaces. For example, if you want to reference an attribute from another namespace in your complex type definition, or you want to derive your type from a type in another namespace, you must import this namespace. This is depicted in Figure 4–4.

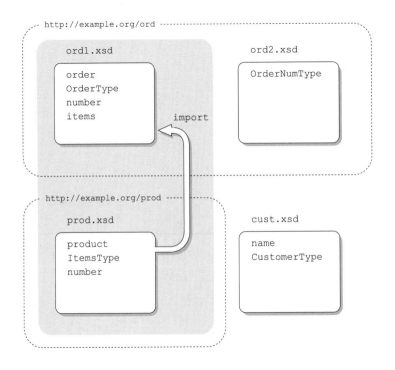

Figure 4–4   Import

Imports differ from includes in two important ways. First, includes only take place within a namespace, while imports take place across namespaces. The second, subtler distinction, is their general purpose. The purpose of include is specifically to pull in other schema documents, while the purpose of import is to record a dependency on another namespace, not necessarily another schema document. Import does allow you to specify the location of a schema document for that namespace, but it is just a hint, and the processor is not required to try to resolve it.

In XSDL, imports are represented by an `import` element, whose syntax is shown in Table 4–3.

Table 4–3   XSDL syntax: import

Name			
`import`			

Parents			
`schema`			

Attribute name	Type	Required/ default	Description
`id`	`ID`		unique ID
`namespace`	`anyURI`		namespace to be imported
`schemaLocation`	`anyURI`		location of a schema document which describes components in the imported namespace

Content			
`annotation?`			

The `import` elements may only appear at the top level of a schema document, and must appear at the beginning (along with the `include` and `redefine` elements).

The `namespace` attribute indicates the namespace that you wish to import. If you do not specify a namespace, it means that you are importing components that are not in any namespace. The imported namespace cannot be the same as the target namespace of the importing schema document. If the importing schema document has no target namespace, the `import` element must have a `namespace` attribute.

The `schemaLocation` attribute provides a hint to the processor as to where to find a schema document that declares components for that

Example 4–5. Import

ord1.xsd:

```
<xsd:schema xmlns:xsd="http://www.w3.org/2001/XMLSchema"
            xmlns="http://example.org/ord"
            xmlns:prod="http://example.org/prod"
            targetNamespace="http://example.org/ord">

  <xsd:import namespace="http://example.org/prod"
              schemaLocation="prod.xsd"/>

  <xsd:element name="order" type="OrderType"/>
  <xsd:complexType name="OrderType">
    <xsd:sequence>
      <xsd:element name="number" type="OrderNumType"/>
      <xsd:element name="items" type="prod:ItemsType"/>
      <!--...-->
    </xsd:sequence>
  </xsd:complexType>
</xsd:schema>
```

prod.xsd:

```
<xsd:schema xmlns:xsd="http://www.w3.org/2001/XMLSchema"
        xmlns="http://example.org/prod"
        targetNamespace="http://example.org/prod">

  <xsd:complexType name="ItemsType">
    <xsd:sequence>
      <xsd:element name="product" type="ProductType"/>
    </xsd:sequence>
  </xsd:complexType>
</xsd:schema>
```

namespace. If you do not specify a schemaLocation, it is assumed that the processor somehow knows where to find the schema document, perhaps through one of the methods described in Section 4.3.1, "Assembling schemas from multiple documents." When schemaLocation is present, and the processor is able to resolve the location to some resource, it must resolve to a schema document. That schema document's target namespace must be equal to the value of the `namespace` attribute of the `import` element.

It is legal to have multiple imports of the same namespace. Even looping references (`ord1.xsd` imports `prod.xsd`'s namespace, and `prod.xsd` imports `ord1.xsd`'s namespace) are acceptable, because this just indicates the interdependence of the components.

Example 4–5 shows the use of `import` in a schema document. The schema author wants to use the type `ItemsType` in an element declaration. However, `ItemsType` is defined in a different namespace. The import statement references the namespace and location of the schema document that contains `ItemsType`. The declaration of `items` is then able to reference `ItemsType` using the appropriate prefix.

Instances and schemas

Chapter 5

T here is a many-to-many relationship between instances and schemas. A schema can describe many valid instances, possibly with different root element types. Likewise, an instance may be described by many schemas, depending on the circumstances. For example, you may have multiple schemas for an instance, with different levels of validation. One may just validate the structure, while another checks every data item against a data type. There may also be multiple schemas with different application information to be used at processing time. This chapter explains the interaction between schemas and instances.

5.1 | Using the instance attributes

There are four attributes that can apply to any element in an instance. These four attributes, which are described in Table 5-1, are all in the

XML Schema Instance Namespace, `http://www.w3.org/2001/XMLSchema-instance`. This namespace is commonly mapped to the prefix `xsi`.[1]

Table 5–1   XSDL instance attributes

Attribute name	*Type*	*Required/ default*	*Description*
`nil`	`boolean`	`false`	whether the element's value is nil, see Section 7.4
`type`	`QName`		the name of a data type that is being substituted for the element's declared data type, see Section 14.6
`schemaLocation`	list of `anyURI`		list of the locations of schema documents for designated namespaces, see Section 5.4.1
`noNamespace-SchemaLocation`	`anyURI`		location of a schema document with no target namespace, see Section 5.4.2

Example 5–1 shows the use of `xsi:type` in an instance.

Example 5–1. Using an instance attribute

```
<product xmlns="http://example.org/prod"
         xmlns:xsi="http://www.w3.org/2001/XMLSchema-instance">
  <number xsi:type="ShortProdNumType">557</number>
  <size>10</size>
</product>
```

---

1. While any prefix may be mapped to the namespace, this book uses the prefix `xsi` as a shorthand, sometimes without explicitly stating that it is mapped to `http://www.w3.org/2001/XMLSchema-instance`.

Because these four attributes are globally declared, their names must be prefixed in instances. You are required to declare the XML Schema Instance Namespace and map a prefix (preferably `xsi`) to it. However, you are not required to specify a schema location for these four attributes. You are also *not* required or even permitted to declare `xsi:type` as an attribute in the data type definition for `number`. The attributes in the XML Schema Instance Namespace, like namespace declarations, are special attributes that a schema processor always recognizes without explicit declarations.

In fact, the `number` element in this example can have a simple type, even though elements with simple types are normally not allowed to have attributes.

5.2 | Schema processing

5.2.1 *Validation*

Validation is an important part of schema processing. Validation determines whether an instance conforms to all of the constraints described in the schema. It involves checking all of the elements and attributes in an instance to determine that they have declarations, and that they conform to those declarations and to the corresponding data type definitions.

The validation process verifies:

- *Correctness of the data.* Validating against a schema does not provide a 100% guarantee that the data is correct, but it can signal invalid formats or out-of-range values.

- *Completeness of data.* Validation can check that all required information is present.

- *Shared understanding of the data.* Validation can make sure that the way you perceive the document is the same way that the sender perceives it.

Whether to validate your instances on a regular basis depends on a number of factors:

- *Where the instances originated.* Within your organization, perhaps you have control over the application that generates instances. After some initial testing, you may trust that all documents coming from that application are valid, without performing validation. However, often the instances you are processing are originating outside your organization. You may be less likely to trust these documents.

- *Whether the instances were application-generated or user-generated.* Human involvement can introduce typographical and other errors. Even with validating XML editors, it is still possible to introduce errors inadvertently during the handling of the documents.

- *Data quality.* If the instances are generated directly from a legacy database, for example, they may not be complete or 100% correct.

- *Performance.* Obviously, it takes extra time to validate. If performance is critical, you may want to avoid some validation, or write application-specific code that can validate more efficiently than a schema processor.

5.2.2   *Augmenting the instance*

In addition to validating the instance, a schema processor may alter the instance by:

- adding default and fixed values for elements and attributes,
- normalizing whitespace in element and attribute values that have simple types.

Because of this, it is important that the sender and receiver of the document agree on the schema to use. If the receiver processes an element with a declaration that has a default value different from that of the sender's declaration, it can alter the data of the element in ways unintended by the sender.

5.3 | Relating instances to schemas

Instances can be related to schemas in a number of ways:

- *Using hints in the instance.* The `xsi:schemaLocation` and `xsi:noNamespaceSchemaLocation` attributes can be used in the instance to provide a hint to the processor where to find the schema documents. These attributes are covered in Section 5.4, "Using XSDL hints in the instance."

- *Application's choice.* Most applications will be processing the same type of instances repeatedly. These applications may already know where the appropriate schema documents are on the web, or locally, or even have them built in. In this case, the processor could either (1) ignore `xsi:schemaLocation`, or (2) reject documents containing `xsi:schemaLocation` attributes, or (3) reject documents in which the `xsi:schema-Location` does not match the intended schema document.

- *User's choice.* The location of the schema document(s) can be specified at processing time, by a command line instruction or user dialog.

- *Dereferencing the namespace.* The namespace name can be dereferenced to retrieve a schema document or resource directory. This is covered in more detail in Section 5.5, "Dereferencing namespaces."

5.4 | Using XSDL hints in the instance

XSDL provides two attributes that act as hints to where the processor might find the schema document(s) for the instance. Different processors may ignore or acknowledge these hints in different ways. This section describes the use of these attributes, while Section 5.8, "Using specific schema processors," describes how different schema processors treat these hints.

These two attributes are: xsi:schemaLocation, for use with schema documents that have target namespaces, and xsi:noNamespace-SchemaLocation, for use with schema documents without target namespaces.

5.4.1   *The* xsi:schemaLocation *attribute*

The xsi:schemaLocation attribute allows you to specify a list of pairs that match namespace names with schema locations. Example 5–2 shows an instance that uses xsi:schemaLocation. The default namespace for the document is http://example.org/prod. The xsi prefix is assigned to the XML Schema Instance Namespace, so that the processor will recognize the xsi:schemaLocation attribute. Then, the xsi:schemaLocation attribute is specified to relate the namespace http://example.org/prod to the schema location prod.xsd.

Example 5–2. Using xsi:schemaLocation

```
<product xmlns="http://example.org/prod"
         xmlns:xsi="http://www.w3.org/2001/XMLSchema-instance"
         xsi:schemaLocation="http://example.org/prod prod.xsd">
  <number>557</number>
  <size>10</size>
</product>
```

The value of the xsi:schemaLocation attribute is actually at least two values separated by whitespace. The first value is the namespace name and the second value is the URL for the schema location. The processor will retrieve the schema document from the schema location and make sure that its target namespace matches that of the namespace it is paired with in xsi:schemaLocation.

If multiple namespaces are used in the document, xsi:schema-Location can contain more than one pair of values, as shown in Example 5–3.

Example 5–3. Using xsi:schemaLocation with multiple pairs

```
<order xmlns="http://example.org/ord"
       xmlns:xsi="http://www.w3.org/2001/XMLSchema-instance"
       xsi:schemaLocation="http://example.org/prod prod.xsd
                           http://example.org/ord ord1.xsd">
  <items>
    <product xmlns="http://example.org/prod">
      <number>557</number>
      <size>10</size>
    </product>
  </items>
</order>
```

If you have a schema document that imports schema documents with different target namespaces, you do not have to specify schema locations for all the namespaces (if the processor has some other way of finding the schema documents, such as the schemaLocation attribute of import). For example, if ord1.xsd imports prod.xsd, it is not necessary to specify prod.xsd in the xsi:schemaLocation. You do still need to declare multiple namespaces in the instance, as shown in the example.

It is generally a good practice to use one main schema document that includes or imports the other schema documents needed for validation. This simplifies the instance and makes name collisions more obvious.

According to XML Schema, the `xsi:schemaLocation` attribute may appear anywhere in an instance, in the tags of any number of elements. Its appearance in a particular tag does not signify its scope. However, it must appear before any elements that it would validate.

It is important to keep in mind that different processors are entitled to use or ignore any or all `xsi:schemaLocation` attributes. For example, the current version of the Xerces parser ignores any `xsi:schemaLocation` attribute that does not appear in the root tag. MSXML ignores `xsi:schemaLocation` attributes completely. It is important to understand the behavior of the processor you use before you decide whether to use these hints and where to put them. In Section 5.8, "Using specific schema processors," we will look at how four schema processors use these hints.

5.4.2 *The* `xsi:noNamespaceSchemaLocation` *attribute*

The `xsi:noNamespaceSchemaLocation` attribute is used to reference a schema document with no target namespace. `xsi:noNamespaceSchemaLocation` does not take a list of values; only one schema location may be specified. The schema document referenced cannot have a target namespace. Example 5–4 shows the use of `xsi:noNamespaceSchemaLocation` in an instance.

Example 5–4. Using `xsi:noNamespaceSchemaLocation`

```
<product xmlns:xsi="http://www.w3.org/2001/XMLSchema-instance"
       xsi:noNamespaceSchemaLocation="prod.xsd">
  <number>557</number>
  <size>10</size>
</product>
```

It is legal according to XML Schema to have both `xsi:noNamespaceSchemaLocation` and `xsi:schemaLocation` specified, but once again, you should check with your processor to see what it will accept.

5.5 | Dereferencing namespaces

Another method of locating the schema document(s) for an instance is by dereferencing the namespace. Namespace names are often HTTP URLs (Uniform Resource Locators), such as `http://exam-ple.org/prod`. This leads a logical person to believe that if he or she types `http://example.org/prod` into a web browser, a web page or other resource will be retrieved associated with that namespace. This is known as dereferencing a namespace, and there is much debate about whether namespaces should be dereferenced or not. The *Namespaces in XML* Recommendation is flexible on this topic:

- You may choose to use URLs as your namespace names, or not.
- You may put a resource at the location the URL points to, or not.
- The resource you put at that location may be a schema document, an HTML document of any kind, a resource directory, or any other type of resource.
- You may require your individual application to dereference namespaces, or not.

In other words, whether you make your namespaces dereferencable is your choice. It is generally a good idea to use URLs for namespace names, and to put a resource at the location referenced by the URL. There are many reasons not to require your application to dereference a namespace name, including security, performance, and network availability. However, a person might want to dereference the namespace in order to find out more information about it.

Having a namespace name resolve to a schema document, though, is not ideal because:

- Many schemas may describe that namespace. Which one do you choose?

- A variety of documents in other formats may also describe that namespace, including DTDs, human-readable documentation, schemas written in other schema languages, and stylesheets. Each may be applicable in different circumstances.

- Schema documents are not particularly human-readable, even by humans who write them!

A better choice is a resource directory, which lists all the resources related to a namespace. Such a directory can be both human- and application-readable. It can also allow different resources to be used depending on the application or purpose.

One language that can be used to define a resource directory is RDDL (Resource Directory Description Language). RDDL is an extension of XHTML that is used to define a resource directory. It does not only apply to namespaces, but it is an excellent choice for dereferencing a namespace. Example 5–5 shows an RDDL document that might be placed at the location `http://example.org/prod`.

This document defines three related resources. Each resource has a *role*, which describes the nature of the resource (e.g., schema, DTD, stylesheet) and an *arcrole*, which indicates the purpose of the resource (e.g., validation, reference). An application that wants to do schema validation, for example, can read this document and extract the location of the schema document to be used for validation. A person could also read this document in a browser, as shown in Figure 5–1.

For more information on RDDL, see `http://www.rddl.org`.

5.6 | The root element

Sometimes you want to be able to specify which element type should be the root element of the instance. For example, you may not want

Example 5–5. RDDL for the product catalog namespace

```
<?xml version='1.0'?>
<!DOCTYPE html PUBLIC "-//XML-DEV//DTD XHTML RDDL 1.0//EN"
                     "rddl/rddl-xhtml.dtd">
<html xml:lang="en" xmlns="http://www.w3.org/1999/xhtml"
     xmlns:xlink="http://www.w3.org/1999/xlink"
     xmlns:rddl="http://www.rddl.org/">
<head><title>Product Catalog</title></head>
<body><h1>Product Catalog</h1>
  <div id="toc"><h2>Table of Contents</h2>
    <ol>
      <li><a href="#intro">Introduction</a></li>
      <li><a href="#related.resources">Resources</a></li>
    </ol>
  </div>
  <div id="intro"><h2>Introduction</h2>
    <p>This document describes the <a href="#xmlschemap1">Product
    Catalog</a> namespace and contains a directory of links to
    related resources.</p>
  </div>
  <div id="related.resources">
    <h2>Related Resources for the Product Catalog Namespace</h2>
    <!-- start resource definitions -->

  <div class="resource" id="DTD">
    <rddl:resource xlink:title="DTD for validation"
     xlink:arcrole="http://www.rddl.org/purposes#validation"
     xlink:role="http://www.isi.edu/in-
               notes/iana/assignments/media-types/text/xml-dtd"
     xlink:href="prod.dtd">
      <h3>DTD</h3>
      <p>A <a href="prod.dtd">DTD</a> for the Product Catalog.</p>
    </rddl:resource>
  </div>

  <div class="resource" id="xmlschema">
    <rddl:resource xlink:title="Products schema"
     xlink:role="http://www.w3.org/2001/XMLSchema"
     xlink:arcrole="http://www.rddl.org/purposes#schema-validation"
     xlink:href="prod.xsd">
      <h3>XML Schema</h3>
      <p>An <a href="prod.xsd">XML Schema</a> for the Product
         Catalog.</p>
    </rddl:resource>
  </div>
```

```
<div class="resource" id="documentation">
  <rddl:resource xlink:title="Application Documentation"
   xlink:role="http://www.w3.org/TR/html4"
   xlink:arcrole="http://www.rddl.org/purposes#reference"
   xlink:href="prod.html">
    <h3>Application Documentation</h3>
    <p><a href="prod.html">Application documentation</a> for
        the Product Catalog application.</p>
  </rddl:resource>
</div>
</div>
</body></html>
```

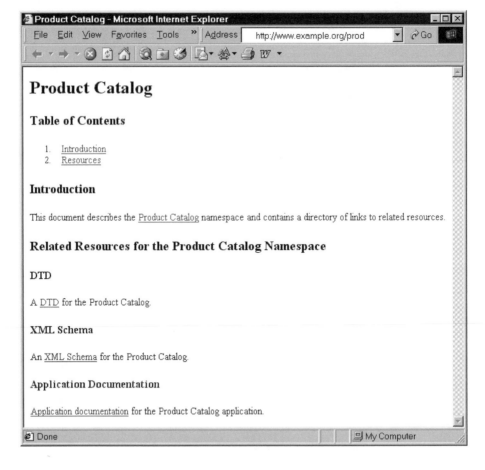

Figure 5–1   Viewing a RDDL document in web browser

the document shown in Example 5–6 to be considered a valid instance, although the element itself is valid according to its declaration.

Example 5–6. A valid instance?

```
<number>557</number>
```

Schemas work similarly to DTDs in this regard. There is no way to designate the root. Any element conforming to a global element declaration can be a root element for validation purposes.

You can work around this by having only one global element declaration. If the number declaration is local, Example 5–6 is not valid on its own. However, there are times that you cannot avoid global element declarations either because you are using substitution groups, or because you are importing element declarations over which you have no control. A better approach is to use the application to verify that the root element is the one you expect.

Using some schema processors, validation may not necessarily start at the root. It is possible to validate sections of instance documents with different schema documents using different xsi:schemaLocation hints, or to validate fragments of instance documents identified by IDs or XPointer expressions. Also, one schema document may describe several related types of instance documents, which may each have different roots (e.g., purchase orders and invoices).

5.7 | Using DTDs and schemas together

There is nothing to prevent an instance from being validated against both a DTD and a schema. In fact, if you wish to use general entities, you must continue to use DTDs alongside schemas. Example 5–7 shows an instance that has both an internal DTD subset and a reference to a schema. Generally, it is recommended to only put entity and notation declarations in the DTD, but there may be cases where you want to also include element declarations in the DTD.

Example 5–7. Using a DTD and a schema

```
<!DOCTYPE catalog [
<!NOTATION jpeg SYSTEM "JPG">
<!ENTITY prod557 SYSTEM "prod557.jpg" NDATA jpeg>
<!ENTITY prod563 SYSTEM "prod563.jpg" NDATA jpeg>]>

<catalog xmlns:xsi="http://www.w3.org/2001/XMLSchema-instance"
         xsi:noNamespaceSchemaLocation="prod.xsd">
  <product>
    <number>557</number>
    <picture location="prod557"/>
  </product>
  <product>
    <number>563</number>
    <picture location="prod563"/>
  </product>
</catalog>
```

Two separate validations will take place; one against the DTD, and one against the schema. The XML 1.0 (DTD) validity will be assessed first. This process will not only validate the instance, but also augment it by resolving the entities, filling in attribute default values, and normalizing whitespace in attribute values. Validity according to the schema is then assessed on the augmented instance. None of the declarations in the DTD override the declarations in the schema. If there are declarations for the same element type in both the DTD and the schema and these declarations are conflicting, an element may be DTD-valid but not schema-valid.

5.8 | Using specific schema processors

This section describes four different schema processors and how they handle validating instances. As we have seen, XML Schema allows some flexibility as to how processors locate the schema documents used for validation. Each of these four processors has a different method of locating schema documents, and each one is legal according to XML Schema.

Because the software described in this section is upgraded frequently, you should not assume this information is up-to-date. Please check the relevant web sites for newer versions of these schema processors.

5.8.1   *XSV*

XSV (XML Schema Validator) is written and maintained by the Language Technology Group at the University of Edinburgh. Unlike the other software described in this section, XSV is not a general-purpose XML parser. Its sole purpose is to validate schemas and instances.

XSV can be executed via the web or downloaded for local installation. As of this writing, the most current version is 1.189/1.95, last modified on May 7, 2001. This version provides support for most of the XML Schema Recommendation, minus a few features that are listed on the website. To use or download XSV or to find out more, see `http://www.w3.org/2001/03/webdata/xsv`.

To locate schema documents for an instance, XSV will attempt three different methods (in this order):

1. Accepting command line parameters. XSV allows you to specify the locations of one or more schema documents on the command line.

2. Looking at `xsi:schemaLocation` and `xsi:noNamespaceSchemaLocation` attributes. XSV will read these attributes anywhere they appear in the instance. XSV will attempt to validate the entire instance, regardless of where the attributes appear.

3. Dereferencing the namespace URI. If a declaration cannot be found using either of the previous two methods, XSV will

dereference the namespace in an attempt to locate the schema document.

If XSV finds a declaration for the root element, it will use strict validation, reporting errors for all invalid or missing components. If it cannot find a declaration for the root element, XSV attempts to validate the other elements in the instance using lax validation. This means that it will report errors in components whose declarations it can find, and ignore the others.

If XSV encounters multiple schema documents (through any of the three methods above), it will join them together and treat them as one schema. However, it does not accept multiple schema documents for the same namespace, except through include. That is, if you specify two pairs of values for the same namespace in the xsi: schemaLocation attribute, it will ignore the second one. Instead, you should have the first schema document include the second one.

If you provide a schema location for a particular namespace both via the command line and an xsi:schemaLocation attribute, the command line parameter takes precedence, *for that particular namespace.* The rest of the xsi:schemaLocation values are still used for the other namespaces.

When using the import mechanism, XSV will attempt to locate the resource identified by the schemaLocation attribute of import. If the import element has no schemaLocation attribute, it will attempt to dereference the namespace. If neither of these results in a schema document, it will not necessarily consider this an error. It is possible that these other-namespace components are declared in another schema document that is retrieved by other means (e.g. a command line parameter or an xsi:schemaLocation hint in the instance).

5.8.2 *Xerces*

Xerces is an open source, general purpose XML parser that is maintained by the Apache Software Foundation. At the time of this writing, its current version is 1.4.0, released on May 22, 2001. This version provides beta support for the XML Schema Recommendation, with a few minor limitations that are listed on the website. To download Xerces or to find out more, see `http://xml.apache.org`.

Xerces uses the `xsi:schemaLocation` and `xsi:noName-spaceSchemaLocation` attributes to locate schema documents for a particular instance. It will only acknowledge those attributes if they appear in the root tag of the instance.

Like XSV, Xerces only accepts one `schemaLocation` hint per namespace. If you have multiple schema documents in the same namespace, you must use the include mechanism to join them together.

When using the import mechanism, Xerces requires that the `schemaLocation` attribute of `import` be present and contain the location of a valid schema document.

Example 5–8 shows Java code that could be used to turn on schema validation in the parser.

Example 5–8. Java code to set schema validation in Xerces

```
SAXParser p=new SAXParser();
try {

// Turn schema validation on
p.setFeature
  ("http://xml.org/sax/features/validation", true);
p.setFeature
  ("http://apache.org/xml/features/validation/schema", true);
p.setFeature
  ("http://apache.org/xml/features/validation/schema-full-checking",
   true);
} catch (SAXException e) {
  System.out.println("error turning on validation");
}
```

Xerces has three separate features that are relevant:

- `http://xml.org/sax/features/validation` is a general validation feature that must be set to `true` for schema validation to take place.

- `http://apache.org/xml/features/validation/schema`
  allows most schema validation to take place.

- `http://apache.org/xml/features/validation/schema-full-checking` is reserved for resource-intensive validation
  like checking for non-deterministic content models and complex
  type restriction validation.

5.8.3 *Oracle XDK*

The Oracle XML Schema processor, developed by Oracle Corporation,
is part of the Oracle XML Developer's Kit (XDK). At the time of this
writing, the current version of the XDK is 9.0.1.0.0, released on
May 31, 2001. This version supports the XML Schema Candidate
Recommendation. To download the XDK or to find out more, see
`http://otn.oracle.com/tech/xml/index.htm`.

The Oracle processor will read the `xsi:schemaLocation` and
`xsi:noNamespaceSchemaLocation` attributes anywhere they appear
in an instance. Unlike XSV or Xerces, it will only validate elements
that have an `xsi:schemaLocation` (or `xsi:noNamespaceSchema-Location`) attribute, and their children. Therefore, if `xsi:schema-Location` does not appear in the root tag, no validation is attempted
on the root element or any other elements that are not in the "scope"
of the `schemaLocation` attribute.

Unlike XSV or Xerces, the Oracle processor will accept multiple
`schemaLocation` hints for the same namespace.

The Oracle processor also allows you to specify one or more schema
locations programmatically, as shown in Example 5–9. Two classes,
`XSDSample.java` and `XSDSetSchema.java`, are provided with the
XDK as examples. If a schema location is set programmatically, all
`xsi:schemaLocation` hints in the instance are ignored, regardless of
their namespace.

When using the import mechanism, the Oracle XML Schema processor requires that the `schemaLocation` attribute of `import` be
present and contain the location of a valid schema document. Any

Example 5–9. Java code to launch Oracle XML Parser

```
import oracle.xml.parser.schema.*;
import oracle.xml.parser.v2.*;
...
DOMParser dp = new DOMParser();
...
// Turn schema validation on
dp.setValidationMode(XMLParser.SCHEMA_VALIDATION);
...
// Assign a particular schema
XSDBuilder builder = new XSDBuilder();
XMLSchema schemadoc = (XMLSchema)builder.build("prod.xsd");
dp.setXMLSchema(schemadoc);
```

references across schema documents must be handled by `import` or `include`; the processor will not allow "dangling" references to be resolved by multiple `xsi:schemaLocation` hints. This is in contrast to XSV and Xerces.

5.8.4 *Microsoft MSXML*

The Microsoft XML Schema Processor, developed by Microsoft Corporation, is part of MSXML. The current version of MSXML at the time of this writing is the 4.0 Technology Preview released in April, 2001. This version supports the XML Schema Candidate Recommendation. To download MSXML or to find out more, see `http://msdn.microsoft.com/downloads`. On that page, MSXML is under Web Development/XML.

MSXML does not currently acknowledge `xsi:schemaLocation` attributes. Instead, the schema location(s) and namespace(s) must be specified programmatically, as shown in Example 5–10.

MSXML performs lax validation. This means that it reports any errors in elements and attributes for which it has declarations, but does not report errors when it cannot find a declaration. In this respect, it is similar to XSV.

Example 5–10. JavaScript function to launch MSXML

```
function runParser(xmlFileName,namespace,xsdFileName)
  {
  var xmlschema = new ActiveXObject("Msxml2.XMLSchemaCache.4.0");
  xmlschema.add(namespace,xsdFileName);
  var xmldoc = new ActiveXObject("Msxml2.DOMDocument.4.0");
  xmldoc.async = false;
  xmldoc.schemas = xmlschema;
  xmldoc.load(xmlFileName);

  if(xmldoc.parseError.errorCode != 0)
    output.innerHTML= xmldoc.parseError.errorCode +
                xmldoc.parseError.reason;
  else
    output.innerHTML="No errors.";
  }
```

Schema documentation and extension

X ML Schema is a full-featured language for describing the structure of XML documents. However, it cannot express everything there is to know about an instance or the data it contains. This chapter explains how you can extend XML Schema to include additional information for users and applications.

6.1 | The mechanics

There are two places to include extensions in XSDL: annotations and non-native attributes. In this section, we will discuss the mechanics of defining each of these kinds of extensions. In later sections, we will explore how extensions might best be used.

6.1.1 *Annotations*

In XSDL, annotations are represented by an `annotation` element, whose syntax is shown in Table 6–1. An `annotation` may appear in almost any element belonging to the XSDL vocabulary, with the exception of annotation itself, and its children, appinfo and documentation. The schema and redefine elements can contain multiple annotation elements, anywhere among their children. All other XSDL elements may only contain one annotation, and it must be their first child.

Table 6–1   XSDL syntax: annotation

Name
annotation

Parents
all, any, anyAttribute, attribute, attributeGroup, choice, complex-Content, complexType, element, extension, field, group, import, include, key, keyref, list, notation, redefine, restriction, schema, selector, sequence, simpleContent, simpleType, union, unique

Attribute name	Type	Required/default	Description
id	ID		unique ID

Content
(documentation | appinfo)*

The content model for annotation allows two types of children: documentation and appinfo. A documentation element is intended to be human-readable user documentation, and appinfo is machine-readable for applications. A single annotation may contain multiple documentation and appinfo elements, in any order, which may serve different purposes.

6.1.2   *User documentation*

The syntax for a documentation element is shown in Table 6–2. It uses an element wildcard for its content model, which specifies that it may contain any number of elements from any namespace (or no namespace), in any order. Its content is mixed, so it may contain character data as well as children.

Table 6–2 XSDL syntax: documentation

Name			
documentation			

Parents			
annotation			

Attribute name	Type	Required/ default	Description
source	anyURI		source of further documentation
xml:lang	language		natural language of the documentation

Content			
mixed, with any wildcard (any character data content, any child elements)			

The source attribute can contain a URI reference that points to further documentation. The schema processor does not dereference this URI during validation.

Example 6–1 shows the use of documentation to document the product element declaration.

Although you can put character data content directly in documentation or appinfo, it is preferable to structure it using at least one child element. This allows the type of information (e.g., description) to be uniquely identified in the case of future additions.

Instead of (or in addition to) including the information in the annotation, you can also provide links to one or more external documents. To do this, you can either use the source attribute, or other mechanisms, such as XLink. This allows reuse of documentation that may apply to more than one schema component.

Example 6–1. Documentation

```
<xsd:schema xmlns:xsd="http://www.w3.org/2001/XMLSchema"
            xmlns:doc="http://example.org/doc">
  <xsd:element name="product" type="ProductType">
    <xsd:annotation>
      <xsd:documentation xml:lang="en"
        source="http://example.org/prod.html#product">
        <doc:description>This element represents a product.
        </doc:description>
      </xsd:documentation>
    </xsd:annotation>
  </xsd:element>
</xsd:schema>
```

6.1.3 *Application information*

The syntax for `appinfo`, shown in Table 6–3, is identical to that of `documentation`, minus the `xml:lang` attribute.

Table 6–3   XSDL syntax: application information

Name			
appinfo			

Parents			
annotation			

Attribute name	Type	Required/ default	Description
source	anyURI		source of further documentation

Content			
mixed, with `any` wildcard (any character data content, any child elements)			

Example 6–2 shows the use of `appinfo` to map `product` to a database table.

Example 6–2. Application information

```
<xsd:schema xmlns:xsd="http://www.w3.org/2001/XMLSchema"
            xmlns:app="http://example.org/app">
  <xsd:element name="product" type="ProductType">
    <xsd:annotation>
      <xsd:appinfo>
        <app:dbmapping>
          <app:tb>PRODUCT_MASTER</app:tb>
        </app:dbmapping>
      </xsd:appinfo>
    </xsd:annotation>
  </xsd:element>
</xsd:schema>
```

In this example, we declare a namespace `http://example.org/app` for the `dbmapping` and `tb` elements used in the annotation. This is not required; `appinfo` can contain elements with no namespace. However, it is preferable to use a namespace because it makes the extension easily distinguishable from other information that may be included for use by other applications.

6.1.4 *Validating annotations*

The wildcards in the content models of `appinfo` and `documentation` are processed using lax validation. This means that if the processor can find a declaration of a particular element or attribute, it will validate it and report errors. If it does not find an appropriate declaration, it does not report any errors.

The previous examples did not declare a schema location for the extensions. Because the processor will not find declarations for the extension elements, it will not report any errors for these extensions.

However, you may want to validate your annotations, to ensure that they follow a standard structure that is expected by a user or an application. To do this, specify the `xsi:schemaLocation` attribute, just like you would in an instance. Example 6–3 shows a schema with xsi:schemaLocation specified. It relates the http://example.org/doc namespace to the schema document doc.xsd.

Example 6–3. Validating documentation

```
<xsd:schema xmlns:xsd="http://www.w3.org/2001/XMLSchema"
            xmlns:doc="http://example.org/doc"
            xmlns:xsi="http://www.w3.org/2001/XMLSchema-instance"
            xsi:schemaLocation="http://example.org/doc doc.xsd">

  <xsd:element name="product" type="ProductType">
    <xsd:annotation>
      <xsd:documentation xml:lang="en"
        source="http://example.org/prod.html#product">
        <doc:description>This element represents a product.
        </doc:description>
      </xsd:documentation>
    </xsd:annotation>
  </xsd:element>
</xsd:schema>
```

Most general-purpose schema processors will then validate the extensions against the specified schema document. Remember, xsi:schemaLocation is just a hint to the processor, and not all processors take the xsi:schemaLocation hint.

Example 6–4 shows a schema that declares the description elements that were included in the annotation.

Example 6–4. A schema for user documentation

```
<xsd:schema xmlns:xsd="http://www.w3.org/2001/XMLSchema"
            xmlns="http://example.org/doc"
            targetNamespace="http://example.org/doc">
  <xsd:element name="description" type="TextType"/>
  <xsd:complexType name="TextType" mixed="true">
    <!--...-->
  </xsd:complexType>
</xsd:schema>
```

The schema does not include a new declaration of documentation itself. Rather, it contains global declarations for all elements that may be direct children of documentation.

6.1.5 *Non-native attributes*

In addition to annotations, all XSDL elements (except for documentation and appinfo) are permitted to have additional attributes. These attributes are known as non-native attributes, since they must be in a namespace other than the XML Schema Namespace. Example 6–5 shows an element declaration that has the non-native attribute description.

Example 6–5. Non-native attributes

```
<xsd:schema xmlns:xsd="http://www.w3.org/2001/XMLSchema"
            xmlns:doc="http://example.org/doc"
            xmlns:xsi="http://www.w3.org/2001/XMLSchema-instance"
            xsi:schemaLocation="http://example.org/doc doc.xsd">

  <xsd:element name="product" type="ProductType"
      doc:description="This element represents a product."/>

</xsd:schema>
```

As with appinfo and documentation contents, the non-native attributes are validated through a wildcard with lax validation. If attribute declarations can be found for the attributes, they will be validated, otherwise the processor will ignore them. In this case, the xsi:schemaLocation attribute points to a schema document for the additional attributes. Example 6–6 shows a schema that might be used to validate the non-native attributes.

Example 6–6. A schema for non-native attributes

```
<xsd:schema xmlns:xsd="http://www.w3.org/2001/XMLSchema"
            xmlns="http://example.org/doc"
            targetNamespace="http://example.org/doc">
  <xsd:attribute name="description" type="xsd:string"/>
</xsd:schema>
```

The schema does not include new declarations for XSDL elements. Rather, it contains global declarations of any non-native attributes.

6.1.6 Design hint: Should I use annotations or non-native attributes?

This is roughly the same as the general question of whether to use attributes or elements. Both can convey additional information, and both are made available to the application by the schema processor. Non-native attributes are less verbose, and perhaps more clear because they are closer to the definitions to which they apply. However, they have drawbacks: they cannot be used more than once in a particular element, they cannot be extended in the future, and they cannot contain other elements. For example, if you decide that you want the descriptions to be expressed in XHTML, this cannot be done if the description is an attribute. For more information on attributes vs. elements, see Section 8.1.1, "Design hint: Should I use attributes or elements?"

6.2 | User documentation

6.2.1 Types of user documentation

In the previous examples, we used very simplistic descriptions in the documentation elements. Generally, you will want to store more detailed and descriptive information than "This element represents a product." The types of user information that you might add to a schema include:

- Descriptive information about what the component means. The name and structure of a data type definition or element declaration can explain a lot, but they cannot impart all the semantics of the schema component.

- An explanation of why a component is structured in a particular way, or why certain XSDL mechanisms are used.

- Meta-meta-data such as copyright information, who is responsible for the schema component, its version, and when it was last changed.

- Internationalization and localization parameters, including language translations.

- Examples of valid instances.

The rest of this section provides some examples of user documentation.

6.2.2   *Data element definitions*

When creating reusable schema documents such as type libraries, it is helpful to have a complete definition of each component declared or defined in it. This ensures that schema authors are reusing the correct components, and allows you to automatically generate human-readable documentation about the components. Example 6–7 shows a schema document that includes a complete definition of a simple type CountryType in its documentation. The example is roughly based on ISO 11179, the ISO standard for the specification and standardization of data elements.

Example 6–7. ISO 11179-based type definition

```
<xsd:schema xmlns:xsd="http://www.w3.org/2001/XMLSchema"
            xmlns:doc="http://example.org/doc">

  <xsd:simpleType name="CountryType">
    <xsd:annotation>
      <xsd:documentation>
        <doc:name>Country identifier</doc:name>
        <doc:identifier>3166</doc:identifier>
        <doc:version>1990</doc:version>
        <doc:registrationAuthority>ISO
        </doc:registrationAuthority>
        <doc:definition>A code for the names of countries of the
          world.</doc:definition>
        <doc:keyword>geopolitical entity</doc:keyword>
        <doc:keyword>country</doc:keyword>
        <!--...-->
      </xsd:documentation>
    </xsd:annotation>
    <xsd:restriction base="xsd:token">
    <!--...-->
    </xsd:restriction>
  </xsd:simpleType>

</xsd:schema>
```

6.2.3   *Code documentation*

Another type of user documentation is code-control information such as when it was created and by whom, its version, and its dependencies. This is illustrated in Example 6–8. The element-type names used in the example are similar to the keywords in Javadocs.

6.2.4   *Section comments*

There is a reason that `schema` and `redefine` elements can have multiple annotations anywhere in their content. These annotations can be used to break a schema document into sections, and provide comments relating to that section. Example 6–9 shows annotations that serve as

Example 6–8. Code documentation

```
<xsd:schema xmlns:xsd="http://www.w3.org/2001/XMLSchema"
            xmlns:doc="http://example.org/doc">

  <xsd:simpleType name="CountryType">
    <xsd:annotation>
      <xsd:documentation>
        <doc:author>Priscilla Walmsley</doc:author>
        <doc:version>1.1</doc:version>
        <doc:since>1.0</doc:since>
        <doc:see>
          <doc:label>Country Code Listings</doc:label>
          <doc:link>http://example.org/countries.html</doc:link>
        </doc:see>
        <doc:deprecated>false</doc:deprecated>
      </xsd:documentation>
    </xsd:annotation>
    <xsd:restriction base="xsd:token">
    <!--...-->
    </xsd:restriction>
  </xsd:simpleType>

</xsd:schema>
```

Example 6–9. Section identifiers

```
<xsd:schema xmlns:xsd="http://www.w3.org/2001/XMLSchema">

  <xsd:annotation><xsd:documentation><sectionHeader>
    ********* Product-Related Element Declarations **************
  </sectionHeader></xsd:documentation></xsd:annotation>
  <xsd:element name="product" type="ProductType"/>
  <xsd:element name="size" type="SizeType"/>

  <xsd:annotation><xsd:documentation><sectionHeader>
    ********* Order-Related Element Declarations ***************
  </sectionHeader></xsd:documentation></xsd:annotation>
  <xsd:element name="order" type="OrderType"/>
  <xsd:element name="items" type="ItemsType"/>

</xsd:schema>
```

section comments. Although they are more verbose than regular XML comments (which are also permitted), they are more structured. This means that they can be used, for example, to generate XHTML documentation for the schema.

6.3 | Application information

6.3.1 *Types of application information*

There are a wide variety of use cases for adding application information to schemas. Some of the typical kinds of application information to include are:

- Extra validation rules, such as co-occurrence constraints. XSDL alone cannot express every constraint you might want to impose on your instances.

- Mappings to other structures, such as databases or EDI messages. These mappings are a flexible way to tell an application where to store or extract individual elements.

- Mapping to XHTML forms or other user input mechanisms. The mappings can include special presentation information for each data element, and translations of labels to other languages.

- Formatting information, such as a stylesheet fragment that can convert the instance element to XHTML, making it presentable to the user.

6.3.2 *Schematron for co-occurrence constraints*

XML Schema can be used to specify a wide variety of constraints on XML data. However, there are also many constraints that it cannot express. Example 6–10 shows an instance that represents simplified customer information.

Example 6–10. Instance with co-constraint

```
<customer newCustomer="false">
  <id>A123</id>
  <name>Priscilla Walmsley</name>
</customer>
```

The schema in Example 6–11 can be used to validate this instance. It can express the structure of the document, such as the fact that id and name elements must appear in that order, and that name is required.

Example 6–11. Schema without co-occurrence constraints

```
<xsd:schema xmlns:xsd="http://www.w3.org/2001/XMLSchema">

<xsd:complexType name="CustomerType">
  <xsd:sequence>
    <xsd:element name="id" type="xsd:string" minOccurs="0"/>
    <xsd:element name="name" type="xsd:string"/>
  </xsd:sequence>
  <xsd:attribute name="newCustomer" type="xsd:boolean"/>
</xsd:complexType>

<xsd:element name="customer" type="CustomerType"/>

</xsd:schema>
```

However, XML Schema does not currently support co-constraints, where one data item affects the validity of another. Suppose we want to enforce that if the value of the attribute, newCustomer, is false, there should always be an id child of customer. Conversely, if the value of newCustomer is true, no id child should be present. This constraint cannot be expressed in XSDL, but it can be expressed in Schematron, a language that was introduced in Section 1.4.5.2, "Schematron."

Example 6–12 shows an XSDL element declaration that contains a schema embedded in its appinfo. The Schematron extension validates the constraints described above.

Example 6–12. Schematron embedded in XSDL

```
<xsd:schema xmlns:xsd="http://www.w3.org/2001/XMLSchema"
            xmlns:sch="http://www.ascc.net/xml/schematron">

<xsd:complexType name="CustomerType">
  <xsd:sequence>
    <xsd:element name="id" type="xsd:string" minOccurs="0"/>
    <xsd:element name="name" type="xsd:string"/>
  </xsd:sequence>
  <xsd:attribute name="newCustomer" type="xsd:boolean"/>
</xsd:complexType>

<xsd:element name="customer" type="CustomerType">
  <xsd:annotation>
    <xsd:appinfo>
      <sch:schema>
        <sch:pattern name="customerIDs">
          <sch:rule context="customer[@newCustomer='false']">
            <sch:assert test="id">If not a new customer, should
              have an id.</sch:assert>
          </sch:rule>
          <sch:rule context="customer[id]">
            <sch:assert test="@newCustomer='false'">If has an
                id, should not be a new customer</sch:assert>
          </sch:rule>
        </sch:pattern>
      </sch:schema>
    </xsd:appinfo>
  </xsd:annotation>
</xsd:element>

</xsd:schema>
```

To use the Schematron extension, the schema needs to be pre-processed to extract the Schematron components and perform a separate validation. It is also possible to have two separate schemas for an instance, one in XSDL and one in Schematron. However, combining the two schema languages juxtaposes all the rules for customer elements, and encourages consistent maintenance.

6.3.3 *Schema adjunct framework for RDBMS mappings*

Suppose you are importing and exporting XML from a database and want to map the XML element types to database tables and columns. Adding these mappings to your schema is a way to flexibly process multiple types of XML documents. The application does not have to be hard-coded to a particular schema. It can process documents of different types by accepting these mappings as parameters from the schema.

Schema adjuncts are XML documents that can be used to provide additional information about schemas, such as the database mappings in this example. The Schema Adjunct Framework is a specification for defining a schema adjunct, which can be a separate document, or be embedded in a schema document itself.

Example 6–13 shows a schema adjunct embedded in an XSDL schema document. It uses the Schema Adjunct Framework and some custom database mapping elements to map XML element types to database tables and columns. Each of the `product` elements is mapped to a `PRODUCT_HEADER` table, while the `effDate` attributes and `name` children are mapped to columns.

You will notice that the elements describing the database mappings are in an `example.org` namespace, not in the SAF namespace. The Schema Adjunct Framework does not provide specific recommendations about how to model database mappings or any other kind of schema extensions. Rather, it is a generic framework for extending schemas. More information about the Schema Adjunct Framework can be found at `http://www.extensibility.com/saf`.

6.4 | Notations

Notations are used to indicate the format of non-XML data. For example, notations can be declared to indicate whether certain binary graphics data embedded in a `picture` element is in JPEG or GIF

Example 6–13. Schema Adjunct Framework in XSDL

```
<xsd:schema xmlns:xsd="http://www.w3.org/2001/XMLSchema"
            xmlns:saf="http://www.extensibility.com/namespaces/saf"
            xmlns:db="http://example.org/dbmap">

  <xsd:annotation>
    <xsd:appinfo>
      <saf:schema-adjunct target="prod.xsd">
        <saf:document>
          <db:server>155.210.0.5</db:server>
          <db:database>PROD_MASTER_DB</db:database>
        </saf:document>

        <saf:element context="product">
          <db:table>PRODUCT_HEADER</db:table>
        </saf:element>

        <saf:element context="product/name">
          <db:column>PROD_NAME</db:column>
        </saf:element>

        <saf:attribute context="product/@effDate">
          <db:column>PROD_EFF_DATE</db:column>
        </saf:attribute>
      </saf:schema-adjunct>
    </xsd:appinfo>
  </xsd:annotation>

  <xsd:element name="product" type="ProductType"/>
  <!--...-->
</xsd:schema>
```

format. Notations may describe data embedded in an XML instance, or data in external files that are linked to the instance through unparsed entities.

A notation may have a `system` or `public` identifier. There are no standard notation names or identifiers for well-known formats such as JPEG. Sometimes the identifier points to an application that can be used to process the format, for example `viewer.exe`, and other times it points to documentation about that format. Sometimes it is simply an abbreviation that can be interpreted by an application. Schema processors do not resolve these identifiers; it is up to the consuming application to process the notations as desired.

To indicate that a `picture` element contains JPEG data, it will generally have a notation attribute (for example, `fmt`) that indicates which notation applies. An element should only have one notation attribute.

Example 6–14 shows an instance that uses a notation. The `fmt` attribute contains the name of the notation that applies to the contents of `picture`.

Example 6–14. Using a notation in an instance

```
<picture fmt="jpeg">47494638396132003200F7FF00FFFFFFFFFFCCFFFF99FF
FF66FFFF33FFFF00FF</picture>
```

6.4.1 *Declaring a notation*

In XSDL, notations are declared using a `notation` element, whose syntax is shown in Table 6–4. Notations are always declared globally, with `schema` as their parent. Notations are named components whose qualified names must be unique among all notations in a schema. Like other named, global components, notations take on the target namespace of the schema document.

6.4.2 *Declaring a notation attribute*

As mentioned earlier, elements that contain data described by a notation have a notation attribute. This attribute has a type that restricts the type `NOTATION` by specifying one or more `enumeration` facets. Each of these enumeration values must match the name of a declared `notation`.

Example 6–15 shows two notation declarations that represent graphics formats. A simple type `PictureNotationType` is then defined, based on `NOTATION`, which enumerates the names of the

Table 6–4   XSDL syntax: notation

Name
`notation`

Parents
`schema`

Attribute name	Type	Required/default	Description
`id`	`ID`		unique ID
`name`	`NCName`	required	name of the notation
`public`	`token`	required	public identifier
`system`	`anyURI`		system identifier

Content
`annotation?`

Example 6–15. Declaring notations and notation attributes

```
<xsd:notation name="jpeg" public="JPG"/>
<xsd:notation name="gif" public="GIF"/>

<xsd:simpleType name="PictureNotationType">
  <xsd:restriction base="xsd:NOTATION">
    <xsd:enumeration value="jpeg"/>
    <xsd:enumeration value="gif"/>
  </xsd:restriction>
</xsd:simpleType>

<xsd:element name="picture">
  <xsd:complexType>
    <xsd:simpleContent>
      <xsd:extension base="xsd:hexBinary">
        <xsd:attribute name="fmt" type="PictureNotationType"/>
      </xsd:extension>
    </xsd:simpleContent>
  </xsd:complexType>
</xsd:element>
```

notations. Next, an element declaration for `picture` is provided which declares an attribute `fmt` of type `PictureNotationType`.

The values of NOTATION-based attributes are qualified names. This means that if the relevant notation is in a namespace, all references to it must be qualified. To be qualified they can either be prefixed, or in the scope of a default namespace declaration. In our example, if the schema document shown in Example 6–15 had a target namespace, and that namespace were mapped to a prefix `prod` in the instance, the attribute value would have to be prefixed, e.g. `<picture fmt="prod:jpeg">`.

Example 6–16. A notation with an unparsed entity

Schema:

```
<xsd:element name="picture">
  <xsd:complexType>
    <xsd:attribute name="location" type="xsd:ENTITY"/>
  </xsd:complexType>
</xsd:element>
<!--...-->
```

Instance:

```
<!DOCTYPE catalog [
<!NOTATION jpeg SYSTEM "JPG">
<!ENTITY prod557 SYSTEM "prod557.jpg" NDATA jpeg>
<!ENTITY prod563 SYSTEM "prod563.jpg" NDATA jpeg>
]>

<catalog>
  <product>
    <number>557</number>
    <picture location="prod557"/>
  </product>
  <product>
    <number>563</number>
    <picture location="prod563"/>
  </product>
</catalog>
```

6.4.3   *Notations and unparsed entities*

Example 6–15 showed the graphics data embedded directly in the XML as a binary data type. Notations can also be used to indicate the format of an unparsed general entity. Example 6–16 shows an XML document that lists products and links to pictures of those products. In the schema, `picture` is declared to have an attribute `location` that is of type `ENTITY`. In the instance, each value of the `location` attribute (in this case, `prod557` and `prod563`) matches the name of an entity declared in the internal DTD subset for the instance. The entity, in turn, refers to the notation via the `NDATA` parameter. In this case, the notation must appear in the internal DTD subset of the instance, in order for the entity to be able to reference it.

Element declarations

T his chapter covers the basic building blocks of XML:
elements. It explains how to use element declarations to
assign names and data types to elements. It also describes
element properties that can be set via element declarations,
such as default and fixed values, nillability, and qualified vs. unqualified
name forms.

7.1 | Global and local element declarations

Element declarations are used to assign element-type names and data
types to elements. In XSDL, this is accomplished using an `element`
element. Element declarations may be either global or local.

7.1.1 *Global element declarations*

Global element declarations appear at the top level of the schema
document, meaning that their parent must be `schema`. These global

Table 7–1   XSDL syntax: global element declaration

Name
element

Parents
schema

Attribute name	Type	Required/ default	Description
id	ID		unique ID
name	NCName	required	element-type name
type	QName		data type, see Section 7.2
default	string		default value, see Section 7.3.1
fixed	string		fixed value, see Section 7.3.2
nillable	boolean	false	whether xsi:nil can be used in the instance, see Section 7.4
abstract	boolean	false	whether the declaration can apply to an instance element (as opposed to being just the head of a substitution group), see Section 16.6.3
substitution-Group	QName		head of the substitution group to which it belongs, see Section 16.3

Table 7–1 XSDL syntax: global element declaration

Attribute name	Type	Required/ default	Description
block	`"#all"` | list of (`"substitution"` | `"extension"` | `"restriction"`)	defaults to `blockDefault` of `schema`	whether type and/or element substitutions should be blocked from the instance, see Section 14.7.3 for type substitutions, Section 16.6.2 for element substitutions
final	`"#all"` | list of (`"extension"` | `"restriction"`)	defaults to `finalDefault` of `schema`	whether the declaration can be the head of a substitution group, see Section 16.6.1

Content

`annotation?, (simpleType | complexType)?, (key | keyref | unique)*`

element declarations can then be used in multiple complex types, as described in Chapter 13, "Complex types." Table 7–1 shows the XSDL syntax for a global element declaration.

Example 7–1 shows two global element declarations: `name` and `size`. A complex type is then defined which references those element declarations by name using the `ref` attribute.

The qualified names used by global element declarations must be unique in the schema. This includes not just the schema document in which they are declared, but also any other schema documents that are used with it.

The name specified in an element declaration must be an XML non-colonized name, which means that it must start with a letter or

Example 7–1. Global element declarations

```
<xsd:schema xmlns:xsd="http://www.w3.org/2001/XMLSchema"
            xmlns="http://example.org/prod"
            targetNamespace="http://example.org/prod">

  <xsd:element name="name" type="xsd:string"/>
  <xsd:element name="size" type="xsd:integer"/>

  <xsd:complexType name="ProductType">
    <xsd:sequence>
      <xsd:element ref="name"/>
      <xsd:element ref="size" minOccurs="0"/>
    </xsd:sequence>
  </xsd:complexType>

</xsd:schema>
```

underscore, and may only contain letters, digits, underscores, hyphens, and periods. The qualified element-type name consists of the target namespace of the schema document, plus the local name in the declaration. In Example 7–1, the `name` and `size` element declarations use the target namespace `http://example.org/prod`.

Because element-type names are qualified by the target namespace of the schema document, it is not legal to include a namespace prefix in the value of the `name` attribute, as shown in Example 7–2. If you want your element declaration to apply to a different namespace, you must create a separate schema document with that target namespace and import it into the original schema document.

Example 7–2. Illegal attempt to prefix an element-type name

```
<xsd:schema xmlns:xsd="http://www.w3.org/2001/XMLSchema"
            xmlns:prod="http://example.org/prod"
            targetNamespace="http://example.org/prod">
  <xsd:element name="name" type="xsd:string"/>
  <xsd:element name="prod:size" type="xsd:integer"/>
</xsd:schema>
```

Occurrence constraints (`minOccurs` and `maxOccurs`) appear in an element reference rather than element declaration. This is because they are related to the appearance of a corresponding element in a content model, not to the element itself. Element references are covered in Section 13.4.2, "Element references."

7.1.2   *Local element declarations*

Local element declarations, on the other hand, appear entirely within a complex type definition. Local element declarations can only be used in that type definition, never referenced by other complex types or used in a substitution group. Table 7–2 shows the XSDL syntax for a local element declaration.

Example 7–3 shows two local element declarations, `size` and `color`, which appear entirely within the complex type definition.

Example 7–3. Local element declarations

```
<xsd:schema xmlns:xsd="http://www.w3.org/2001/XMLSchema"
            xmlns="http://example.org/prod"
            targetNamespace="http://example.org/prod">
  <xsd:complexType name="ProductType">
    <xsd:sequence>
      <xsd:element name="name" type="xsd:string"/>
      <xsd:element name="size" type="xsd:integer" minOccurs="0"/>
    </xsd:sequence>
  </xsd:complexType>
</xsd:schema>
```

Occurrence constraints (`minOccurs` and `maxOccurs`) can appear in local element declarations. Some attributes, namely `substitution-Group`, `final`, and `abstract`, are valid in global element declarations but not in local element declarations. This is because these attributes all relate to substitution groups, in which local element declarations cannot participate.

Table 7–2   XSDL syntax: local element declaration

Name
element

Parents
all, choice, sequence

Attribute name	Type	Required/default	Description
id	ID		unique ID
name	NCName	required	element-type name
form	"qualified" | "unqualified"	defaults to elementForm-Default of schema, which defaults to unqualified	whether the element-type name must be qualified in the instance, see Section 20.2
type	QName		data type, see Section 7.2
minOccurs	nonNegative-Integer	1	minimum number of times an element of this type may appear, see Section 13.4.2
maxOccurs	nonNegative-Integer | "unbounded"	1	maximum number of times an element of this type may appear, see Section 13.4.2
default	string		default value, see Section 7.3.1
fixed	string		fixed value, see Section 7.3.2
nillable	boolean	false	whether xsi:nil can be used in the instance, see Section 7.4

Table 7–2 XSDL syntax: local element declaration

Attribute name	Type	Required/default	Description
block	"#all" | list of ("extension" | "restriction")	defaults to blockDefault of schema	whether type substitutions should be blocked from the instance, see Section 14.7.3

Content
annotation?, (simpleType | complexType)?, (key | keyref | unique)*

The name specified in a local element declaration must also be an XML non-colonized name. If its form is qualified, it takes on the target namespace of the schema document. If it is unqualified, it is considered to be in no namespace. See Section 7.5, "Qualified vs. unqualified forms," for more information.

Names used in local element declarations are scoped to the complex type within which they are declared. You can have two completely different local element declarations with the same element-type name, as long as they are in different complex types. You can also have two local element declarations with the same element-type name in the same complex type, provided that they themselves have the same data type. This is explained further in Section 13.4.4, "Duplication of element-type names."

7.1.3 *Design hint: Should I use global or local element declarations?*

Use global element declarations if:

- The element declaration could ever apply to the root element during validation. Such declaration should be global so that the schema processor can access it.

- You want to use the exact same element declaration in more than one complex type.

- You want to use the element declaration in a substitution group. Local element declarations cannot participate in substitution groups (see Chapter 16, "Substitution groups").

Use local element declarations if:

- You want to allow unqualified element-type names in the instance. In this case, make all of the element declarations local except for the declaration of the root element type. If you mix global and local declarations, and you want the element-type names in local declarations to be unqualified, you will require your instance authors to know which element declarations are global and which are local. Global element-type names are always qualified in the instance (see Section 7.5, "Qualified vs. unqualified forms").

- You want to declare several element types with the same name but different data types or other properties. Using local declarations, you can have two element declarations for `size`: one that is a child of `shoe` has the data type `ShoeSizeType`, and one that is a child of `hat` has the data type `HatSizeType`. If the `size` declaration is global, it can only occur once, and therefore use only one data type, in that schema. The same holds true for default and fixed values, and nillability.

7.2 | Declaring the data types of elements

Regardless of whether they are local or global, all element declarations associate an element-type name with a data type, which may be either simple or complex. There are three ways to associate a data type with an element-type name in XSDL:

1. Reference a named data type by specifying the type attribute in the element declaration. This may be either a built-in type or a user-derived type.

2. Define an anonymous type by specifying either a simpleType or a complexType child.

3. Use no particular type, by specifying neither a type attribute nor a simpleType or complexType child. In this case, the actual data type of the declaration is anyType which allows any children and/or character data content, and any attributes, as long as it is well-formed XML.[1]

Example 7–4 shows four element declarations with different data type assignment methods.

Example 7–4. Declaring the data types of elements

```
<xsd:element name="size" type="SizeType"/>

<xsd:element name="name" type="xsd:string"/>

<xsd:element name="product">
  <xsd:complexType>
    <xsd:sequence>
      <xsd:element ref="name"/>
      <xsd:element ref="size"/>
    </xsd:sequence>
  </xsd:complexType>
</xsd:element>

<xsd:element name="anything"/>
```

The first example uses the type attribute to indicate SizeType as the data type of size. The second example also uses the type attribute, this time to assign a built-in type string to name. The xsd prefix is

---

1. Unless it is in a substitution group, as described in Chapter 16, "Substitution groups."

used because built-in types are part of the XML Schema Namespace. For a complete explanation of the use of prefixes in schema documents, see Chapter 3, "Namespaces."

The third example uses an in-line anonymous complex type, which is defined entirely within the `product` declaration. Finally, the fourth element declaration, `anything`, does not specify a particular data type, which means that a corresponding element can have any well-formed content and any attributes in the instance.

For detailed discussion of using named or anonymous data types see Section 9.2.3, "Design hint: Should I use named or anonymous types?"

7.3 | Default and fixed values

Default and fixed values are used to augment an instance by adding values to empty elements. The schema processor will insert a default or fixed value if the element in question is empty. If the element is absent from the instance, it will not be inserted. This is different from the treatment of default and fixed values for attributes.

In XSDL, default and fixed values are specified by the `default` and `fixed` attributes, respectively. Only one of the two attributes (`default` or `fixed`) may appear; they are mutually exclusive. Default and fixed values can be specified in element declarations with:

- simple types,
- complex types with simple content,
- complex types with mixed content, if all children are optional.

The default or fixed value must be valid for the data type of that element declaration. For example, it is not legal to specify a default value of `xyz` if the data type of the element is `integer`.[1]

---

1. This is not considered an error in the schema, but any instance that relied on the value would be in error.

The specification of fixed and default values in element declarations is independent of their occurrence constraints (`minOccurs` and `max-Occurs`). Unlike defaulted attributes, defaulted element declarations or references may be required (i.e., `minOccurs` may be more than 0). If an element declaration or reference with a default value is required, a corresponding element still may appear empty and have its default value filled in.

7.3.1 Default values

The default value is filled in if the element is empty. Example 7–5 shows the declaration of `product` with two children, `name` and `size`, that have default values specified.

Example 7–5. Specifying an element default value

```
<xsd:element name="product">
  <xsd:complexType>
    <xsd:choice minOccurs="0" maxOccurs="unbounded">
      <xsd:element name="name" type="xsd:string" default="N/A"/>
      <xsd:element name="size" type="xsd:integer" default="12"/>
    </xsd:choice>
  </xsd:complexType>
</xsd:element>
```

It is important to note that the definition of "empty" varies based on the data type in an element declaration. Certain data types allow an empty value. This includes `string`, `normalizedString`, `token`, and any types derived from them that allow the empty string as a value. Additionally, unrestricted list types allow empty values. For any type that allows an empty string value, the element will never be considered empty and the default value will *never be filled in*. On the other hand, an empty element with an `integer` data type is considered empty, and the default value is added. Additionally, if an element has the `xsi:nil` attribute set to `true`, its default value is not inserted.

Table 7–3 describes how element default values are inserted in different situations, based on the declaration in Example 7–5. The default value (N/A) for `name` is never filled in, because `name` is of type `string`. You may be surprised by the fourth example, where whitespace is replaced by the default value. This is because the `whiteSpace` facet value for `integer` is `collapse`, and whitespace handling happens *before* default processing.

Table 7–3   Default value behavior for elements

Situation	*Result*	*Before example*	*After example*
value specified	original value kept	`<size>10</size>`	`<size>10</size>`
empty element (`integer`)	value filled in	`<size/>` `<size></size>`	`<size>12</size>` `<size>12</size>`
empty element (`string`)	no value filled in	`<name/>` `<name></name>`	`<name/>` `<name></name>`
value is just whitespace (`integer`)	whitespace collapsed, value filled in	`<size> </size>`	`<size>12</size>`
value is just whitespace (`string`)	whitespace preserved, no value filled in	`<name> </name>`	`<name> </name>`
element is nil	no value filled in	`<size xsi:nil="true"/>`	`<size xsi:nil="true"/>`
element does not appear	no element added	`<product/>`	`<product/>`

If you do want to allow default values to work with string-based types, you must define a new type that does not allow the empty string as a value. Such a type is shown in Example 7–6. It is based on the token data type so that whitespace will be collapsed. With this definition, an empty (or whitespace-only) name element will be replaced by the default value.

Example 7–6. A default value with a string type

```xsd
<xsd:element name="name" default="N/A">
  <xsd:simpleType>
    <xsd:restriction base="xsd:token">
      <xsd:minLength value="1"/>
    </xsd:restriction>
  </xsd:simpleType>
</xsd:element>
```

7.3.2   *Fixed values*

Fixed values are added in all the same situations as default values. The only difference is that if the element has a value, its value must be equivalent to the fixed value. When the schema processor determines whether the value of the element is in fact equivalent to the fixed value, it takes into account the element's data type.

Table 7–4 shows some valid and invalid instances for element declarations with fixed value specifications. The size element has the data type integer, so all forms of the integer 1 are accepted in the instance, including 01, +1, and 1 surrounded by whitespace. The whitespace is acceptable because the whiteSpace facet value for integer is collapse, meaning that whitespace is stripped before validation takes place.

The name element, on the other hand, has the data type string. The string "01" is invalid because it is not considered to be equal to the string "1". The string " 1 " is also invalid because the whiteSpace facet value for string is preserve, meaning that the leading and trailing spaces are kept. For more information on type equality, see Section 12.7, "Type equality."

An empty element is acceptable for elements with data type integer because the value is considered missing. Empty elements with data type

Table 7–4   Elements instances with fixed values

Schema

```
<xsd:element name="name" type="xsd:string" fixed="1"/>
<xsd:element name="size" type="xsd:integer" fixed="1"/>
```

Valid instances	*Invalid instances*
`<size>1</size>`	`<size>2</size>`
`<size>01</size>`	`<name>01</name>`
`<size>+1</size>`	`<name>+1</name>`
`<size> 1 </size>`	`<name> 1 </name>`
`<size/>`	`<name/>`
`<size></size>`	`<name></name>`
`<size> </size>`	`<name> </name>`
`<name>1</name>`	`<name>2</name>`

`string`, however, are not acceptable because the empty string is considered a value, one that is not equal to "`1`".

7.4 | Nils and nillability

In some cases, an element may be either absent from an instance or empty (contain no value). For example, the instance shown in Example 7–7 is a purchase order with some absent and empty elements.

There are many possible reasons for an element value to be missing from an instance:

- The information is not applicable: Umbrellas do not come in different sizes.
- We do not know whether the information is applicable: We do not know whether the customer has a middle name.
- It is not relevant to this particular application of the data: The billing application does not care about product sizes.

Example 7–7. Missing values

```
<order>
  <giftWrap>ADULT BDAY</giftWrap>
  <customer>
    <name>
      <first>Priscilla</first>
      <middle/>
      <last>Walmsley</last>
    </name>
  </customer>
  <items>
    <shirt xsi:type="ProductType">
      <giftWrap/>
      <number>557</number>
      <name>Short-Sleeved Linen Blouse</name>
      <size></size>
    </shirt>
    <umbrella xsi:type="ProductType">
      <number>443</number>
      <name>Deluxe Golf Umbrella</name>
      <size></size>
    </umbrella>
  </items>
</order>
```

- It is the default, so it is not specified: The customer's title should default to "Mr."
- It actually is present and the value is an empty string: The gift wrap value for the shirt is empty, meaning "none", which should override the gift wrap value of the order.
- It is erroneously missing because of a user error or technical bug: We should have a size for the shirt.

Different applications treat missing values in different ways. One application might treat an absent element as not applicable, and an empty element as an error. Another might treat an empty element as not applicable, and an absent element as an error. The treatment of missing values may vary from one element type to another. In our example, we used a combination of absent and empty elements to signify different reasons for missing values.

XML Schema offers a third method of indicating a missing value: *nils*. By marking an element as nil, you are telling the processor "I know this element is empty, but I want it to be valid anyway." The actual reason why it is empty, or what the application should do with it, is entirely up to you. XML Schema does not associate any particular semantics with this absence. It only offers an additional way to express a missing value, with the following benefits:

- You do not have to weaken the data type by allowing empty content and/or making attributes optional.

- You are making a deliberate statement that the information does not exist. This is a clearer message than simply omitting the component declaration, which means that we do not know if it exists.

- If for some reason an application is relying on that element or attribute being there, for example as a placeholder, nil provides a way for it to exist without imparting any additional information.

- You can easily turn off default value processing. Default values for the element will not be added if it is marked as nil.

An approach for our purchase order document is outlined below. It uses nils, derived types, simple type restrictions and default values to better constrain missing values. The resulting instance is shown in Example 7–8.

- The information is not applicable: Give `shirt` and `umbrella` different data types, and do not include the `size` element declaration in `UmbrellaType`.

- We do not know whether the information is applicable: Make `middle` nillable and set `xsi:nil` to `true` if it is not present.

- It is not relevant to this particular application of the data: Give the billing application a separate schema document and insert

Example 7–8. Missing values, revisited

```
<order xmlns:xsi="http://www.w3.org/2001/XMLSchema-instance">
  <giftWrap>ADULT BDAY</giftWrap>
  <customer>
    <name>
      <title/>                  <!--default will be filled in-->
      <first>Priscilla</first>
      <middle xsi:nil="true"/>
      <last>Walmsley</last>
    </name>
  </customer>
  <items>
    <shirt xsi:type="ShirtType">
      <giftWrap/>
      <number>557</number>
      <name>Short-Sleeved Linen Blouse</name>
      <size></size>                    <!--INVALID! -->
    </shirt>
    <umbrella xsi:type="UmbrellaType">
      <number>443</number>
      <name>Deluxe Golf Umbrella</name>
    </umbrella>
  </items>
</order>
```

a wildcard where the `size` and other optional element declarations or references may appear.

- It is the default, so it is not specified: Specify a default value of "Mr." for `title`.

- It actually is present and the value is an empty string: Allow `giftWrap` to appear empty.

- It is erroneously missing because of a user error or technical bug: Make `size` required, make it an `integer` or other type that does not accept empty values.

This is one of many reasonable approaches for handling absent values. The important thing is to define a strategy that provides all the information your application needs, and ensures that all errors are caught.

7.4.1   Using xsi:nil in an instance

To indicate that the value of an instance element is nil, specify the xsi:nil attribute in the tag of that element. Example 7–9 shows four instances of size that use the xsi:nil attribute. The xsi:nil attribute applies to the element in whose tag it appears, not any of the attributes. There is no way to specify that an attribute value is nil.

The xsi:nil attribute is in the XML Schema Instance Namespace (http://www.w3.org/2001/XMLSchema-instance). This namespace must be declared in the instance, but it is not necessary to specify a schema location for it. Any schema processor will recognize the xsi:nil attribute of any XML element.

Example 7–9. xsi:nil in instance elements

```
<size xsi:nil="true"/>
<size xsi:nil="true"></size>
<size xsi:nil="true" system="US-DRESS"/>
<size xsi:nil="false">10</size>
<size xsi:nil="true">10</size> <!--INVALID! -->
```

If the xsi:nil attribute appears in the start-tag of an element, that element must be empty. It cannot contain any child elements or character data, even if its type requires content. The last instance of the size element in Example 7–9 is invalid because xsi:nil is true and it contains data. However, it is valid for a nil element to have other attributes, as long as they are declared for that type.

7.4.2   Making elements nillable

In order to allow an element to appear in the instance with the xsi:nil attribute, its element type must be *nillable*. In XSDL, nillability is indicated by setting the nillable attribute in the element declaration to true. Example 7–10 shows an element declaration illustrating this.

Example 7–10. Making `size` elements nillable

```
<xsd:element name="size" type="xsd:integer" nillable="true"/>
```

Declaring an element type as nillable allows elements to exhibit the `xsi:nil` attribute. Absent such a declaration, the `xsi:nil` attribute cannot appear, even with its value set to `false`. It is not necessary (or even legal) to separately declare the `xsi:nil` attribute for the data type used in the element declaration. In Example 7–10, we gave `size` a simple type. Normally this would mean that it cannot have attributes, but the `xsi:nil` attribute is given special treatment. Nillability can be specified in an element declaration even when the data type is a simple type.

If `nillable` is set to `true`, a fixed value may not be specified in the declaration.[1] However, it is legal to specify a default value. If an element has an `xsi:nil` set to `true`, the default value is not filled in, even though the element is empty.

Elements should not be declared nillable if they will ever be used as fields in an identity constraint, such as a key or a uniqueness constraint. See Section 17.7.2, "Fields," for more information on identity constraint fields.

7.5 | Qualified vs. unqualified forms

Many instances include elements from more than one namespace. This can potentially result in instances with a large number of different prefixes, one for each namespace. However, when an element declaration is local — that is, when it isn't at the top level of a schema document — you have the choice of using either qualified or unqualified element-type names in instances.

---

1. This would be considered an error in the instance, not the schema.

In XSDL, this is indicated by the `form` attribute, which may be set to `qualified` or `unqualified`. If the `form` attribute is not present in a local element declaration, the value defaults to the value of the `elementFormDefault` attribute of the schema document. If neither attribute is present, the default is `unqualified`. The `form` attribute only applies to local element declarations. Instance elements conforming to global element declarations (i.e. those at the top level of the schema document) must always have qualified element-type names.

The issue of whether to use qualified or unqualified local element-type names is covered in detail in Section 20.2, "Qualified vs. unqualified names."

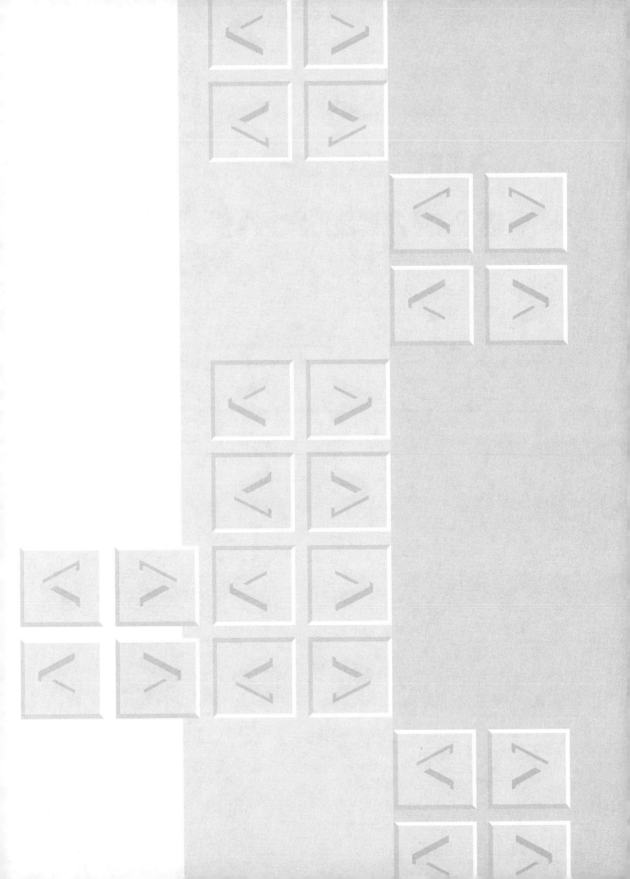

Attribute
declarations

T his chapter covers the other basic building block of XML: attributes. It explains how to declare attributes and assign types to them. It also describes fixed and default values as they apply to attributes.

8.1 | Global and local attribute declarations

Attribute declarations are used to name an attribute and associate it with a particular simple type. In XSDL, this is accomplished using an `attribute` element. Attribute declarations may be either global or local.

8.1.1 *Design hint: Should I use attributes or elements?*

Whether to model data values as elements or attributes is an often-discussed question. XML Schema, with its ability to define data types for elements, eliminates many of the advantages of attributes in XML 1.0. The advantages of using attributes are:

- They are less verbose.
- If you plan to validate using DTDs as well as schemas, you can perform some minimal type checking on attribute values. For example, color can be constrained to a certain set of values. Element character data content cannot be validated using DTDs.
- Attributes can be added to the instance by specifying default values; elements cannot (they must appear to receive a default value).

The advantages of using elements are:

- They are more extensible because attributes can later be added to them without affecting a processing application. For example, if you realized that you needed to keep track of what currency a price is expressed in, you can declare a currency attribute in the price element declaration. If price is an attribute, this is not possible.
- They can contain other elements. For example, if you want to express a textual description using XHTML tags, this is not possible if description is an attribute.
- They can be repeated. An element may only appear once now, but later you may wish to extend it to appear multiple times. For example, if you decide later that a product can have multiple colors, you can allow a color child to appear more than once. Attributes may only appear once per element.

- You have more control over the rules of their appearance. For example, you can say that a `product` can either have a `number` or a `productCode` child. This is not possible for attributes.
- They can be used in substitution groups.
- They can be given nil values.
- They can use type substitution to substitute derived types in the instance.
- Their order is significant, while the order of attributes is not. Obviously, this is only an advantage if you care about the order.
- When the values are lengthy, elements tend to be more readable than attributes.

As you can see, there are many more advantages to using elements than attributes, but attributes are useful in some cases. A general recommendation is to use attributes for meta data and elements for data. For example, use an attribute to describe the units, language, or time-dependence of an element value. Additionally, attributes should be used for `ID` and `IDREF` values, and XLink expressions. Elements should be used for everything else.

8.1.2 *Global attribute declarations*

Global attribute declarations appear at the top level of the schema document, meaning that their parent must be the `schema` element. These globally declared attributes can then be used in multiple complex types, as described in Chapter 13, "Complex types." Table 8–1 shows the XSDL syntax for a global attribute declaration.

Example 8–1 shows the global declarations of two attributes: `system` and `dim`. A complex type is then defined which references those attributes by name using the `ref` attribute.

The qualified names of globally declared attributes must be unique in the schema. This includes not just the schema document in which it is declared, but also any other schema documents that are used with it.

Table 8–1   XSDL syntax: global attribute declaration

Name
attribute

Parents
schema

Attribute name	Type	Required/default	Description
id	ID		unique ID
name	NCName	required	unique name
type	QName		data type, see Section 8.2
default	string		default value, see Section 8.3.1
fixed	string		fixed value, see Section 8.3.2

Content
annotation?, simpleType?

Example 8–1. Global attribute declarations

```
<xsd:schema xmlns:xsd="http://www.w3.org/2001/XMLSchema"
            xmlns="http://example.org/prod"
            targetNamespace="http://example.org/prod">

  <xsd:attribute name="system" type="xsd:string"/>
  <xsd:attribute name="dim" type="xsd:integer"/>

  <xsd:complexType name="SizeType">
    <xsd:attribute ref="system" use="required"/>
    <xsd:attribute ref="dim"/>
  </xsd:complexType>

</xsd:schema>
```

The use attribute, which indicates whether an attribute is required or optional, appears in the attribute reference rather than the attribute declaration. This is because it is related to the appearance of that attribute in a complex type, not the attribute itself. Attribute references are covered in Chapter 13, "Complex types."

The name specified in an attribute declaration must be an XML non-colonized name, which means that it must start with a letter or under-score, and may only contain letters, digits, underscores, hyphens and periods. The qualified name of a globally declared attribute consists of the target namespace of the schema document plus the local name in the declaration. In Example 8–1, the system and dim attributes take on the target namespace http://example.org/prod.

Since global attribute names are qualified by the target namespace of the schema document, it is not legal to include a namespace prefix in the value of the name attribute. If you want to declare attributes in another namespace, you must create a separate schema document with that namespace as target and import it into the original schema document. If you simply want to specify an attribute from another namespace, such as xml:lang, use the ref attribute to reference it in a complex type.

8.1.3 *Local attribute declarations*

Local attribute declarations, on the other hand, appear entirely within a complex type definition. They may only be used in that type definition, and are never reused by other types. Table 8–2 shows the XSDL syntax for a local attribute declaration.

Example 8–2 shows the local declarations of two attributes, system and dim, which appear entirely within the complex type definition.

The name specified in a local attribute declaration must also be an XML non-colonized name. If its form is qualified, it takes on the target namespace of the schema document. If it is unqualified, it is considered to be in no namespace. See Section 8.4, "Qualified vs. unqualified forms," for more information on qualified vs. unqualified attribute names.

Locally declared attribute names are scoped to the complex type in which they are declared. It is illegal to have two attributes with the

Table 8–2   XSDL syntax: local attribute declaration

Name
`attribute`

Parents
`complexType, restriction, extension, attributeGroup`

Attribute name	*Type*	*Required/default*	*Description*
`id`	`ID`		unique ID
`name`	`NCName`	required	unique name
`type`	`QName`		simple type, see Section 8.2
`form`	`"qualified"` | `"unqualified"`	defaults to `attributeForm-Default` of `schema`, which defaults to "`unqualified`"	whether the attribute name must be qualified in the instance, see Section 8.4
`use`	`"optional"` | `"prohibited"` | `"required"`	optional	whether it is required or optional, see Section 13.6.2
`default`	`string`		default value, see Section 8.3.1
`fixed`	`string`		fixed value, see Section 8.3.2

Content
`annotation?, simpleType?`

same qualified name in the same complex type definition. This is explained further in Section 13.6, "Using attributes."

Example 8–2. Local attribute declarations

```
<xsd:schema xmlns:xsd="http://www.w3.org/2001/XMLSchema"
            xmlns="http://example.org/prod"
            targetNamespace="http://example.org/prod">

  <xsd:complexType name="SizeType">
    <xsd:attribute name="system" type="xsd:string" use="required"/>
    <xsd:attribute name="dim" type="xsd:integer"/>
  </xsd:complexType>

</xsd:schema>
```

8.1.4 *Design hint: Should I declare attributes globally or locally?*

Global attribute declarations are discouraged unless the attribute is used in a variety of element declarations which are in a variety of namespaces. This is because globally declared attribute names must be prefixed in instances, resulting in an instance element that looks like this:

```
<prod:size prod:system="US-DRESS" prod:dim="1"/>
```

Prefixing every attribute is not what users generally expect, and it adds a lot of extra text without any additional meaning.

Two examples of global attributes are the `xml:lang` attribute that is part of XML 1.0, and the `xsi:type` attribute in XSDL. Virtually any element in any namespace may have these two attributes, so in this case it is desirable to distinguish them by their namespace.

If you are tempted to declare an attribute globally because you want to be able to reuse it multiple times, consider these two alternatives:

- Put it into an attribute group. This makes it effectively a local attribute declaration, while still allowing you to reuse it.
- Declare it locally, but give it a named simple type that can be reused by multiple local attribute declarations.

8.2 | Assigning types to attributes

Regardless of whether they are local or global, all attribute declarations assign a simple type to an attribute. All attributes have simple types rather than complex types, which make sense since they cannot themselves have child elements or attributes. There are three ways to assign a simple type to an attribute in XSDL:

1. Assign a named simple type by specifying the `type` attribute in the attribute declaration. This may be either a built-in type or a user-derived type.

2. Assign an anonymous type by specifying a `simpleType` child.

3. Assign no particular type, by specifying neither a `type` attribute nor a `simpleType` child. In this case, the attribute has the type `anySimpleType`, which may have any value, so long as it is well-formed XML.

Example 8–3 shows four attribute declarations with different type assignment methods.

Example 8–3. Assigning types to attributes

```
<xsd:attribute name="color" type="ColorType"/>

<xsd:attribute name="dim" type="xsd:integer"/>

<xsd:attribute name="system">
  <xsd:simpleType>
    <xsd:restriction base="xsd:string">
      <xsd:enumeration value="US-DRESS"/>
      <!--...-->
    </xsd:restriction>
  </xsd:simpleType>
</xsd:attribute>

<xsd:attribute name="anything"/>
```

The first example uses the `type` attribute to assign `ColorType` to the attribute `color`. The second example also uses the `type` attribute, this time to assign the built-in type `xsd:integer` to the attribute `dim`. The `xsd` prefix is used because the built-in types are part of the XML Schema Namespace. For a complete explanation of the use of prefixes in schema documents, see Chapter 3, "Namespaces."

The third example uses an in-line anonymous simple type, which is defined entirely within the `system` attribute declaration. Finally, the fourth attribute, `anything`, does not specify a particular type, which means that any value is valid.

For detailed discussion of using named or anonymous types see Section 9.2.3, "Design hint: Should I use named or anonymous types?"

8.3 | Default and fixed values

Default and fixed values are used to augment an instance by adding attributes when they are not present. If an attribute is absent, and a default or fixed value is specified in its declaration, the schema processor will insert the attribute and give it the default or fixed value.

In XSDL, default and fixed values are specified by the `default` and `fixed` attributes, respectively. Only one of the two attributes (`default` or `fixed`) may appear; they are mutually exclusive. If an attribute has a default value specified, it cannot be a required attribute. This makes sense, because if the attribute is required, it will always appear in the instance, and the default value will never be used.

The default or fixed value must be valid for the type of that attribute. For example, it is not legal to specify a default value of `xyz` if the type of the attribute is `integer`. This is not considered an error in the schema, but any instance that relied on the value would be in error.

8.3.1 *Default values*

A default value is filled in if the attribute is absent from the element. If the attribute appears, with any value, it is left alone. Example 8–4 shows the declaration of `size` with one attribute, `dim`, that has a default value specified.

Example 8–4. Declaring a default value for an attribute

```
<xsd:element name="size">
  <xsd:complexType>
    <xsd:attribute name="dim" type="xsd:integer" default="1"/>
  </xsd:complexType>
</xsd:element>
```

Table 8–3 describes how attribute default values are inserted in different situations, based on the declaration in Example 8–4. Note that the only time the default value is inserted is when the attribute is absent. If the attribute's value is the empty string, it is left as is, even though this is not a valid value for the `integer` data type. This is different from the behavior of default values for elements, as described in Section 7.3.1, "Default values."

Table 8–3   Default value behavior for attributes

Situation	Result	Before example	After example
attribute is absent	attribute is added with default value	`<size/>`	`<size dim="1"/>`
attribute appears with a value	original value is kept	`<size dim="2"/>`	`<size dim="2"/>`
attribute appears with empty string as its value	empty string is kept	`<size dim=""/>`	`<size dim=""/>`

8.3.2 *Fixed values*

Fixed values are inserted in all the same situations as default values. The only difference is that if the attribute appears, its value must be equal to the fixed value. When the schema processor determines whether the value of the attribute is in fact equal to the fixed value, it takes into account the attribute's type.

Table 8–4 shows some valid and invalid instances for attributes declared with fixed values. The `dim` attribute has the type `integer`, so all forms of the integer 1 are accepted in the instance, including "01", "+1", and " 1 " surrounded by whitespace. The whitespace is acceptable because the `whiteSpace` facet value for `integer` is `collapse`, meaning that leading and trailing whitespace is stripped before validation takes place.

The `system` attribute, on the other hand, has the type `string`. The string "01" is invalid because it is not considered to be equal to the string "1". The string " 1 " is also invalid because the `whiteSpace` facet value for `string` is preserve, meaning that the leading and trailing spaces are kept. For more information on type equality, please see Section 12.7, "Type equality."

Table 8–4 Instances of attributes with fixed values

Schema

```
<xsd:element name="size">
  <xsd:complexType>
    <xsd:attribute name="system" type="xsd:string" fixed="1"/>
    <xsd:attribute name="dim" type="xsd:integer" fixed="1"/>
  </xsd:complexType>
</xsd:element>
```

Valid instances	*Invalid instances*
`<size system="1" dim="1"/>`	`<size system="3" dim="3"/>`
`<size/>`	`<size dim=""/>`
`<size dim="01"/>`	`<size system="01"/>`
`<size dim="+1"/>`	`<size system="+1"/>`
`<size dim=" 1 "/>`	`<size system=" 1 "/>`
	`<size system=""/>`

8.4 | Qualified vs. unqualified forms

XML Schema allows you to exert some control over whether to have namespace-qualified or unqualified attribute names in the instance. Since default namespace declarations do not apply to attributes, this is essentially a question of whether you want the attribute names to be prefixed or unprefixed.

In XSDL, this is indicated by the `form` attribute, which may be set to `qualified` or `unqualified`. If the `form` attribute is not present in a local attribute declaration, the value defaults to the value of the `attributeFormDefault` attribute of the `schema` element. If neither attribute is present, the default is `unqualified`. The `form` attribute only applies to locally declared attributes. If an attribute is declared globally (at the top level of the schema document), it must always be qualified in the instance.

The issue of whether to use qualified or unqualified local attribute names is covered in detail in Section 20.2.7, "Qualified vs. unqualified attribute names."

Simple types

Chapter

9

 oth element and attribute declarations can use simple types to describe the data content of the components. This chapter introduces simple types, and explains how to define your own atomic simple types for use in your schemas.

9.1 | Simple type varieties

There are three varieties of simple type: atomic types, list types, and union types.

1. *Atomic types* have values that are indivisible, such as 10 and large.

2. *List types* have values that are whitespace-separated lists of atomic values, such as `<availableSizes>10 large 2</availableSizes>`.

3. *Union types* may have values that are either atomic values or list values. What differentiates them is that the set of valid values,

or "value space," for the type is the union of the value spaces of two or more other simple types. For example, to represent a dress size, you may define a union type that allows a value to be either an integer from 2 through 18, or one of the string values `small`, `medium`, or `large`.

List and union types are covered in Chapter 11, "Union and list types."

9.1.1   *Design hint: How much should I break down my data values?*

Data values should be broken down to the most atomic level possible. This allows them to be processed in a variety of ways for different uses, such as display, mathematical operations, and validation. It is much easier to concatenate two data values back together than it is to split them apart. In addition, more granular data is much easier to validate.

It is a fairly common practice to put a data value and its units in the same element, for example `<length>3cm</length>`. However, the preferred approach is to have a separate data value, preferably an attribute, for the units, for example `<length units="cm">3</length>`.

Using a single concatenated value is limiting because:

- It is extremely cumbersome to validate. You have to apply a complicated pattern that would need to change every time a unit type is added.

- You cannot perform comparisons, conversions, or mathematical operations on the data without splitting it apart.

- If you want to display the data item differently (for example, as "3 centimeters" or "3 cm" or just "3", you have to split it apart. This complicates the stylesheets and applications that process the instance document.

It is possible to go too far, though. For example, you may break a date down as follows:

```
<orderDate>
  <year>2001</year>
  <month>06</month>
  <day>15</day>
</orderDate>
```

This is probably an overkill unless you have a special need to process these items separately.

9.2 | Simple type definitions

9.2.1 *Named simple types*

Simple types can be either named or anonymous. Named simple types are always defined globally (i.e., their parent is always schema or redefine) and are required to have a name that is unique among the data types (both simple and complex) in the schema. The XSDL syntax for a named simple type definition is shown in Table 9–1.

The name of a simple type must be an XML non-colonized name, which means that it must start with a letter or underscore, and may only contain letters, digits, underscores, hyphens, and periods. You cannot include a namespace prefix when defining the type; it takes its namespace from the target namespace of the schema document.

All of the examples of named types in this book have the word "Type" at the end of their names, to clearly distinguish them from element-type names and attribute names. However, this is not a requirement; you may in fact have a data type definition and an element declaration using the same name.

Example 9–1 shows the definition of a named simple type Dress-SizeType, along with an element declaration that references it. Named types can be used in multiple element and attribute declarations.

Table 9–1   XSDL syntax: named simple type definition

Name
`simpleType`

Parents
`schema, redefine`

Attribute name	Type	Required/ default	Description
`id`	`ID`		unique ID
`name`	`NCName`	required	simple type name
`final`	`"#all"` | list of (`"extension"` | `"restriction"` | `"list"` | `"union"`)	defaults to `finalDefault` of `schema`	whether other types can be derived from this one, see Section 9.5

Content
`annotation?, (restriction | list | union)`

Example 9–1. Defining and referencing a named simple type

```
<xsd:simpleType name="DressSizeType">
  <xsd:restriction base="xsd:integer">
    <xsd:minInclusive value="2"/>
    <xsd:maxInclusive value="18"/>
  </xsd:restriction>
</xsd:simpleType>

<xsd:element name="size" type="DressSizeType"/>
```

9.2.2   *Anonymous simple types*

Anonymous types, on the other hand, must not have names. They are always defined entirely within an element or attribute declaration, and may only be used once, by that declaration. Defining a type anonymously prevents it from ever being restricted, used in a list or union, or redefined. The XSDL syntax to define an anonymous simple type is shown in Table 9–2.

Table 9–2 XSDL syntax: anonymous simple type definition

Name			
simpleType			

Parents			
element, attribute, restriction, list, union			

Attribute name	Type	Required/default	Description
id	ID		unique ID

Content			
annotation?, (restriction | list | union)			

Example 9–2 shows the definition of an anonymous simple type within an element declaration.

Example 9–2. Defining an anonymous simple type

```
<xsd:element name="size">
  <xsd:simpleType>
    <xsd:restriction base="xsd:integer">
      <xsd:minInclusive value="2"/>
      <xsd:maxInclusive value="18"/>
    </xsd:restriction>
  </xsd:simpleType>
</xsd:element>
```

9.2.3 *Design hint: Should I use named or anonymous types?*

The advantage of named types is that they may be defined once and used many times. For example, you may define a type named Product-CodeType that lists all of the valid product codes in your organization.

This type can then be used in many element and attribute declarations in many schemas. This has the advantages of:

- encouraging consistency throughout the organization,
- reducing the possibility of error,
- requiring less time to define new schemas,
- simplifying maintenance, because new product codes need only be added in one place.

Named types can also make the schema more readable, when the type definitions are complex.

An anonymous type, on the other hand, can be used only in the element or attribute declaration that contains it. It can never be redefined, have types derived from it, or be used in a list or union type. This can seriously limit its reusability, extensibility, and ability to change over time.

However, there are cases where anonymous types are preferable to named types. If the type is unlikely to ever be reused, the advantages listed above no longer apply. Also, there is such a thing as too much reuse. For example, if an element can contain the values 1 through 10, it does not make sense to try to define a data type named OneToTen-Type that is reused by other unrelated element declarations with the same value space. If the value space for one of the element declarations that uses the named data type changes, but the other element declarations do not change, it actually makes maintenance more difficult, because a new data type needs to be defined at that time.

In addition, anonymous types can be more readable when they are relatively simple. It is sometimes desirable to have the definition of the data type right there with the element or attribute declaration.

9.3 | Simple type restrictions

Every simple type is a restriction of another simple type, known as its base type. It is not possible to extend a simple type, except to add attributes, which results in a complex type. This is described in Section 14.4.1, "Simple content extensions."

Every new simple type restricts the value space of its base type in some way. Example 9–3 shows a definition of DressSizeType that restricts the built-in type integer.

Example 9–3. Deriving a simple type from a built-in simple type

```
<xsd:simpleType name="DressSizeType">
  <xsd:restriction base="xsd:integer">
    <xsd:minInclusive value="2"/>
    <xsd:maxInclusive value="18"/>
    <xsd:pattern value="\d{1,2}"/>
  </xsd:restriction>
</xsd:simpleType>
```

Simple types may also restrict user-derived simple types that are defined in the same schema document, or even in a different schema document. For example, you could further restrict DressSizeType by defining another simple type, MediumDressSizeType, as shown in Example 9–4.

Example 9–4. Deriving a simple type from a user-derived simple type

```
<xsd:simpleType name="MediumDressSizeType">
  <xsd:restriction base="DressSizeType">
    <xsd:minInclusive value="8"/>
    <xsd:maxInclusive value="12"/>
  </xsd:restriction>
</xsd:simpleType>
```

A simple type restricts its base type by applying facets to restrict its values. In Example 9–4, the facets minInclusive and maxInclusive are used to restrict the value of MediumDressSizeType to be between 8 and 12 inclusive.

9.3.1 Defining a restriction

The syntax for a restriction element is shown in Table 9–3. You must specify one base type either by using the base attribute, or by defining the simple type anonymously using a simpleType child. The alternative of using a simpleType child is generally only useful when restricting list types, as described in Chapter 11, "Union and list types."

Table 9–3 XSDL syntax: simple type restriction

Name
restriction

Parents
simpleType

Attribute name	Type	Required/default	Description
id	ID		unique ID
base	QName	either a base attribute or a simpleType child is required	simple type that is being restricted

Content
annotation? , simpleType? , (minExclusive | minInclusive | maxExclusive | maxInclusive | length | minLength | maxLength | totalDigits | fractionDigits | enumeration | pattern | whiteSpace)*

Within a restriction element, you can specify any of the facets, in any order. However, the only facets that may appear more than once in the same restriction are pattern and enumeration. It is legal to define a restriction that has no facets specified. In this case, the derived type allows the same values as the base type.

9.3.2   Overview of the facets

The available facets are listed in Table 9–4.

The XSDL syntax for applying a facet is shown in Table 9–5. All facets must have a `value` attribute, which has different valid values

Table 9–4   Facets

Facet	Meaning
minExclusive	value must be greater than x
minInclusive	value must be greater than or equal to x
maxInclusive	value must be less than or equal to x
maxExclusive	value must be less than x
length	the length of the value must be equal to x
minLength	the length of the value must be greater than or equal to x
maxLength	the length of the value must be less than or equal to x
totalDigits	the number of significant digits must be less than or equal to x
fractionDigits	the number of fractional digits must be less than or equal to x
whiteSpace	the schema processor should either preserve, replace, or collapse whitespace depending on x
enumeration	x is one of the valid values
pattern	x is one of the regular expressions that the value may match

depending on the facet. Most facets may also have a `fixed` attribute, as described in Section 9.3.4, "Fixed facets."

Certain facets are not applicable to some types. For example, it does not make sense to apply the `fractionDigits` facet to a character string type. There is a defined set of applicable facets for each of the built-in types[1]. If a facet is applicable to a built-in type, it is also applicable to atomic types that are derived from it. For example, since the `length` facet is applicable to `string`, if you derive a new type from `string`, the `length` facet is also applicable to your new type. Section 9.4, "Facets," describes each of the facets in detail and lists the built-in types to which the facet can apply.

9.3.3   *Inheriting and restricting facets*

When a simple type restricts its base type, it inherits all of the facets of its base type, its base type's base type, and so on back through its ancestors. Example 9–4 showed a simple type `MediumDressSizeType` whose base type is `DressSizeType`. `DressSizeType` has a `pattern` facet which restricts its value space to one or two-digit numbers. Because `MediumDressSizeType` inherits all of the facets from `DressSizeType`, this same `pattern` facet applies to `MediumDressSizeType` also. Example 9–5 shows an equivalent definition of `MediumDressSize-Type`, where it restricts `integer` and has the pattern facet applied.

Sometimes a simple type definition will include facets that are also specified for one of its ancestors. In Example 9–4, `MediumDressSize-Type` includes `minInclusive` and `maxInclusive`, which are also applied to its base type, `DressSizeType`. The `minInclusive` and `maxInclusive` facets of `MediumDressSizeType` (whose values are

---

1.   Technically, it is the primitive types that have applicable facets, with the rest of the built-in types inheriting that applicability from their base types. However, since most people do not have the built-in type hierarchy memorized, it is easier to list applicable facets for all the built-in types.

Table 9–5   XSDL syntax: facet

Name

minExclusive, minInclusive, maxExclusive, maxInclusive, length,
minLength, maxLength, totalDigits, fractionDigits, enumeration,
pattern, whiteSpace

Parents

restriction

Attribute name	Type	Required/default	Description
id	ID		unique ID
value	various	required	value of the restricting facet
fixed	boolean	false; n/a for pattern, enumeration	whether the facet is fixed and therefore cannot be restricted further, see Section 9.3.4

Content

annotation?

Example 9–5. Effective definition of MediumDressSizeType

```
<xsd:simpleType name="MediumDressSizeType">
  <xsd:restriction base="xsd:integer">
    <xsd:minInclusive value="8"/>
    <xsd:maxInclusive value="12"/>
    <xsd:pattern value="\d{1,2}"/>
  </xsd:restriction>
</xsd:simpleType>
```

8 and 12, respectively) override those of DressSizeType (2 and 18,
respectively).

It is a requirement that the facets of the derived type (in this case
MediumDressSizeType) be more restrictive than those of the base
type. In Example 9–6, we define a new restriction of DressSizeType,

called `SmallDressSizeType`, and set `minInclusive` to 0. This type definition is illegal, because it attempts to expand the value space by allowing 0, which was not valid for `DressSizeType`.

Example 9–6. Illegal attempt to extend a simple type

```
<xsd:simpleType name="SmallDressSizeType">
  <xsd:restriction base="DressSizeType">
    <xsd:minInclusive value="0"/>
    <xsd:maxInclusive value="6"/>
  </xsd:restriction>
</xsd:simpleType>
```

This rule also applies when you are restricting the built-in types. For example, the `short` data type has a `maxInclusive` value of 32767. It is illegal to define a restriction of `short` that sets `maxInclusive` to 32768.

Although `enumeration` facets can appear multiple times in the same type definition, they are treated in much the same way. If both a derived type and its ancestor have a set of `enumeration` facets, the values of the derived type must be a subset of the values of the ancestor. An example of this is provided in Section 9.4.4, "Enumeration."

Likewise, the `pattern` facets specified in a derived type must allow a subset of the values allowed by the ancestor types. Schema processors will not necessarily check that the regular expressions represent a subset, but it will instead validate instances against the patterns of both the derived type and all the ancestor types, effectively taking the intersection of the pattern values.

9.3.4   *Fixed facets*

When you define a simple type, you can fix one or more of the facets. This means that further restrictions of this type cannot change the value of the facet. Any of the facets may be fixed, with the exception of `pattern` and `enumeration`. Example 9–7 shows our `DressSize-`

Type with fixed `minExclusive` and `maxInclusive` facets, as indicated by a `fixed` attribute that is set to `true`.

Example 9–7. Fixed facets

```
<xsd:simpleType name="DressSizeType">
  <xsd:restriction base="xsd:integer">
    <xsd:minInclusive value="2" fixed="true"/>
    <xsd:maxInclusive value="18" fixed="true"/>
    <xsd:pattern value="\d{1,2}"/>
  </xsd:restriction>
</xsd:simpleType>
```

With this definition of `DressSizeType`, it would have been illegal to define the `MediumDressSizeType` as shown in Example 9–4 because it attempts to override the `minInclusive` and `maxInclusive` facets, which are now fixed. Some of the built-in types have fixed facets that cannot be overridden. For example, the built-in type `integer` has its `fractionDigits` facet fixed at `0`, so it is illegal to derive a type from `integer` and specify a `fractionDigits` that is not `0`.

9.3.4.1 Design hint: When should I fix a facet?

Fixing facets makes your type less flexible, and discourages other schema authors from reusing it. Keep in mind that any types that may be derived from your type must be more restrictive, so you are not at risk that your type will be dramatically changed if its facets are unfixed.

A justification for fixing facets might be that changing that facet value would significantly alter the meaning of the type. For example, suppose you want to define a simple type that represents price. You define a `Price` type, and fix the `fractionDigits` at `2`. This still allows other schema authors to restrict `Price` to define other types, such as, for example, a `SalePrice` type whose values must end in `99`. However, they cannot modify the `fractionDigits` of the type, because this would result in a type not representing a price with both dollars and cents.

9.4 | Facets

9.4.1   *Bounds facets*

The four bounds facets (`minInclusive`, `maxInclusive`, `minExclusive`, and `maxExclusive`) restrict a value to a specified range. Our previous examples apply `minInclusive` and `maxInclusive` to restrict the value space of `DressSizeType`. While `minInclusive` and `maxInclusive` specify boundary values that are included in the valid range, `minExclusive` and `maxExclusive` specify values that are outside the valid range.

There are several constraints associated with the bounds facets:

- `minInclusive` and `minExclusive` cannot both be applied to the same type. Likewise, `maxInclusive` and `maxExclusive` cannot both be applied to the same type. You may, however, mix and match, applying `minInclusive` and `maxExclusive` together. You may also apply just one end of the range, such as `minInclusive` only.

- The value for the lower bound (`minInclusive` or `minExclusive`) must be less than or equal to the value for the upper bound (`maxInclusive` or `maxExclusive`).

- The facet value must be a valid value for the base type. For example, when restricting `integer`, it is illegal to specify a `maxInclusive` value of `18.5`, because `18.5` is not a valid integer.

The four bounds facets can be applied only to the date/time and numeric types, and types derived from them. Special consideration should be given to time zones when applying bounds facets to date and time types. For more information, see Section 12.4.12, "Date and time ordering."

9.4.2 *Length facets*

The `length` facet allows you to limit values to a specific length. If it is a string-based type, length is measured in number of characters. This includes the legacy types and `anyURI`. If it is a binary type, length is measured in octets of binary data. If it is a list type, length is measured in number of items in the list. The facet value for `length` must be a non-negative integer.

The `minLength` and `maxLength` facets allow you to limit a value's length to a specific range. Either of both of these facets may be applied. If they are both applied, `minLength` must be less than or equal to `maxLength`. If the `length` facet is applied, neither `minLength` nor `maxLength` may be applied. The facet values for `minLength` and `maxLength` must be non-negative integers.

The three length facets (`length`, `minLength`, `maxLength`) can be applied to any of the string-based types (including the legacy types), the binary types, `QName`, and `anyURI`. They cannot be applied to the date/time types, numeric types, or `boolean`.

9.4.2.1   Design hint: What if I want to allow empty values?

Many of the built-in types do not allow empty values. Types other than `string`, `normalizedString`, `token`, `hexBinary`, and `base64-Binary` do not allow an empty value, unless `xsi:nil` appears in the element tag.

There may be a case where you have an integer that you want to be either between 2 and 18, or empty. First, consider whether you want to make the element (or attribute) optional. In this case, if the data is absent, the element will not appear at all. However, sometimes it is desirable for the element to appear, as a placeholder, or perhaps it is unavoidable because of the technology used to generate the instance.

If you do determine that the elements must be able to appear empty, you must define a union data type that includes both the integer type and an empty string. For example:

```
<xsd:simpleType name="DressSizeType">
  <xsd:union>
    <xsd:simpleType>
      <xsd:restriction base="xsd:integer">
        <xsd:minInclusive value="2"/>
        <xsd:maxInclusive value="18"/>
      </xsd:restriction>
    </xsd:simpleType>
    <xsd:simpleType>
      <xsd:restriction base="xsd:token">
        <xsd:enumeration value=""/>
      </xsd:restriction>
    </xsd:simpleType>
  </xsd:union>
</xsd:simpleType>
```

9.4.2.2   Design hint: What if I want to restrict the length of an integer?

The `length` facet only applies to the string-based types, the legacy types, the binary types, and `anyURI`. It does not make sense to try to limit the length of the date and time types because they have fixed lexical representations. But what if you want to restrict the length of an integer value?

You can restrict the lower and upper bounds of an integer by applying bounds facets, as discussed in Section 9.4.1, "Bounds facets." You can also control the number of significant digits in an integer using the `totalDigits` facet, as discussed in Section 9.4.3, "`totalDigits` and `fractionDigits`." However, these facets do not consider leading zeros to be significant. Therefore, they cannot force the integer to appear in the instance as a specific number of digits. To do this, you need a pattern. For example, the pattern `\d{1,2}` used in our `Dress-SizeType` example forces the size to be one or two digits long, so `012` would be invalid.

Before taking this approach, however, you should reconsider whether it is really an integer or a string. See Section 12.3.3.1, "Design hint: Is it an integer or a string?" for a discussion of this issue.

9.4.3   `totalDigits` *and* `fractionDigits`

The `totalDigits` facet allows you to specify the maximum number of digits in a number. The facet value for `totalDigits` must be a positive integer.

The `fractionDigits` facet allows you to specify the maximum number of digits in the fractional part of a number. The facet value for `fractionDigits` must be a non-negative integer, and it must not exceed the value for `totalDigits`, if one exists.

The `totalDigits` facet can be applied to `decimal` or any of the integer types, and types derived from them. The `fractionDigits` facet may only be applied to `decimal`, because it is fixed at 0 for all integer types.

9.4.4   *Enumeration*

The `enumeration` facet allows you to specify a distinct set of valid values for a type. Unlike most other facets (except `pattern`), the `enumeration` facet can appear multiple times in a single restriction. Each enumerated value must be unique, and must be valid for that type. If it is a string-based or binary data type, you may also specify the empty string in an enumeration value, which allows elements or attributes of that type to have empty values.

Example 9–8 shows a simple type `SMLXSizeType` that allows the values `small`, `medium`, `large`, and `extra large`.

When restricting types that have enumerations, it is important to note that you must *restrict*, rather than *extend*, the set of enumeration values. For example, if you want to restrict the valid values of `SMLSizeType` to only be `small`, `medium`, and `large`, you could define a simple type as in Example 9–9.

Note that you need to repeat all of the enumeration values that apply to the new type. This example is legal because the values for `SMLSizeType` (`small`, `medium`, and `large`) are a subset of the values for `SMLXSizeType`. By contrast, Example 9–10 attempts to add an enumeration facet to allow the value `extra small`. This type definition

Example 9–8. Applying the enumeration facet

```
<xsd:simpleType name="SMLXSizeType">
  <xsd:restriction base="xsd:token">
    <xsd:enumeration value="small"/>
    <xsd:enumeration value="medium"/>
    <xsd:enumeration value="large"/>
    <xsd:enumeration value="extra large"/>
  </xsd:restriction>
</xsd:simpleType>
```

Example 9–9. Restricting an enumeration

```
<xsd:simpleType name="SMLSizeType">
  <xsd:restriction base="SMLXSizeType">
    <xsd:enumeration value="small"/>
    <xsd:enumeration value="medium"/>
    <xsd:enumeration value="large"/>
  </xsd:restriction>
</xsd:simpleType>
```

is illegal because it attempts to extend rather than restrict the value space of SMLXSizeType.

Example 9–10. Illegal attempt to extend an enumeration

```
<xsd:simpleType name="XSMLXSizeType">
  <xsd:restriction base="SMLXSizeType">
    <xsd:enumeration value="extra small"/>
    <xsd:enumeration value="small"/>
    <xsd:enumeration value="medium"/>
    <xsd:enumeration value="large"/>
    <xsd:enumeration value="extra large"/>
  </xsd:restriction>
</xsd:simpleType>
```

The only way to add an enumeration value to a type is by defining a union type. Example 9–11 shows a union type that adds the value extra small to the set of valid values. Union types are described in detail in Chapter 11, "Union and list types."

Example 9–11. Using a union to extend an enumeration

```
<xsd:simpleType name="XSMLXSizeType">
  <xsd:union memberTypes="SMLXSizeType">
    <xsd:simpleType>
      <xsd:restriction base="xsd:token">
        <xsd:enumeration value="extra small"/>
      </xsd:restriction>
    </xsd:simpleType>
  </xsd:union>
</xsd:simpleType>
```

When enumerating numbers, it is important to note that the enumeration facet works on the actual value of the number, not its lexical representation as it appears in an XML instance. Example 9–12 shows a simple type `NewSmallDressSizeType` that is based on `integer`, and specifies an enumeration of 2, 4, and 6. The two instance elements shown, which contain 2 and 02, are both valid. This is because 02 is equivalent to 2 for integer-based types. However, if the base type of `NewSmallDressSizeType` had been `string`, the value 02 would not be valid, because the strings 2 and 02 are not the same. If you wish to constrain the lexical representation of a numeric type, you should apply the `pattern` facet instead. For more information on type equality in XML Schema, see Section 12.7, "Type equality."

The `enumeration` facet can be applied to any type except `boolean`.

9.4.5 Pattern

The `pattern` facet allows you to restrict values to a particular pattern, represented by a regular expression. Chapter 10, "Regular expressions," provides more detail on the rules for the regular expression syntax. Unlike most other facets (except `enumeration`), the `pattern` facet can be specified multiple times in a single restriction. If multiple `pattern` facets are specified in the same restriction, the instance value must match at least one of the patterns. It is not required to match all of the patterns.

Example 9–12. Enumerating numeric values

Schema:

```
<xsd:simpleType name="NewSmallDressSizeType">
  <xsd:restriction base="xsd:integer">
    <xsd:enumeration value="2"/>
    <xsd:enumeration value="4"/>
    <xsd:enumeration value="6"/>
  </xsd:restriction>
</xsd:simpleType>
```

Valid instances:

```
<size>2</size>
<size>02</size>
```

Example 9–13 shows a simple type `DressSizeType` that includes the pattern `\d{1,2}`, which restricts the size to one or two digits.

Example 9–13. Applying the pattern facet

```
<xsd:simpleType name="DressSizeType">
  <xsd:restriction base="xsd:integer">
    <xsd:minInclusive value="2"/>
    <xsd:maxInclusive value="18"/>
    <xsd:pattern value="\d{1,2}"/>
  </xsd:restriction>
</xsd:simpleType>
```

When restricting types that have patterns, it is important to note that you must *restrict*, rather than *extend*, the set of valid values that the patterns represent. In Example 9–14, we define a simple type `SmallDressSizeType` that is derived from `DressSizeType`, and add an additional `pattern` facet that restricts the size to one digit.

Example 9–14. Restricting a pattern

```
<xsd:simpleType name="SmallDressSizeType">
  <xsd:restriction base="DressSizeType">
    <xsd:minInclusive value="2"/>
    <xsd:maxInclusive value="6"/>
    <xsd:pattern value="\d{1}"/>
  </xsd:restriction>
</xsd:simpleType>
```

It is not technically an error to apply a pattern facet that does not represent a subset of the ancestors' pattern facets. However, the schema processor tries to match the instance value against the pattern facet of both the type and its ancestors, ensuring that it is in fact a subset. Example 9–15 shows an illegal attempt to define a new size type that allows the size value to be up to three digits long. While the schema is not in error, it will not have the desired effect because the schema processor will check values against both the pattern of `LongerDress-SizeType` and the pattern of `DressSizeType`. The value `004` would not be considered a valid instance of `LongerDressSizeType` because it does not conform to the pattern of `DressSizeType`.

Unlike the `enumeration` facet, the `pattern` facet applies to the lexical representation of the value. If the value `02` appears in an instance, the pattern is applied to the digits `02`, not `2` or `+2` or any other form of the integer.

The `pattern` facet can be applied to any type.

Example 9–15. Illegal attempt to extend a pattern

```
<xsd:simpleType name="LongerDressSizeType">
  <xsd:restriction base="DressSizeType">
    <xsd:pattern value="\d{1,3}"/>
  </xsd:restriction>
</xsd:simpleType>
```

9.4.6 *Whitespace*

The `whiteSpace` facet allows you to specify the whitespace normalization rules which apply to this value. Unlike the other facets, which restrict the value space of the type, the `whiteSpace` facet is an instruction to the schema processor as to what to do with whitespace. The valid values for the `whiteSpace` facet are:

- `preserve`: All whitespace is preserved; the value is not changed. This is how XML 1.0 processors handle whitespace in the character data content of elements.

- `replace`: Each occurrence of a tab (#x9), line feed (#xA), and carriage return (#xD) is replaced with a single space (#x20). This is how XML 1.0 processors handle whitespace in attributes of type `CDATA`.

- `collapse`: As with replace, each occurrence of tab (#x9), line feed (#xA) and carriage return (#xD) is replaced with a single space (#x20). After the replacement, all consecutive spaces are collapsed into a single space. In addition, leading and trailing spaces are deleted. This is how XML 1.0 processors handle whitespace in all attributes that are not of type `CDATA`.

Table 9–6 shows examples of how values of a string-based type will be handled depending on its `whiteSpace` facet.

Table 9–6   Handling of string values depending on `whiteSpace` facet

Original string	string (preserve)	normalizedString (replace)	token (collapse)
a string	a string	a string	a string
on two lines	on two lines	on two lines	on two lines
has spaces	has spaces	has spaces	has spaces
leading tab	leading tab	leading tab	leading tab
leading spaces	leading spaces	leading spaces	leading spaces

The whitespace processing, if any, will happen first, before any validation takes place. In Example 9–8, the base type of SMLXSizeType is token, which has a whiteSpace facet of collapse. Example 9–16 shows valid instances of SMLXSizeType. They are valid because the leading and trailing spaces are removed, and the line feed is turned into a space. If the base type of SMLXSizeType had been string, the whitespace would have been left as is, and these values would have been invalid.

Example 9–16. Valid instances of SMLXSizeType

```
<size> small </size>

<size>extra
large</size>
```

Although you should understand what the whiteSpace facet represents, it is unlikely that you will ever apply it directly in your schemas. The whiteSpace facet is fixed at collapse for most built-in types. Only the string-based types can be restricted by a whiteSpace facet, but this is not recommended. Instead, select a base type that already has the whiteSpace facet you want. The data types string, normalizedString, and token have the whiteSpace values preserve, replace, and collapse, respectively. For example, if you wish to define a string-based type that will have its whitespace collapsed, base your type on token, instead of basing your type on string and applying a whiteSpace facet. Section 12.2.1, "string, normalizedString, and token," provides a discussion of these three types.

9.5 | Preventing simple type derivation

XML Schema allows you to prevent derivation of other types from your type. By specifying the final attribute in your simple type definition, you may prevent derivation of any kind (restriction, extension, list, or union) by specifying a value of `#all`. If you want more specific control, the value of `final` can be a whitespace-separated list of any of the keywords `restriction`, `extension`, `list`, or `union`. Extension refers to the extension of simple types to derive complex types, described in Chapter 14, "Deriving complex types." Example 9–17 shows some valid values for `final`.

Example 9–17. Valid values for the `final` attribute in simple type definitions

```
final="#all"
final="restriction list union"
final="list restriction extension"
final="union"
final=""
```

Example 9–18 shows a simple type that cannot be restricted by any other type, or used as the item type of a list. With this definition of `DressSizeType`, it would have been illegal to define `MediumDressSizeType` in Example 9–4 because it attempts to restrict `DressSizeType`.

Example 9–18. Preventing type derivation

```
<xsd:simpleType name="DressSizeType" final="restriction list">
  <xsd:restriction base="xsd:integer">
    <xsd:minInclusive value="2"/>
    <xsd:maxInclusive value="18"/>
  </xsd:restriction>
</xsd:simpleType>
```

If no `final` attribute is specified, it defaults to the value of the `finalDefault` attribute of the `schema` element. If neither `final` nor `finalDefault` are specified, there are no restrictions on derivation from that type. You can specify the empty string (`""`) for the `final` value if you want to override the `finalDefault` value.

Regular
expressions

Chapter

10

P atterns are used to restrict the values of simple types to certain
sequences of characters. For example, a pattern could specify
that an SKU must be three digits, followed by a dash, followed by two uppercase letters. These patterns are described
by regular expressions. This chapter explains the XML Schema syntax
for regular expressions.

10.1 | The structure of a regular expression

The XML Schema's regular expression language is very similar to that
of the Perl programming language. Regular expressions are made up
of branches, which are in turn made up of pieces. Each piece consists
of one atom and an optional quantifier.

For example, suppose the product number in your organization can
either be an SKU or a 7-digit number. Remember, an SKU is three
digits, followed by a dash, followed by two uppercase letters, such as

123-AB. We could represent such a pattern by defining the simple type shown in Example 10–1.

Example 10–1. A simple type with a pattern

```
<xsd:simpleType name="ProdNumType">
  <xsd:restriction base="xsd:string">
    <xsd:pattern value="\d{3}-[A-Z]{2} | \d{7}"/>
  </xsd:restriction>
</xsd:simpleType>
```

Figure 10–1 shows the structure of this regular expression.

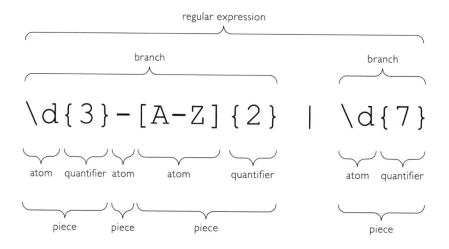

Figure 10–1   Structure of a regular expression

It has two branches separated by a vertical bar (|): the first to represent an SKU, and the second to represent a seven-digit number. If there is more than one branch in a regular expression, a matching string must match at least one of the branches; it is not required to match all of the branches. In this case, the first branch consists of three pieces:

- \d{3} represents the initial three digits. The atom, \d, is a character class escape that represents any digit. The quantifier, {3}, indicates how many times the atom (a digit) may appear.

- - represents the dash. The atom in this case is the dash, which represents itself as a normal character. This piece does not contain a quantifier, so the dash must appear once and only once.

- [A-Z]{2} represents the two letters. The atom, [A-Z], is a character class expression which represents any one of the letters A through Z. The quantifier, {2}, indicates how many times the atom (a letter) may appear.

The second branch, \d{7}, consists of only one piece, which represents the seven digits.

The rest of this chapter explains these concepts in detail.

10.2 | Atoms

An atom describes one or more characters. It may be any one of the following:

- A normal character, such as a.
- A parenthesized regular expression, evidenced by parentheses, such as (a|b).
- An escape, evidenced by a backslash, such as \d or \p{Is-BasicLatin}.
- A character class expression, evidenced by square brackets, such as [A-Z].

Each of these types of atoms is described in the sections that follow.

10.2.1 *Normal characters*

An atom can be a single character, as shown in Table 10–1. Each of the characters a, b, and c is an atom.

Table 10–1   Using normal characters

Regular expression	Matching strings	Non-matching strings
a	a	b
a|b|c	a, b, c	abc

Most characters that can be entered on a keyboard can be represented directly in a regular expression. The following characters have special meaning and must be escaped in order to be treated like normal characters: ., \, ?, *, +, |, {, }, (,), [, and]. This is explained in Section 10.2.2.1, "Single-character escapes."

Characters that are not easily entered on a keyboard may also be represented as they are in any XML document, by character entities that specify the character's Unicode code point. XML character entities take two forms:

- "&#" plus a sequence of decimal digits representing the character's code point, followed by ";",
- "&#x" plus a sequence of hexadecimal digits representing the character's code point, followed by ";".

For example, a space can be represented as . It is also possible to include the standard XML entities for the "less than," "greater than," ampersand, apostrophe, and quote characters. Table 10–2 lists some common XML character entities.

Table 10–3 illustrates the inclusion of character entity references in regular expressions.

Table 10–2   Common XML character entities

Entity	Meaning
&#x20;	space
&#xA;	newline (also represented by \n)
&#xD;	carriage return (also represented by \r)
&#x9;	tab (also represented by \t)
&lt;	less than (<)
&gt;	greater than (>)
&amp;	ampersand (&)
&apos;	apostrophe (')
&quot;	quote (")

Table 10–3   Using character entity references

Regular expression	Matching strings	Non-matching strings
a z	a z	az
a *z	az, a z, a z, a z	a *z
PB&J	PB&J	PBJ

10.2.2 *Character class escapes*

A character class escape uses an escape character, the backslash (\), to indicate any one of several characters. There are four categories of character class escapes:

- single character escapes, which represent one specific character,
- multi-character escapes, which represent any one of several characters,
- category escapes, which represent any one of a group of characters with similar characteristics (such as "Punctuation"), as defined in the Unicode standard,

- block escapes, which represent any one character in a range of code points, as defined in the Unicode standard.

Note that each escape may be replaced by only one character. You must apply a quantifier such as * to an escape to allow it to appear multiple times.

This section describes each of the four types of character class escapes.

10.2.2.1 Single-character escapes

Single-character escapes are used for characters that are either difficult to read and write in their natural form, or have special meaning in regular expressions. Each escape represents only one possible replacement character. Table 10–4 provides a complete list of single-character escapes.

Table 10–5 illustrates single-character escapes in regular expressions. The first example has an unescaped plus sign (+). Since the plus sign has another meaning in regular expressions, it is treated as a quantifier on the atom consisting of the character 1. The second example escapes the plus sign, which results in it being treated as an atom itself, allowing it to appear in the matching string. The third example escapes the first plus sign, but not the second, resulting in the first one being interpreted as an atom, and the second one being interpreted as a quantifier.

10.2.2.2 Multi-character escapes

A multi-character escape may represent any one of several characters. Table 10–6 provides a complete list of multi-character escapes. Note that the period, which represents any character, is not preceded by a backslash.

Table 10–7 illustrates multi-character escapes in regular expressions.

Table 10–4   Single-character escapes

Escape	Meaning
\n	newline (#xA)
\r	carriage return (#xD)
\t	tab (#x9)
\\	\
|	|
\.	.
\-	–
\^	^
\?	?
*	*
\+	+
\{	{
\}	}
\(	(
\)	)
\[	[
\]	]

Table 10–5   Using single-character escapes

Regular expression	Matching strings	Non-matching strings
1+2	12, 112, 1112	1+2
1\+2	1+2	12, 1\+2
1\++2	1+2, 1++2, 1+++2	12

Table 10–6   Multi-character escapes

Escape	Meaning
.	any character that is not a carriage return () or newline (
)
\d	any decimal digit (0 through 9)
\D	any character that is not a decimal digit
\s	a whitespace character (space, tab, carriage return, or newline)
\S	any character that is not a whitespace character
\i	any character that may be the first character of an XML name, namely a letter, an underscore (_), or a colon (:)
\I	any character that is not permitted as the first character of an XML name
\c	any character that may be part of an XML name, namely a letter, a digit, an underscore (_), a colon (:), a hyphen (-), or a period (.)
\C	any character that cannot be part of an XML name
\w	any character *not* in one of the categories "Punctuation", "Separators", and "Other", described in the next section
\W	any character in one of the categories "Punctuation", "Separators", and "Other", described in the next section

Table 10–7   Using multi-character escapes

Regular expression	Matching strings	Non-matching strings
a\dz	a0z, a1z	az, adz, a12z
a.z	a1z, axz	az, axxz

10.2.2.3 Category escapes

Category escapes provide convenient groupings of characters, based on their characteristics. These categories are defined by the Unicode stan-

dard. More information about the Unicode standard can be found at
`http://www.unicode.org`. Table 10–8 provides a complete list of
category escapes.

Table 10–8   Category escapes

Category	Property	Meaning
Letters	L	all letters
	Lu	uppercase
	Ll	lowercase
	Lt	titlecase
	Lm	modifier
	Lo	other
Marks	M	all marks
	Mn	non-spacing
	Mc	spacing combining
	Me	enclosing
Numbers	N	all numbers
	Nd	decimal digit
	Nl	letter
	No	other
Punctuation	P	all punctuation
	Pc	connector
	Pd	dash
	Ps	open
	Pe	close
	Pi	initial quote
	Pf	final quote
	Po	other

Table 10–8   Category escapes

Category	Property	Meaning
Separators	Z	all separators
	Zs	space
	Zl	line
	Zp	paragraph
Symbols	S	all symbols
	Sm	math
	Sc	currency
	Sk	modifier
	So	other
Other	C	all others
	Cc	control
	Cf	format
	Co	private use
	Cn	not assigned

The syntax to use one of these escapes is \p{*xx*} where *xx* is the one- or two-character property. For example, \p{Nd} represents any decimal digit. It is also possible to represent the complement, that is, any character that is *not* part of the category, using a capital P. For example, \P{Nd} represents any character that is not a decimal digit. Table 10–9 illustrates category escapes in regular expressions.

10.2.2.4 Block escapes

Block escapes represent a range of characters based on their Unicode code points. The Unicode standard provides names for these ranges, such as Basic Latin, Greek, Thai, Mongolian, etc. The block names

Table 10–9   Using category escapes

Regular expression	Matching strings	Non-matching strings
\p{Lu}	A, B, C	a, b, c, 1, 2, 3
\P{Lu}	a, b, c, 1, 2, 3	A, B, C
\p{Nd}	1, 2, 3	a, b, c, A, B, C
\P{Nd}	a, b, c, A, B, C	1, 2, 3

used in regular expressions are these same names, with the spaces removed. Table 10–10 provides a complete list of the block escapes.

Table 10–10   Block escapes

Start code	End code	Block name
#x0000	#x007F	BasicLatin
#x0080	#x00FF	Latin-1Supplement
#x0100	#x017F	LatinExtended-A
#x0180	#x024F	LatinExtended-B
#x0250	#x02AF	IPAExtensions
#x02B0	#x02FF	SpacingModifierLetters
#x0300	#x036F	CombiningDiacriticalMarks
#x0370	#x03FF	Greek
#x0400	#x04FF	Cyrillic
#x0530	#x058F	Armenian
#x0590	#x05FF	Hebrew
#x0600	#x06FF	Arabic
#x0700	#x074F	Syriac
#x0780	#x07BF	Thaana
#x0900	#x097F	Devanagari
#x0980	#x09FF	Bengali

Table 10–10 Block escapes

Start code	End code	Block name
#x0A00	#x0A7F	Gurmukhi
#x0A80	#x0AFF	Gujarati
#x0B00	#x0B7F	Oriya
#x0B80	#x0BFF	Tamil
#x0C00	#x0C7F	Telugu
#x0C80	#x0CFF	Kannada
#x0D00	#x0D7F	Malayalam
#x0D80	#x0DFF	Sinhala
#x0E00	#x0E7F	Thai
#x0E80	#x0EFF	Lao
#x0F00	#x0FFF	Tibetan
#x1000	#x109F	Myanmar
#x10A0	#x10FF	Georgian
#x1100	#x11FF	HangulJamo
#x1200	#x137F	Ethiopic
#x13A0	#x13FF	Cherokee
#x1400	#x167F	UnifiedCanadianAboriginalSyllabics
#x1680	#x169F	Ogham
#x16A0	#x16FF	Runic
#x1780	#x17FF	Khmer
#x1800	#x18AF	Mongolian
#x1E00	#x1EFF	LatinExtendedAdditional
#x1F00	#x1FFF	GreekExtended
#x2000	#x206F	GeneralPunctuation
#x2070	#x209F	SuperscriptsandSubscripts

Table 10–10 Block escapes

Start code	End code	Block name
#x20A0	#x20CF	CurrencySymbols
#x20D0	#x20FF	CombiningMarksforSymbols
#x2100	#x214F	LetterlikeSymbols
#x2150	#x218F	NumberForms
#x2190	#x21FF	Arrows
#x2200	#x22FF	MathematicalOperators
#x2300	#x23FF	MiscellaneousTechnical
#x2400	#x243F	ControlPictures
#x2440	#x245F	OpticalCharacterRecognition
#x2460	#x24FF	EnclosedAlphanumerics
#x2500	#x257F	BoxDrawing
#x2580	#x259F	BlockElements
#x25A0	#x25FF	GeometricShapes
#x2600	#x26FF	MiscellaneousSymbols
#x2700	#x27BF	Dingbats
#x2800	#x28FF	BraillePatterns
#x2E80	#x2EFF	CJKRadicalsSupplement
#x2F00	#x2FDF	KangxiRadicals
#x2FF0	#x2FFF	IdeographicDescriptionCharacters
#x3000	#x303F	CJKSymbolsandPunctuation
#x3040	#x309F	Hiragana
#x30A0	#x30FF	Katakana
#x3100	#x312F	Bopomofo
#x3130	#x318F	HangulCompatibilityJamo
#x3190	#x319F	Kanbun

Table 10–10   Block escapes

Start code	End code	Block name
#x31A0	#x31BF	BopomofoExtended
#x3200	#x32FF	EnclosedCJKLettersandMonths
#x3300	#x33FF	CJKCompatibility
#x3400	#x4DB5	CJKUnifiedIdeographsExtensionA
#x4E00	#x9FFF	CJKUnifiedIdeographs
#xA000	#xA48F	YiSyllables
#xA490	#xA4CF	YiRadicals
#xAC00	#xD7A3	HangulSyllables
#xE000	#xF8FF	PrivateUse
#xF900	#xFAFF	CJKCompatibilityIdeographs
#xFB00	#xFB4F	AlphabeticPresentationForms
#xFB50	#xFDFF	ArabicPresentationForms-A
#xFE20	#xFE2F	CombiningHalfMarks
#xFE30	#xFE4F	CJKCompatibilityForms
#xFE50	#xFE6F	SmallFormVariants
#xFE70	#xFEFE	ArabicPresentationForms-B
#xFEFF	#xFEFF	Specials
#xFF00	#xFFEF	HalfwidthandFullwidthForms
#xFFF0	#xFFFD	Specials

The syntax to use one of the block escapes is \p{Is*XX*} where *XX* is the block name. For example, \p{IsBasicLatin} represents any character in the range #x0000 to #x007F. It is also possible to represent the complement, that is, any character that is not part of the block, using a capital P. For example, \P{IsBasicLatin} represents any character that is not in that range. Table 10–11 illustrates block escapes in regular expressions.

Table 10–11   Using block escapes

Regular expression	Matching strings	Non-matching strings
\p{IsBasicLatin}	a, b, c	â, ß, ç
\P{IsBasicLatin}	â, ß, ç	a, b, c

10.2.3 *Character class expressions*

A character class expression allows you to specify a choice among a set of characters. The expression, which appears in square brackets, may include a list of characters or character escapes, or a character range, or both. It is also possible to negate the specified set of characters, or subtract values from it. Like an escape, a character class expression may only represent one character in the matching string. To allow a matching character to appear multiple times, a quantifier may be applied to it.

10.2.3.1 Specifying a list of characters

The simplest case of a character class expression is a list of the characters or escapes that may be used. The expression represents one and only one of the characters listed. Table 10–12 illustrates a list of characters inside an expression. The first example can be read as "a or b or c, followed by z." The character class expression in the second example uses escapes to represent one character that is either an uppercase letter or a decimal digit.

Table 10–12   Specifying a list of characters

Regular expression	Matching strings	Non-matching strings
[abc]z	az, bz, cz	abz, z, abcz, abc
[\p{Lu}\d]z	Az, Bz, 1z, 2z	az, bz, cz, A1z

10.2.3.2 Specifying a range

A range of characters may be specified in a character class expression. The lower and upper bounds are inclusive, and they are separated by a dash. For example, to allow the letters a through f, you can specify [a-f]. The bounds must be single characters, or single character escapes. It is not valid to specify a range using multi-character strings, such as [(aa)-(fe)], or multi-character escapes, such as [\p{Lu}-\p{Ll}]. The lower bound must have a code point that is less than or equal to that of the upper bound.

Multiple ranges may be specified in the same expression. If multiple ranges are specified, the character must match one of the ranges.

Table 10–13 illustrates ranges in expressions. The first example can be read as "a letter between a and f (inclusive), followed by z." The second example provides three ranges, namely the digits 0 to 9, lower-case a to f, and uppercase A to F. The first character of a matching string must conform to at least one of these ranges. The third example uses character entities to represent the bounds.

Table 10–13   Specifying a range

Regular expression	*Matching strings*	*Non-matching strings*
[a-f]z	az, fz	z, abz, gz, hz
[0-9a-fA-F]z	1z, az, Bz	z, gz, Gz, 1aBz
[&#x0000;-&#x007F;]z	az, bz, cz	âz

10.2.3.3 Combining characters and ranges

It is also possible to combine ranges, single characters, and escapes in an expression, in any order. Table 10–14 illustrates this. The first example allows the first character of the matching string to be either a digit 0 through 9, or one of the letters p, q, or r. The second example represents the exact same thing, with the range on the letters instead of the numbers, and the escape \d to represent the digits.

Table 10–14   Combining characters and ranges

Regular expression	Matching strings	Non-matching strings
[0-9pqr]z	1z, 2z, pz, rz	cz,dz,0sz
[p-r\d]z	1z, 2z, pz, rz	cz,dz,0sz

10.2.3.4 Negating a character class expression

A character class expression can be negated, meaning that it represents any character that is not in the specified set of characters. You can negate any expression, regardless of whether it is a range, a list of characters, or both. The negation character (^) must appear directly after the left bracket, signifying that the entire expression is negated.

Table 10–15 illustrates this negation. The character class expression in the first example represents "any character except a or b". In the second example it is "any character that is not a digit." In the third, it is "any character that does not fall in the range 1 through 3, or a through c." Note that the negation in the third example applies to both ranges. It is *not* possible to negate one range but not another in the same expression. To represent this, use subtraction, which is described in the next section.

Table 10–15   Negating a character class expression

Regular expression	Matching strings	Non-matching strings
[^ab]z	cz, dz, 1z	az, bz
[^\d]z	az, bz, cz	1z, 2z, 3z
[^1-3a-c]z	dz, 4z	1z, az

10.2.3.5 Subtracting from a character class expression

It is possible to subtract individual values or ranges of values from a specified set of characters. The values being subtracted must themselves be in square brackets. Table 10–16 illustrates subtractions from character class expressions. The first example represents "any character between a and z, except for c, followed by z." The second is "any character between a and z, except for c and d, followed by z." The third example subtracts a range, namely c through e, from the range a through z. The net result is that the allowed values are a through b, and f through z. The fourth example is a negation of a subtraction; remember, this is a negation of the entire character class expression, so the matching set is the complement of that in the third example. That is, anything but a, b, or f through z, followed by z, is legal.

Table 10–16   Subtracting from a character class expression

Regular expression	Matching strings	Non-matching strings
[a-z-[c]]z	az, dz, ez, zz	cz
[a-z-[cd]]z	az, ez, zz	cz, dz
[a-z-[c-e]]z	az, zz	cz, dz, ez, 1z
[^a-z-[c-e]]z	cz, dz, ez, 1z	az, zz

10.2.4 *Parenthesized regular expressions*

A parenthesized regular expression may be used as an atom in a larger regular expression. This is useful when you want to allow a choice between several different patterns, or to repeat certain sequences of characters. Any regular expression may be included in parentheses, including those containing normal characters, characters entities, escapes, and character class expressions. Table 10–17 shows some examples of parenthesized regular expressions within regular expressions.

10.3 | Quantifiers

A quantifier indicates how many times the atom may appear in a matching string. Table 10–18 lists the quantifiers.

Table 10–17   Using parenthesized regular expressions

Regular expression	Matching strings	Non-matching strings
(a|b)z	az, bz	abz, z
(ab)*z	z, abz, ababz	az, bz, aabbz
(a+b)*z	z, abz, aabz, abaabz	az, abbz
([a-f]x)*z	z, axz, bxfxfxz	gxz, xz
(\db)*z	z, 1bz, 1b2bz	1z, bz

Table 10–18   Quantifiers

Quantifier	Meaning
none	must appear once
?	may appear 0 or 1 times
*	may appear 0 to many times
+	may appear 1 to many times
$\{n\}$	must appear n times
$\{n,\}$	may appear n to many times
$\{n,m\}$	may appear n to m times

Table 10–19 illustrates quantifiers in regular expressions. The first seven examples illustrate the seven types of quantifiers. They each have three atoms: a, b, and z, with the quantifier applying only to b. The remaining three examples show how quantifiers can apply not just to normal character atoms, but also to character class expressions, character class escapes, and parenthesized regular expressions, respectively.

Table 10-19   Using quantifiers

Regular expression	Matching strings	Non-matching strings
abz	abz	az, abbz
ab?z	az, abz	abbz
ab*z	az, abz, abbz, abbbz, ...	a1z
ab+z	abz, abbz, abbbz, ...	az
ab{2}z	abbz	abz, abbbz
ab{2,}z	abbz, abbbz, abbbbz, ...	az, abz
ab{2,3}z	abbz, abbbz	az, abz, abbbbz
a[b-d]+z	abz, abdz, addbccdddz	az, aez, abez
a\p{Nd}+z	a1z, a11z, a234z	az, abcz
a(bc)+z	abcz, abcbcz, abcbcbcz, ...	az, abz

Union and list types

n Chapter 9, "Simple types," we learned how to define atomic simple types. This chapter covers the other two varieties of simple types: union types and list types.

11.1 | Varieties and derivation types

As we saw in Chapter 9, "Simple types," there are three varieties of simple type: atomic types, list types, and union types.

- *Atomic types* have values that are indivisible, such as 10 and large.
- *List types* have values that are whitespace-separated lists of atomic values, such as `<availableSizes>10 large 2</availableSizes>`.
- *Union types* may have values that are either atomic values or list values. What differentiates them is that the set of valid values,

or "value space," for the type is the union of the value spaces of two or more other simple types. For example, to represent a dress size, you may define a union type that allows a value to be either an integer from 2 through 18, or one of the string values small, medium, or large.

Each newly defined simple type must be derived from an existing type, using one of the following derivation types:

- A restriction of another type, known as the base type of the restriction. This results in a type of the same variety as the base type, with a restricted set of valid values. For example, you can define a SmallInteger type that restricts the value space of the integer type.

- A list of another type (either an atomic or union type), known as the item type of the list. This results in a type that allows a whitespace-separated list of values of the item type. For example, you can define an IntegerList type that is a list of integers.

- A union of one or more other types, known as the member types of the union. This results in a type that allows values that are valid for any of its member types. For example, you can define an IntegerOrString type that allows either an integer or a string.

The variety of the resulting type depends on both the derivation type and the variety of the original type. Table 11–1 shows all possible combinations of derivation types and original type varieties. The important thing to understand is that when you restrict, for example, a list type the resulting type is still a list type. All the rules for list types, such as applicable facets, also apply to this new type.

Table 11–1 Varieties of derived types

		Derivation type		
		restriction	*list*	*union*
	atomic	atomic	list	union
Base type variety	*list*	list	*not legal*	union
	union	union	list[†]	union

† Legal only if the union type does not itself contain a list.

11.2 | Union types

11.2.1 *Defining union types*

Union types allow a value to conform to any one of several different simple types. The syntax to define a union type is shown in Table 11–2.

Table 11–2 XSDL syntax: union type

Name

union

Parents

simpleType

Attribute name	Type	Required/default	Description
id	ID		unique ID
memberTypes	list of QName values	either a memberTypes attribute or a simpleType child is required	member types that make up the union type

Content

annotation? , simpleType*

To continue with our `DressSizeType` example, perhaps we want to allow a value to be either an integer from 2 to 18, or one of the specific values `small`, `medium`, or `large`. Example 11–1 shows the definition of a union type that accomplishes this.

Example 11–1. Defining a union type

```xsd
<xsd:simpleType name="SizeType">
  <xsd:union>
    <xsd:simpleType>
      <xsd:restriction base="xsd:integer">
        <xsd:minInclusive value="2"/>
        <xsd:maxInclusive value="18"/>
      </xsd:restriction>
    </xsd:simpleType>
    <xsd:simpleType>
      <xsd:restriction base="xsd:token">
        <xsd:enumeration value="small"/>
        <xsd:enumeration value="medium"/>
        <xsd:enumeration value="large"/>
      </xsd:restriction>
    </xsd:simpleType>
  </xsd:union>
</xsd:simpleType>
```

The simple types that compose a union type are known as its member types. Member types must always be simple types; there is no such thing as a union of complex types. There must be at least one member type, and there is no limit of how many member types may exist.

In Example 11–1, the member types are defined anonymously within the `union`, as `simpleType` children. It is also possible to specify the member types using a `memberTypes` attribute of the `union` element, as shown in Example 11–2. It is assumed that `DressSizeType` and `SMLSizeType` are defined elsewhere in the schema.

You can also combine the `memberTypes` attribute with `simpleType` children, as shown in Example 11–3.

Example 11–2. Using the `memberTypes` attribute

```
<xsd:simpleType name="SizeType">
  <xsd:union memberTypes="DressSizeType SMLSizeType"/>
</xsd:simpleType>
```

Example 11–3. Combining `memberTypes` and `simpleType`

```
<xsd:simpleType name="SizeType">
  <xsd:union memberTypes="DressSizeType">
    <xsd:simpleType>
      <xsd:restriction base="xsd:token">
        <xsd:enumeration value="small"/>
        <xsd:enumeration value="medium"/>
        <xsd:enumeration value="large"/>
      </xsd:restriction>
    </xsd:simpleType>
  </xsd:union>
</xsd:simpleType>
```

11.2.2 *Restricting union types*

It is possible to restrict a union type. The XSDL syntax for restricting a union type is shown in Table 11–3.

Of all the facets, only two may be applied to union types: `pattern` and `enumeration`. These restrictions are considered to be in addition to the restrictions of the individual member types. Example 11–4 shows a restriction of `SizeType` that only allows integers 2, 4, and 6, and the

Example 11–4. Restricting a union

```
<xsd:simpleType name="SmallSizeType">
  <xsd:restriction base="SizeType">
    <xsd:enumeration value="2"/>
    <xsd:enumeration value="4"/>
    <xsd:enumeration value="6"/>
    <xsd:enumeration value="small"/>
  </xsd:restriction>
</xsd:simpleType>
```

Table 11–3   XSDL syntax: union type restriction

Name			
restriction			

Parents			
simpleType			

Attribute name	Type	Required/default	Description
id	ID		unique ID
base	QName	either a base attribute or a simpleType child is required	base type of the restriction (in this case, the union type)

Content
annotation? , simpleType? , (enumeration | pattern)*

value small. Values of the type SmallSizeType are first validated against the enumerations defined in SmallSizeType, then validated against each of the member types of SizeType until it is successfully validated against one.

11.2.3 *Unions of unions*

It is possible to define a union type that has another union type as its member type. For example, if we want to expand our size type yet again, to include non-US sizes, we might define a new type International-SizeType that is the union of SizeType (which is itself a union) and a new anonymous type, as shown in Example 11–5.

11.2.4 *Specifying the member type in the instance*

An instance element can exhibit the xsi:type attribute to specify its type. In the case of union types, you can use xsi:type to specify which

Example 11–5. A union of a union

```
<xsd:simpleType name="InternationalSizeType">
  <xsd:union memberTypes="SizeType">
    <xsd:simpleType>
      <xsd:restriction base="xsd:integer">
        <xsd:minInclusive value="24"/>
        <xsd:maxInclusive value="54"/>
      </xsd:restriction>
    </xsd:simpleType>
  </xsd:union>
</xsd:simpleType>
```

of the member types the element conforms to. This allows more targeted validation, and provides a clue to the application that processes the instance about what type of value to expect. Example 11–6 shows what an instance element might look like.

Example 11–6. Specifying the member type in the instance

```
<size xsi:type="DressSizeType">12</size>
```

Naturally, this technique only works for elements, not attributes. In the previous example, if `size` were an attribute, you would have no way of specifying its member type, because attributes cannot have attributes.

11.3 | List types

11.3.1 *Defining list types*

List types are whitespace-separated lists of atomic values. A list type is defined by designating another simple type (an atomic or union type) as its item type. Table 11–4 shows the syntax for defining a list type.

Table 11–4   XSDL syntax: list type

Name			
list			

Parents			
simpleType			

Attribute name	Type	Required/default	Description
id	ID		unique ID
itemType	QName	either an itemType attribute or a simple-Type child is required	the simple type of each item in the list

Content			
annotation? , simpleType?			

For example, suppose we wanted to define a simple type that is a list of available dress sizes. Example 11–7 shows such a simple type.

Example 11–7. Defining a list type using an itemType attribute

```
<xsd:simpleType name="AvailableSizesType">
  <xsd:list itemType="DressSizeType"/>
</xsd:simpleType>
```

An instance element of the type AvailableSizesType is shown in Example 11–8.

Example 11–8. List instance

```
<availableSizes>10 12  14</availableSizes>
```

Example 11–7 uses the itemType attribute to designate a global simple type named DressSizeType as its item type. Alternatively, the item type can be specified anonymously in a `simpleType` child within the list type definition, as shown in Example 11–9. Either the `itemType` attribute or the `simpleType` child must appear, not both.

Example 11–9. Defining a list type using a `simpleType` child

```
<xsd:simpleType name="AvailableSizesType">
  <xsd:list>
    <xsd:simpleType>
      <xsd:restriction base="xsd:integer">
        <xsd:minInclusive value="2"/>
        <xsd:maxInclusive value="18"/>
      </xsd:restriction>
    </xsd:simpleType>
  </xsd:list>
</xsd:simpleType>
```

There is no way to represent an absent or nil item in a list. The `whiteSpace` facet for all list types is fixed at `collapse`, which means that if multiple whitespace characters appear consecutively, they are collapsed into one space. In Example 11–8, even though there are two spaces between the values 12 and 14, there are only three items in the list.

11.3.2 *Design hint: When should I use lists?*

When representing sequences of like values, you are faced with a decision whether to use a list, such as:

```
<availableSizes>10 12 14</availableSizes>
```

or use markup to separate the distinct values, such as:

```
<availableSizes>
  <size>10</size>
  <size>12</size>
  <size>14</size>
</availableSizes>
```

The advantage of using a list is obvious: it is less verbose. However, there are a number of disadvantages of lists:

- They are not appropriate for values that may contain whitespace (see Section 11.3.4, "Lists and strings").
- If you later wish to expand the values by adding children or attributes, this will not be possible if you use a list. For example, if you use markup, you can later add an attribute to `size` to indicate the measurement system, e.g. `<size system="US-DRESS">`.
- There is no way to represent nil values.
- There may be limited support for lists in other XML technologies. Currently, individual values in a list cannot be accessed via XPath or XSLT.

11.3.3 *Restricting list types*

The XSDL syntax for restricting a list type is shown in Table 11–5. A limited number of facets may be applied to list types. These facets have slightly different behavior when applied to a list type, because they apply to the list as a whole, not to the individual items in the list. To restrict the values of each item in the list, you should restrict the item type, not the list type itself.

When applying facets to a list type, you do not specify the facets directly in the list type definition. Instead, you define the list type, then define a restriction of that list type. This can be done with two separate, named simple types, or it can be accomplished all in one definition as shown in Example 11–10.

11.3.3.1 Length facets

Length facets `length`, `minLength`, and `maxLength` may be used to restrict list types. The length is measured in number of items in the

Table 11–5   XSDL syntax: list type restriction

Name

restriction

Parents

simpleType

Attribute name	*Type*	*Required/default*	*Description*
id	ID		unique ID
base	QName	either a base attribute or a simpleType child is required	the base type of the restriction (in this case, the list type)

Content

annotation? , simpleType? , (length | minLength | maxLength
| pattern | enumeration)*

Example 11–10. Length facet applied to a list

```
<xsd:simpleType name="AvailableSizesType">
  <xsd:restriction>
    <xsd:simpleType>
      <xsd:list itemType="SMLSizeType"/>
    </xsd:simpleType>
    <xsd:maxLength value="3"/>
  </xsd:restriction>
</xsd:simpleType>
```

list, not the length of each item. Example 11–10 shows a list that is restricted by a maxLength facet.

Example 11–11 shows a valid instance of AvailableSizesType. It is valid because the number of items in the list is not more than three. The fact that the strings medium and large are longer than three characters is not relevant. To restrict the length of each item in the list, apply the maxLength facet to the item type itself (SMLSizeType), not to the list type.

Example 11–11. Valid instance of a length-restricted list

```
<availableSizes>medium large</availableSizes>
```

When you define a list type, there are no automatic restrictions on the length of the list. Therefore, lists with zero items (i.e., empty elements or just whitespace) are considered valid. If you do not want a list to be valid if it is empty, restrict the list type by setting its `minlength` to 1.

11.3.3.2 Enumeration facet

The `enumeration` facet may also be used to restrict list types. However, the enumeration specified applies to the whole list, not to each item in the list. For example, to restrict the values in a list to a specific set, you may be tempted to define a simple type like the one shown in Example 11–12.

Example 11–12. Enumeration applied inappropriately to a list type

---

```
<xsd:simpleType name="AvailableSizesType">
  <xsd:restriction>
    <xsd:simpleType>
      <xsd:list itemType="xsd:token"/>
    </xsd:simpleType>
    <xsd:enumeration value="small"/>
    <xsd:enumeration value="medium"/>
    <xsd:enumeration value="large"/>
  </xsd:restriction>
</xsd:simpleType>
```

However, this would not behave as you expect. It would restrict the value of the entire list to only one of the values: `small`, `medium`, or `large`. Therefore, `<availableSizes>small</availableSizes>` would be valid, but `<availableSizes>small medium</availableSizes>` would not. Instead, apply the `enumeration` to the item type, as shown in Example 11–13.

Example 11–13. Enumeration applied to item type of a list

```xsd
<xsd:simpleType name="AvailableSizesType">
  <xsd:list>
    <xsd:simpleType>
      <xsd:restriction base="xsd:token">
        <xsd:enumeration value="small"/>
        <xsd:enumeration value="medium"/>
        <xsd:enumeration value="large"/>
      </xsd:restriction>
    </xsd:simpleType>
  </xsd:list>
</xsd:simpleType>
```

There may be cases where you do want to restrict the entire list to certain values. Example 11–14 shows a list that may only have two values, as shown.

Example 11–14. Enumeration correctly applied to a list type

Schema:

```xsd
<xsd:simpleType name="ApplicableSizesType">
  <xsd:restriction>
    <xsd:simpleType>
      <xsd:list itemType="SizeType"/>
    </xsd:simpleType>
    <xsd:enumeration value="small medium large"/>
    <xsd:enumeration value="2 4 6 8 10 12 14 16 18"/>
  </xsd:restriction>
</xsd:simpleType>
```

Instance:

```xml
<applicableSizes>small medium large</applicableSizes>
<applicableSizes>2 4 6 8 10 12 14 16 18</applicableSizes>
```

11.3.3.3 Pattern facet

The pattern facet may also be applied to list types. Like the length and enumeration facets, the pattern facets in this case apply to the entire list, not the items in the list. For example, suppose you want to represent vector information as a list of integers. You want your list to always contain zero or more groups of three integers each, separated by white space. The restriction shown in Example 11–15 enforces this constraint.

Example 11–15. Pattern applied to a list type

```
<xsd:simpleType name="VectorType">
  <xsd:restriction>
    <xsd:simpleType>
      <xsd:list itemType="xsd:unsignedInt"/>
    </xsd:simpleType>
    <xsd:pattern value="((\d+\s*){3})*"/>
  </xsd:restriction>
</xsd:simpleType>
```

11.3.4 *Lists and strings*

Be careful when deriving list types from the string-based types, whose values may contain whitespace. This includes the built-in types `string`, `normalizedString`, and `token`, and any types derived from them. Because the list items are separated by whitespace, strings that contain whitespace may give unexpected results when included as items in a list. Example 11–16 shows the definition of `AvailableSizesType` as a list of `SMLXSizeType`, which is derived from `xsd:token` and allows the values `small`, `medium`, `large`, and `extra large`.

Example 11–17 shows an invalid instance of `AvailableSizes-Type`. The schema processor would consider this instance to be a list of three items ("`small`", "`extra`", and "`large`") rather than the expected two items ("`small`" and "`extra large`"). When it attempts to validate the value "`extra`" against the enumerated values, it will determine that it is an invalid list item.

Example 11–16. Defining a list of a string-based type

```
<xsd:simpleType name="AvailableSizesType">
  <xsd:list itemType="SMLXSizeType"/>
</xsd:simpleType>
<xsd:simpleType name="SMLXSizeType">
  <xsd:restriction base="xsd:token">
    <xsd:enumeration value="small"/>
    <xsd:enumeration value="medium"/>
    <xsd:enumeration value="large"/>
    <xsd:enumeration value="extra large"/>
  </xsd:restriction>
</xsd:simpleType>
```

Example 11–17. Invalid instance of `AvailableSizesType`

```
<availableSizes>
small
extra large
</availableSizes>
```

11.3.5 *Lists of unions*

Lists of union types are no different from lists of atomic types. Each item in the list must simply be a valid value of one of the member types of the union type. Example 11–18 defines our now familiar union type `SizeType`, then defines a list type `AvailableSizesType` whose item type is `SizeType`.

Example 11–18. Defining a list of a union

```
<xsd:simpleType name="SizeType">
  <xsd:union memberTypes="DressSizeType SMLXSizeType"/>
</xsd:simpleType>

<xsd:simpleType name="AvailableSizesType">
  <xsd:list itemType="SizeType"/>
</xsd:simpleType>
```

Example 11–19 shows a valid instance of `AvailableSizesType`. Note that both the integers and the enumerated `small`, `medium`, and `large` are valid list items, in any order.

Example 11–19. Instance of a list of a union

```
<availableSizes>10 large 2</availableSizes>
```

The only restriction on lists of unions is that the union type cannot have any list types among its member types. That would equate to a list of a list, which is not legal.

11.3.6 *Lists of lists*

Lists of lists are not legal. The item type of a list type cannot be a list type itself, nor can it be derived at any level from another list type (for example, as a restriction of a list, or a union of a list). Example 11–20 is illegal as it attempts to define a simple type `TwoDimensionalArray-Type` as a list of lists.

Example 11–20. Illegal list of lists

```
<xsd:simpleType name="RowType">
  <xsd:list itemType="xsd:integer"/>
</xsd:simpleType>

<xsd:simpleType name="TwoDimensionalArrayType">
  <xsd:list itemType="RowType"/>
</xsd:simpleType>
```

Instead, you should put markup around the items in the lists. Example 11–21 shows a complex type definition that accomplishes this, and a valid instance.

Example 11–21. An array using markup

Schema:

```
<xsd:complexType name="VectorType">
  <xsd:sequence maxOccurs="unbounded">
    <xsd:element name="e" type="xsd:integer"/>
  </xsd:sequence>
</xsd:complexType>

<xsd:complexType name="ArrayType">
  <xsd:sequence maxOccurs="unbounded">
    <xsd:element name="r" type="VectorType"/>
  </xsd:sequence>
</xsd:complexType>

<xsd:element name="array" type="ArrayType"/>
```

Instance:

```
<array>
  <r>  <e>1</e>   <e>12</e>  <e>15</e> </r>
  <r>  <e>44</e>  <e>2</e>   <e>3</e>   </r>
</array>
```

11.3.7 *Restricting the item type*

Once you have defined a list type, you cannot derive another list type from it that restricts the item type. For example, it is impossible to derive a list of MediumDressSizeType from a list of DressSizeType. Instead, you must restrict the item type (in this case DressSizeType), then define a new list type of the new restricted atomic type (e.g., MediumDressSizeType).

Built-in simple types

12

This chapter describes the 44 built-in simple types that are included in XML Schema. These simple types represent common data types that can be used directly in schemas. They are also the foundation for deriving other simple types, as described in Chapter 9, "Simple types." A complete reference to the built-in simple types and the facets that apply to them can be found in Appendix B, "Built-in simple types."

12.1 | Built-in types

There are 44 simple types built into XML Schema. They are specified in Part 2 of the XML Schema Recommendation. This part of the Recommendation makes a distinction between "datatypes" and "simple types." Datatypes are abstract concepts of data, such as "integer." Simple types are the concrete representations of these datatypes. The term "datatype" (one word) used in the Recommendation should not be confused with the term "data type" (two words), used throughout this book to mean "simple or complex type." In fact, a schema author does not need to be concerned with "datatypes" at all.

Most of the built-in types are atomic types, although there are three list types (NMTOKENS, ENTITIES, and IDREFS). Figure 12–1 depicts their hierarchy, showing that many of the built-in types are derived from other built-in types. At the top of the hierarchy is anySimpleType, which is an unrestricted type that cannot actually be used in a schema.

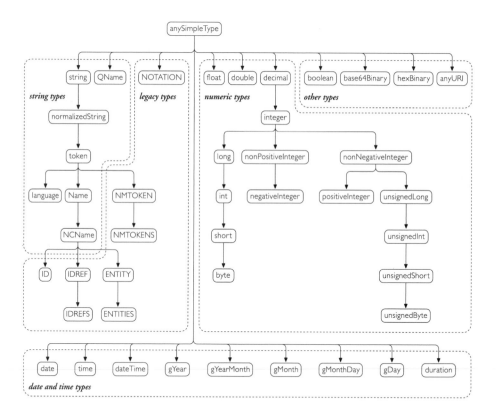

Figure 12–1   The built-in type hierarchy

The types at the next level of the hierarchy, directly under anySimpleType, are known as *primitive* types, while the rest are *derived* built-in types. The primitive types represent basic data type concepts, and all other built-in types are either restrictions or lists of those types. When you define new simple types, they can never be primitive; they must be derived from another type.

As we saw in Chapter 9, "Simple types," simple types inherit the facets of their ancestors. For example, the `integer` data type has a `fractionDigits` facet that is set to 0. This means that all of the twelve types derived (directly and indirectly) from `integer` also have a `fractionDigits` of 0.

However, it is not just the facet *value* that is inherited, but also the *applicability* of a facet. Each primitive type has certain facets that are applicable to it. For example, the `string` type has `length` as an applicable facet, but not `totalDigits`, because it does not make sense to apply `totalDigits` to a string. Therefore, the `totalDigits` facet cannot be applied to `string`, or any of its descendants, whether they are built-in types, or ones you derive.

It is not necessary to remember which types are primitive and which are derived. This chapter lists the applicable facets for *all* of the built-in types, not just the primitive types. When you derive new types from the built-in types, you may simply check which facets are applicable to the built-in type, regardless of whether it is primitive or derived.

12.2 | String-based types

12.2.1 `string`, `normalizedString`, *and* `token`

The data types `string`, `normalizedString`, and `token` represent a character string that may contain any Unicode character. Certain characters, namely the "less than" symbol (<) and the ampersand (&), must be escaped (using the entities `&lt;` and `&amp;`, respectively) when used in strings in XML instances. The only difference between the three types is in the way whitespace is handled by a schema-aware processor, as shown in Table 12–1.

Table 12–1   Whitespace handling of string data types

Original string	string *(preserve)*	normalizedString *(replace)*	token *(collapse)*
A string	A string	A string	A string
On two lines	On two lines	On two lines	On two lines
Has spaces	Has spaces	Has spaces	Has spaces
Leading tab	Leading tab	Leading tab	Leading tab
Leading spaces	Leading spaces	Leading spaces	Leading spaces

The `string` type has a `whiteSpace` facet of `preserve`, which means that all whitespace characters (spaces, tabs, carriage returns, and line feeds) are preserved by the processor.

The `normalizedString` type has a `whiteSpace` facet of `replace`, which means that the processor replaces each carriage return, line feed, and tab by a single space. This processing is equivalent to the processing of CDATA attribute values in XML 1.0. There is no collapsing of multiple consecutive spaces into a single space.

The `token` type represents a tokenized string. The name `token` may be slightly confusing because it implies that there may be only one token with no whitespace. In fact, there can be whitespace in a `token` value. The `token` data type has a `whiteSpace` facet of `collapse`, which means that the processor replaces each carriage return, line feed, and tab by a single space. After this replacement, each group of consecutive spaces is collapsed into one space character, and all leading and trailing spaces are removed. This processing is equivalent to the processing of non-CDATA attribute values in XML 1.0.

Table 12–2 shows some valid and invalid values of the string types.

The facets indicated in Table 12–3 can restrict `string`, `normalizedString`, and `token`, and their descendants.[1]

---

1.   A — applicable, V — value specified, F — fixed value specified.

Table 12–2   Values of string data types

Valid values	Comment
`This is a string!`	
`Édition française.`	
`12.5`	
	an empty string is valid
`PB&amp;J`	when parsed, it will become "PB&J"
`   Separated   by   3   spaces.`	
`This` `is on two lines.`	

Invalid values[†]	Comment
`AT&T`	ampersand must be escaped
`3 < 4`	the "less than" symbol must be escaped

[†]   In physical XML files.

Table 12–3   Facets applicable to `string`, `normalizedString`, and `token` types

`length`	A	`minExclusive`		`totalDigits`	
`minLength`	A	`minInclusive`		`fractionDigits`	
`maxLength`	A	`maxInclusive`		`pattern`	A
`whiteSpace`	V	`maxExclusive`		`enumeration`	A

`whiteSpace` is `preserve` for `string`, `replace` for `normalizedString`, and `collapse` for `token`.

12.2.1.1 Design hint: Should I use `string`, `normalizedString`, or `token`?

First, consider whether to use a string-based simple type at all. If it is a long string of general text, such as a letter or a long description of an item, this may not be wise. This is because simple types are not extensible. Later, you may want to allow XHTML markup in the letter, or break the item description down into more structured components. It will be impossible to do this without altering the schema in a way that is not backwards compatible.

Additionally, simple types cannot support internationalization requirements such as Ruby annotations and BIDI (bidirectionality) elements.

In these cases, you should instead declare a complex type with mixed content, and include a wildcard to allow for future extensions. The following complex type definition accomplishes this purpose. The character data content of an element of this type will have its whitespace preserved.

```
<xsd:complexType name="TextType" mixed="true">
  <xsd:sequence>
    <xsd:any namespace="##any" processContents="lax"
            minOccurs="0" maxOccurs="unbounded"/>
  </xsd:sequence>
  <xsd:attribute ref="xml:lang"/>
</xsd:complexType>
```

For short, atomic items, such as a postal code or a gender, it does make sense to use string, normalizedString, or token. But which one? Here are some general guidelines:

- string should be used for text where formatting, such as tabs and line breaks, is significant. However, as mentioned above, it may be better to use mixed complex type in this case.

- normalizedString is used when formatting is not significant but consecutive whitespace characters are significant. This can be used when the information in the string is positional.

- token should be used for most short, atomic strings, especially ones that have an enumerated set of values. Basing your enumerated types on token means that <gender>M </gender> will be valid as well as <gender>M</gender>.

12.2.2 Name

The data type `Name` represents an XML name, which can be used as an element-type name or attribute name, among other things. Specifically, this means that values must start with a letter, underscore(_), or colon (:), and may contain only letters, digits, underscores (_), colons (:), hyphens (-), and periods (.). Colons should only be used to separate namespace prefixes from local names.

Table 12–4 shows some valid and invalid values of the `Name` type.

Table 12–4 Values of `Name` data type

Valid values	Comment
myElement	
_my.Element	
my-element	
pre:myelement3	this is recommended only if `pre` is a namespace prefix; otherwise, colons should not be used

Invalid values	Comment
-myelement	a `Name` must not start with a hyphen
3rdElement	a `Name` must not start with a number
	an empty value is not valid, unless `xsi:nil` is used

The facets indicated in Table 12–5 can restrict `Name` and its descendants.

12.2.3 NCName

The data type `NCName` represents an XML non-colonized name, which is simply a name that does not contain colons. An `NCName` must start with either a letter or underscore (_) and may contain only letters,

Table 12–5   Facets applicable to `Name` data type

length	A	minExclusive		totalDigits	
minLength	A	minInclusive		fractionDigits	
maxLength	A	maxInclusive		pattern	V
whiteSpace	V	maxExclusive		enumeration	A

`whiteSpace` is `collapse`, `pattern` is `\i\c*`

digits, underscores (_), hyphens (–), and periods (.). This is equivalent to the `Name` type, except that colons are not permitted.

Table 12–6 shows some valid and invalid values of the `NCName` type.

Table 12–6   Values of `NCName` data type

Valid values	Comment
`myElement`	
`_my.Element`	
`my-element`	

Invalid values	Comment
`pre:myElement`	an `NCName` must not contain a colon
`-myelement`	an `NCName` must not start with a hyphen
	an empty value is not valid, unless `xsi:nil` is used

The facets indicated in Table 12–7 can restrict `NCName` and its descendants.

12.2.4 `language`

The data type `language` represents a natural language identifier, generally used to indicate the language of a document or a part of a document. Before creating a new attribute of type `language`, consider using

Table 12–7 Facets applicable to `NCName` data type

`length`	A	`minExclusive`		`totalDigits`	
`minLength`	A	`minInclusive`		`fractionDigits`	
`maxLength`	A	`maxInclusive`		`pattern`	V
`whiteSpace`	V	`maxExclusive`		`enumeration`	A

`whiteSpace` is `collapse`, pattern is `[\i-[:]][\c-[:]]*`

the `xml:lang` attribute that is intended to indicate the natural language of the element and its content.

Values of the `language` data type conform to RFC 1766, *Tags for the Identification of Languages.* The three most common formats are:

- For ISO-recognized languages, the format is a two-letter, lower-case language code that conforms to ISO 639, optionally followed by a hyphen and a two-letter, uppercase country code that conforms to ISO 3166. For example, `en` or `en-US`.

- For languages registered by the Internet Assigned Numbers Authority (IANA), the format is `i-`*langname*, where *langname* is the registered name. For example, `i-navajo`.

- For unofficial languages, the format is `x-`*langname*, where *langname* is a name of up to eight characters agreed upon by the two parties sharing the document. For example, `x-Newspeak`.

Any of these three formats may have additional parts, each preceded by a hyphen, which identify additional countries or dialects.

Table 12–8 shows some valid and invalid values of the `language` type.

The facets indicated in Table 12–9 can restrict `language` and its descendants.

Table 12–8   Values of `language` data type

Valid values	Comment
en	English
en-GB	UK English
en-US	US English
fr	French
de	German
es	Spanish
it	Italian
nl	Dutch
zh	Chinese
ja	Japanese
ko	Korean
i-navajo	IANA-registered language
x-Newspeak	private, unregistered language
Invalid values	**Comment**
english	
	an empty value is not valid, unless `xsi:nil` is used

Table 12–9   Facets applicable to `language` data type

length	A	minExclusive		totalDigits	
minLength	A	minInclusive		fractionDigits	
maxLength	A	maxInclusive		pattern	V
whiteSpace	V	maxExclusive		enumeration	A

`whiteSpace` is `collapse`, `pattern` is
`([a-zA-Z]{2}|[iI]-[a-zA-Z]+|[xX]-[a-zA-Z]{1,8})(-[a-zA-Z]{1,8})*`

12.3 | Numeric types

12.3.1 `float` *and* `double`

The data type `float` represents an IEEE single-precision 32-bit floating-point number, and `double` represents an IEEE double-precision 64-bit floating-point number. The lexical representation of both `float` and `double` values is a mantissa (a number which conforms to the type `decimal` described in the next section) followed, optionally, by the character "E" or "e" followed by an exponent. The exponent must be an integer. In addition, the following values are valid: `INF` (infinity), `-INF` (negative infinity), `0` (positive 0), `-0` (negative zero), and `NaN` (Not a Number).

When comparing two `float` or `double` values, positive zero is evaluated as being greater than negative zero. Not-a-number is greater than all other values, including positive infinity.

Table 12–10 shows some valid and invalid values of the `float` and `double` types.

The facets indicated in Table 12–11 can restrict `float` and `double`, and their descendants.

12.3.2 `decimal`

The data type `decimal` represents a decimal number of arbitrary precision. Schema processors vary in the number of significant digits they support, but a conforming processor must support a minimum of 18 significant digits. The lexical representation of `decimal` is a sequence of digits optionally preceded by a sign ("+" or "-") and optionally containing a period. The value may start or end with a period. If the fractional part is 0 then the period and trailing zeros may be omitted. Leading and trailing zeros are permitted, but they are not considered significant. That is, the decimal values 3.0 and 3.0000 are considered equal.

Table 12–12 shows some valid and invalid values of the `decimal` type.

Table 12–10 Values of `float` and `double` data types

Valid values	Comment
-3E2	
4268.22752E11	
+24.3e-3	
12	
+3.5	any value valid for `decimal` is also valid for `float` and `double`
-INF	negative infinity
-0	negative 0
NaN	Not a Number
Invalid values	**Comment**
-3E2.4	the exponent must be an integer
12E	an exponent must be specified if "E" is present
	an empty value is not valid, unless `xsi:nil` is used

Table 12–11 Facets applicable to `float` and `double` data types

length		minExclusive	A	totalDigits	
minLength		minInclusive	A	fractionDigits	
maxLength		maxInclusive	A	pattern	A
whiteSpace	F	maxExclusive	A	enumeration	A

whiteSpace is `collapse`

The facets indicated in Table 12–13 can restrict `decimal` and its descendants.

Table 12–12   Values of `decimal` data type

Valid values	Comment
3.0	
-3.0	a negative sign is permitted
+3.5	a positive sign is permitted
3	a decimal point is not required
.3	the value can start with a decimal point
3.	the value can end with a decimal point
0	
-.3	
0003.0	leading zeros are permitted
3.0000	trailing zeros are permitted

Invalid values	Comment
3,5	commas are not permitted; the decimal separator must be a period
	an empty value is not valid, unless `xsi:nil` is used

Table 12–13   Facets applicable to `decimal` data type

length		minExclusive	A	totalDigits	A
minLength		minInclusive	A	fractionDigits	A
maxLength		maxInclusive	A	pattern	A
whiteSpace	F	maxExclusive	A	enumeration	A

`whiteSpace` is `collapse`

12.3.3 *Integer types*

The data type `integer` represents an arbitrarily large integer, from which twelve other built-in integer types are derived (directly or indirectly). The lexical representation of the integer data types is a sequence of digits. Some of the integer types allow or require a sign ("+" or "-") to precede the numbers, others prohibit it. Leading zeros are permitted, but decimal points are not.

Table 12–14 lists all of the integer types, with their bounds and their rules for preceding signs.

Table 12–15 shows some valid and invalid values of the integer types.

The facets indicated in Table 12–16 can restrict the integer types and their descendants.

12.3.3.1 Design hint: Is it an integer or a string?

When defining types for values that are sequences of digits, it may be difficult to determine whether the type should be based on an integer or a string. For example, U.S. zip codes are valid integers, but they can also be interpreted as strings. Here are some general guidelines:

Use `integer` (or, more likely, `nonNegativeInteger`) if:

- You will ever compare two values of that type. For example, zip code 49685 is more than 49684. Strings are not ordered, so they are not intended to be compared. While you could still programmatically compare them, future XML technologies such as new versions of XSLT and XML Query, will not support the comparison of unordered types.

- You will ever perform mathematical operations on a value of that type. For example, 49684 + 1 may be a zip code in a neighboring town.

- You want to restrict their values bounds. For example, you may require that zip codes must not be less than 49600 or more than 49700. While it is technically possible to restrict a string in this way, by applying a pattern, it is more cumbersome.

Use `string` (or, more likely, `token`) if:

Table 12–14 Integer types

Type name	minInclusive	maxInclusive	Preceding sign
integer	n/a	n/a	+ (optional for positive values) or -
positive-Integer	1	n/a	+ (optional)
non-Positive-Integer	n/a	0	- (optional if the value is 0)
negative-Integer	n/a	-1	- (required)
non-Negative-Integer	0	n/a	+ (optional)
long	-9223372036854775808	9223372036854775807	+ (optional for positive values) or -
int	-2147483648	2147483647	+ (optional for positive values) or -
short	-32768	32767	+ (optional for positive values) or -
byte	-128	127	+ (optional for positive values) or -
unsignedLong	0	18446744073709551615	prohibited
unsignedInt	0	4294967295	prohibited
unsignedShort	0	65535	prohibited
unsignedByte	0	255	prohibited

Table 12–15   Values of integer data types

Valid values	Comment
122	valid for all integer types except `negativeInteger` and `nonPositiveInteger`
00122	leading zeros are permitted
0	0 is permitted for most integer types (except `positiveInteger` and `negativeInteger`)
-3	a negative sign is permitted for some integer types, see Table 12–14
+3	a positive sign is permitted for some integer types, see Table 12–14

Invalid values	Comment
3.	an integer must not contain a decimal point
3.0	an integer must not contain a decimal point
	an empty value is not valid, unless `xsi:nil` is used

Table 12–16   Facets applicable to integer data types

length	minExclusive	A	totalDigits	A
minLength	minInclusive	V	fractionDigits	F
maxLength	maxInclusive	V	pattern	A
whiteSpace	F	maxExclusive	A	enumeration	A

`whiteSpace` is `collapse`, `fractionDigits` is 0, `minInclusive` and `maxInclusive` are as specified in Table 12–14

- You want to restrict their lexical length. For example, zip codes must be five digits long; "8540" is not a valid zip code, but "08540" is valid. While it is technically possible to restrict an integer to five digits, by applying a pattern, it is more cumbersome.

- You will ever take a substring. For example, the state code is the first two digits of the zip code.

- You plan to derive non-numeric types from this type, or use it in a substitution group with non-numeric types. For example, if you are likely to also define types for international postal codes, which may contain letters or other characters, it is safer to base your U.S. zip code elements on a string data type, so that they can be used in a substitution group with other postal code elements.

12.4 | Date and time types

XML Schema provides a number of built-in date and time data types, whose formats are based on ISO 8601. This section explains each of the date and time types and provides general information that applies to all date and time types.

12.4.1 `date`

The data type `date` represents a Gregorian calendar date. The lexical representation of `date` is CCYY-MM-DD where CC represents the century, YY the year, MM the month and DD the day. No left truncation is allowed for any part of the date. To represent years later than 9999, additional digits can be added to the left of the year value, but extra leading zeros are not permitted. To represent years before 0000, a preceding minus sign ("-") is allowed. An optional time zone expression may be added at the end, as described in Section 12.4.10, "Representing time zones."

Table 12–17 shows some valid and invalid values of the `date` type.

Table 12–17   Values of `date` data type

Valid values	Comment
1968-04-02	April 2, 1968
-0045-01-01	January 1, 45 BC
11968-04-02	April 2, 11968
1968-04-02+05:00	April 2, 1968 on Eastern Standard Time
1968-04-02Z	April 2, 1968 on Coordinated Universal Time (UTC)
Invalid values	*Comment*
68-04-02	left truncation of the century is not allowed
1968-4-2	month and day must be two digits each
1968/04/02	slashes are not valid separators
04-02-1968	the value must be in CCYY-MM-DD order
1968-04-31	the date must be a valid date (April has 30 days)
	an empty value is not valid, unless `xsi:nil` is used

12.4.2 `time`

The data type `time` represents a time of day. The lexical representation of `time` is `hh:mm:ss.sss` where `hh` represents the hour, `mm` the minutes, and `ss.sss` the seconds. An unlimited number of additional digits can be used to increase the precision of fractional seconds if desired. The time is based on a 24-hour time period, so hours should be represented as 00 through 23, where 00 is midnight. An optional time zone expression may be added at the end, as described in Section 12.4.10, "Representing time zones."

Table 12–18 shows some valid and invalid values of the `time` type.

Table 12–18   Values of `time` data type

Valid values	Comment
13:20:00	1:20 PM
13:20:30.5555	1:20 PM and 30.5555 seconds
13:20:00-05:00	1:20 PM on Eastern Standard Time
13:20:00Z	1:20 PM on Coordinated Universal Time (UTC)
Invalid values	*Comment*
5:20:00	hours, minutes, and seconds must be two digits each
13:20:	seconds must be specified, even if it is 00
13:20.5:00	values for hours and minutes must be integers
13:65:00	the value must be a valid time of day
	an empty value is not valid, unless `xsi:nil` is used

12.4.3 `dateTime`

The data type `dateTime` represents a specific date and time. The lexical representation of `dateTime` is `CCYY-MM-DDThh:mm:ss.sss`, which is a concatenation of the `date` and `time` forms, separated by a literal letter "T". All of the same rules that apply to the `date` and `time` data types are applicable to `dateTime` as well. An optional time zone expression may be added at the end, as described in Section 12.4.10, "Representing time zones."

Table 12–19 shows some valid and invalid values of the `dateTime` type.

12.4.4 `gYear`

The data type `gYear` represents a specific Gregorian calendar year. The letter g at the beginning of most date and time types signifies "Gregorian." The lexical representation of `gYear` is `CCYY`. No left truncation is allowed. To represent years later than 9999, additional digits can be

Table 12–19   Values of `dateTime` data type

Valid values	Comment
1968-04-02T13:20:00	1:20 pm on April 2, 1968
1968-04-02T13:20:15.5	1:20 pm and 15.5 seconds on April 2, 1968
1968-04-02T13:20:00-05:00	1:20 pm on April 2, 1968 on Eastern Standard Time which is 5 hours behind Coordinated Universal Time (UTC)
1968-04-02T13:20:00Z	1:20 pm on April 2, 1968 on Coordinated Universal Time (UTC)

Invalid values	Comment
1968-04-02T13:00	seconds must be specified
1968-04-0213:20:00	the letter T is required
68-04-02T13:00	the century must not be left truncated
1968-04-02	the time is required
	an empty value is not valid, unless `xsi:nil` is used

added to the left of the year value. To represent years before 0000, a preceding minus sign ("-") is allowed. An optional time zone expression may be added at the end, as described in Section 12.4.10, "Representing time zones."

Table 12–20 shows some valid and invalid values of the `gYear` type.

12.4.5 gYearMonth

The data type `gYearMonth` represents a specific month of a specific year. The lexical representation of `gYearMonth` is `CCYY-MM`. No left truncation is allowed on either part. To represents years later than 9999, additional digits can be added to the left of the year value. To represent years before 0000, a preceding minus sign ("-") is permitted.

Table 12–20   Values of `gYear` data type

Valid values	Comment
1968	1968
1968-05:00	1968 on Eastern Standard Time
11968	the year 11968
0968	the year 968
-0045	45 BC

Invalid values	Comment
68	the century must not be truncated
968	no left truncation is allowed; leading zeros should be added if necessary
	an empty value is not valid, unless `xsi:nil` is used

An optional time zone expression may be added at the end, as described in Section 12.4.10, "Representing time zones."

Table 12–21 shows some valid and invalid values of the `gYearMonth` type.

Table 12–21   Values of `gYearMonth` data type

Valid values	Comment
1968-04	April 1968
1968-04-05:00	April 1968 on Eastern Standard Time

Invalid values	Comment
68-04	the century must not be truncated
1968	the month is required
1968-4	the month must be two digits
1968-13	the month must be a valid month
	an empty value is not valid, unless `xsi:nil` is used

12.4.6 gMonth

The data type `gMonth` represents a specific month that recurs every year. It can be used to indicate, for example, that fiscal year-end processing occurs in September of every year. To represent a duration of months, use the `duration` data type instead. The lexical representation of `gMonth` is `--MM`. An optional time zone expression may be added at the end, as described in Section 12.4.10, "Representing time zones." No preceding sign is allowed.

Table 12–22 shows some valid and invalid values of the `gMonth` type.

Table 12–22   Values of `gMonth` data type

Valid values	Comment
`--04`	April
`--04-05:00`	April on Eastern Standard Time
Invalid values	*Comment*
`1968-04`	the year must not be specified; use `gYearMonth` instead
`04`	the leading hyphens are required
`--4`	the month must be 2 digits
`--13`	the month must be a valid month
	an empty value is not valid, unless `xsi:nil` is used

12.4.7 gMonthDay

The data type `gMonthDay` represents a specific day that recurs every year. It can be used to say, for example, that your birthday is on the 2nd of April every year. The lexical representation of `gMonthDay` is `--MM-DD`. An optional time zone expression may be added at the end, as described in Section 12.4.10, "Representing time zones."

Table 12–23 shows some valid and invalid values of the `gMonthDay` type.

Table 12–23   Values of `gMonthDay` data type

Valid values	Comment
--04-02	April 2
--04-02Z	April 2 on Coordinated Universal Time (UTC)

Invalid values	Comment
04-02	the leading hyphens are required
--04-31	it must be a valid day of the year (April has 30 days)
--4-2	the month and day must be 2 digits each
	an empty value is not valid, unless `xsi:nil` is used

12.4.8 gDay

The data type `gDay` represents a day that recurs every month. It can be used to say, for example, that checks are paid on the 5th of each month. To represent a duration of days, use the `duration` data type instead. The lexical representation of `gDay` is `---DD`. An optional time zone expression may be added at the end, as described in Section 12.4.10, "Representing time zones."

Table 12–24 shows some valid and invalid values of the `gDay` type.

Table 12–24   Values of `gDay` data type

Valid values	Comment
---02	the 2nd of the month

Invalid values	Comment
02	the leading hyphens are required
---2	the day must be 2 digits
---32	the day must be a valid day of the month; no month has 32 days
	an empty value is not valid, unless `xsi:nil` is used

12.4.9 `duration`

The data type `duration` represents a duration of time expressed as a number of years, months, days, hours, minutes, and seconds. The lexical representation of `duration` is `PnYnMnDTnHnMnS`, where `P` is a literal value that starts the expression, `nY` is the number of years followed by a literal `Y`, `nM` is the number of months followed by a literal `M`, `nD` is the number of days followed by a literal `D`, `T` is a literal value that separates the date and time, `nH` is the number of hours followed by a literal `H`, `nM` is the number of minutes followed by a literal `M`, and `nS` is the number of seconds followed by a literal `S`. The following rules apply to `duration` values:

- Any of these numbers and corresponding designators may be absent if they are equal to 0, but at least one number and designator must appear.

- The numbers may be any integer, with the exception of the number of seconds, which may be a decimal number.

- A minus sign may appear before the `P` to specify a negative duration.

- If no time items (hour, minute, second) are present, the letter `T` must not appear.

Table 12–25 shows some valid and invalid values of the `Name` type. When deriving data types from `duration`, applying the bounds facets (`minExclusive`, `minInclusive`, `maxInclusive`, and `maxExclusive`) can have unexpected results. For example, if the `maxInclusive` value for a duration-based data type is `P1M`, and an instance value contains `P30D`, it is ambiguous. Months may have 28, 29, 30, or 31 days, so is 30 days less than a month or not?

It is best to avoid the ambiguity, by always specifying bounds for durations in the same unit in which the instance values will appear, in this case setting `maxExclusive` to `P32D` instead of `P1M`. You can use the `pattern` facet to force a particular unit of duration. For example,

Table 12–25   Values of `duration` data type

Valid values	Comment
`P2Y6M5DT12H35M30S`	2 years, 6 months, 5 days, 12 hours, 35 minutes, 30 seconds
`P1DT2H`	1 day, 2 hours
`P20M`	20 months (the number of months can be more than 12)
`P0Y20M0D`	20 months (0 is permitted as a number, but is not required)
`-P60D`	minus 60 days

Invalid values	Comment
`P-20M`	the minus sign must appear first
`P20MT`	no time items are present, so "`T`" must not be present
`P1YM5D`	no value is specified for months, so "`M`" must not be present
`P15.5Y`	only the seconds can be expressed as a decimal
`P1D2H`	"`T`" must be present to separate days and hours
`1Y2M`	"`P`" must always be present
`P2M1Y`	year must appear before month
`P`	at least one number and designator are required
	an empty value is not valid, unless `xsi:nil` is used

the pattern `P\d+D` applied to the `duration` type would force the duration to be expressed in days only.

12.4.10 *Representing time zones*

All of the date and time types, with the exception of duration, allow an optional time zone indicator at the end. The letter `Z` is used to indicate Coordinated Universal Time (UTC). All other time zones are represented by their difference from Coordinated Universal Time in the format +hh:mm, or -hh:mm. For example, Eastern Standard Time, which is five hours behind UTC, is represented as -05:00. If no time zone value is present, it is considered unknown; it is not assumed to be UTC.

Table 12–26 shows some valid and invalid values of time zones.

Table 12–26   Values of time zones

Valid values	Comment
z	Coordinated Universal Time (UTC)
-05:00	Eastern Standard Time which is 5 hours behind UTC
+09:00	UTC plus 9 hours, Japan's time zone
	unknown time zone

Invalid values	Comment
z+05:00	the value may be "z" or a time zone, but not both
+25:00	the range is limited to -24:00 through +24:00
-05	minutes are required

12.4.11 *Facets*

The facets indicated in Table 12–27 can restrict the date and time data types, and their descendants.

Table 12–27   Facets applicable to date and time data types

length		minExclusive	A	totalDigits	
minLength		minInclusive	A	fractionDigits	
maxLength		maxInclusive	A	pattern	A
whiteSpace	F	maxExclusive	A	enumeration	A

whiteSpace is collapse

12.4.12 *Date and time ordering*

When deriving data types from date and time data types (other than duration), it is important to note that applying the bounds facets (minExclusive, minInclusive, maxInclusive, and maxExclusive) can have unexpected results. If the values of the bounds facets specify time zones, and the instance values do not, or vice versa, it may be impossible to compare the two. For example, if maxInclusive for a time-based type is 14:30:00Z, this means that the maximum value is 2:30 PM in UTC. If the value 13:30:00 appears in an instance, which is 1:30 PM with no time zone specified, it is impossible to tell if this value is valid. It could be 1:30 PM in UTC, which would be valid, or 1:30 PM Eastern Standard Time, which would be 6:30 PM UTC, and therefore invalid. Because this is indeterminate, the schema processor will consider it an invalid value.

To avoid this problem, either use time zones in both bounds facet values and instance values, or do not use time zones at all. If both bounds and instance values have a time zone, the two values can be compared. Likewise, if neither has a time zone, the two values are assumed to be in the same time zone and compared as such.

12.5 | Legacy types

The legacy types described in this section are attribute types that are specified in the XML 1.0 Recommendation. It is recommended that these data types only be used for attributes, in order to maintain compatibility with XML 1.0. However, it is not an error to use these data types in element declarations.

12.5.1 ID

The data type ID is used for an attribute that uniquely identifies an element in an XML document. An ID value must be an NCName, as described in Section 12.2.3, "NCName." This means that it must start with a letter or underscore, and can only contain letters, digits, underscores, hyphens, and periods.

ID carries several additional constraints. Their values must be unique within an XML instance, regardless of the attribute's name or its element-type name. Example 12–1 is invalid if attributes custID and orderID are both declared to be of type ID.

Example 12–1. Invalid non-unique IDs

```
<order orderID="A123">
  <customer custID="A123">...</customer>
</order>
```

A complex type cannot include more than one attribute of type ID, or any type derived from ID. The type definition in Example 12–2 is illegal.

Example 12–2. Illegal duplication of ID attributes

```
<xsd:complexType name="CustType">
  <xsd:attribute name="id" type="xsd:ID" use="required"/>
  <xsd:attribute name="custSSN" type="xsd:ID" use="required"/>
</xsd:complexType>
```

ID attributes cannot have default or fixed values specified. The attribute declarations in Example 12–3 are illegal.

Example 12–3. Illegal attribute declarations

```
<xsd:attribute name="id" type="xsd:ID" fixed="A123"/>
<xsd:attribute name="id" type="xsd:ID" default="A123"/>
```

The facets indicated in Table 12–28 can restrict ID and its descendants.

Table 12–28   Facets applicable to `ID` data type

`length`	A	`minExclusive`		`totalDigits`	
`minLength`	A	`minInclusive`		`fractionDigits`	
`maxLength`	A	`maxInclusive`		`pattern`	V
`whiteSpace`	F	`maxExclusive`		`enumeration`	A

`whiteSpace` is `collapse`, pattern is `[\i-[:]][\c-[:]]*`

12.5.2 `IDREF`

The data type `IDREF` is used for an attribute that references an ID. A common use case for `IDREF` is to create a cross-reference to a particular section of a document. Like `ID`, an `IDREF` value must be an `NCName`, as described in Section 12.2.3, "`NCName`."

All attributes of type `IDREF` must reference an `ID` in the same XML document. In Example 12–4, the `ref` attribute of `quote` is of type `IDREF`, and the `id` attribute of `footnote` is of type `ID`. The instance contains a reference between them.

`ID` and `IDREF` are best used for referencing unique locations in document-oriented XML. To enforce complex uniqueness of data values, and primary and foreign key references, consider using identity constraints, which are described in Chapter 17, "Identity constraints."

The facets indicated in Table 12–29 can restrict `IDREF` and its descendants.

Table 12–29   Facets applicable to `IDREF` data type

`length`	A	`minExclusive`		`totalDigits`	
`minLength`	A	`minInclusive`		`fractionDigits`	
`maxLength`	A	`maxInclusive`		`pattern`	V
`whiteSpace`	F	`maxExclusive`		`enumeration`	A

`whiteSpace` is `collapse`, pattern is `[\i-[:]][\c-[:]]*`

Example 12–4. Using IDREF

Schema:

```
<xsd:element name="quote">
  <xsd:complexType>
    <!--content model-->
    <xsd:attribute name="ref" type="xsd:IDREF"/>
  </xsd:complexType>
</xsd:element>
<xsd:element name="footnote">
  <xsd:complexType>
    <!--content model-->
    <xsd:attribute name="id" type="xsd:ID" use="required"/>
  </xsd:complexType>
</xsd:element>
```

Instance:

```
<quote ref="fn1">...</quote>
<footnote id="fn1">...</footnote>
```

12.5.3 IDREFS

The data type IDREFS represents a list of IDREF values separated by whitespace. There must be at least one IDREF in the list. Each of the IDREF values must match an ID contained in the same XML document.

The facets indicated in Table 12–30 can restrict IDREFS and its descendants.

Table 12–30 Facets applicable to IDREFS data type

length	A	minExclusive	totalDigits	
minLength	V	minInclusive	fractionDigits	
maxLength	A	maxInclusive	pattern	A
whiteSpace	F	maxExclusive	enumeration	A

whiteSpace is collapse, minLength is 1

Because IDREFS is a list data type, restricting an IDREFS value with these facets may not behave as you expect. The facets length, min-Length, and maxLength apply to the number of items in the IDREFS list, not the length of each item. The enumeration facet applies to the whole list, not the individual items in the list. For more information, see Section 11.3.3, "Restricting list types."

12.5.4 ENTITY

The data type ENTITY represents a reference to an unparsed entity. The ENTITY data type is most often used to include information from another location that is not in XML format, such as graphics. An ENTITY value must be an NCName, as described in Section 12.2.3, "NCName." An ENTITY value carries the additional constraint that it must match the name of an unparsed entity in a document type definition (DTD) for the instance.

Example 12–5 shows an XML document that links product numbers to pictures of the products. In the schema, the picture element declaration declares an attribute location that has the data type ENTITY. In the instance, each value of the location attribute (in this case, prod557 and prod563) matches the name of an entity declared in the internal DTD subset of the instance.

The facets indicated in Table 12–31 can restrict ENTITY and its descendants.

Table 12–31   Facets applicable to ENTITY data type

length	A	minExclusive		totalDigits	
minLength	A	minInclusive		fractionDigits	
maxLength	A	maxInclusive		pattern	V
whiteSpace	F	maxExclusive		enumeration	A

whiteSpace is collapse, pattern is [\i-[:]][\c-[:]]*

Example 12–5. Using an unparsed entity

Schema:

```
<xsd:element name="picture">
  <xsd:complexType>
    <xsd:attribute name="location" type="xsd:ENTITY"/>
  </xsd:complexType>
</xsd:element>
<!--...-->
```

Instance:

```
<!DOCTYPE catalog [
<!NOTATION jpeg SYSTEM "JPG">
<!ENTITY prod557 SYSTEM "prod557.jpg" NDATA jpeg>
<!ENTITY prod563 SYSTEM "prod563.jpg" NDATA jpeg>
]>

<catalog>
  <product>
    <number>557</number>
    <picture location="prod557"/>
  </product>
  <product>
    <number>563</number>
    <picture location="prod563"/>
  </product>
</catalog>
```

12.5.5 ENTITIES

The data type ENTITIES represents a list of ENTITY values separated by whitespace. There must be at least one ENTITY in the list. Each of the ENTITY values must match the name of an unparsed entity that has been declared in a document type definition (DTD) for the instance.

Expanding on the example from the previous section, Example 12–6 shows the declaration of an attribute named location that is of type ENTITIES. In the instance, the location attribute can include a list of entity names. Each value (in this case there are two: prod557a and prod557b) matches the name of an entity that is declared in the internal DTD subset for the instance.

Example 12–6. Using ENTITIES

Schema:

```
<xsd:element name="pictures">
  <xsd:complexType>
    <xsd:attribute name="location" type="xsd:ENTITIES"/>
  </xsd:complexType>
</xsd:element>
```

Instance:

```
<!DOCTYPE catalog [
<!NOTATION jpeg SYSTEM "JPG">
<!ENTITY prod557a SYSTEM "prod557a.jpg" NDATA jpeg>
<!ENTITY prod557b SYSTEM "prod557b.jpg" NDATA jpeg>
]>

<catalog>
  <product>
    <number>557</number>
    <pictures location="prod557a prod557b"/>
  </product>
</catalog>
```

The facets indicated in Table 12–32 can restrict ENTITIES and its descendants.

Table 12–32 Facets applicable to ENTITIES data type

length	A	minExclusive		totalDigits	
minLength	V	minInclusive		fractionDigits	
maxLength	A	maxInclusive		pattern	A
whiteSpace	F	maxExclusive		enumeration	A

whiteSpace is collapse, minLength is 1

Because ENTITIES is a list data type, restricting an ENTITIES value with these facets may not behave as you expect. The facets length, minLength, and maxLength apply to the number of items in the ENTITIES list, not the length of each item. The enumeration facet applies to the whole list, not the individual items in the list. For more information, see Section 11.3.3, "Restricting list types."

12.5.6 NMTOKEN

The data type NMTOKEN represents a single string token. NMTOKEN values may consist of letters, digits, periods (.), hyphens (-), underscores (_), and colons (:). They may start with any of these characters. NMTOKEN has a whiteSpace facet value of collapse, so any leading or trailing whitespace will be removed. However, no whitespace may appear within the value itself. Table 12–33 shows some valid and invalid values of the NMTOKEN type.

Table 12–33   Values of NMTOKEN data type

Valid values	*Comment*
ABCD	
123_456	
starts_with_a_space	when parsed, leading spaces will be removed
Invalid values	*Comment*
contains a space	value must not contain a space
	an empty value is not valid, unless xsi:nil is used

The facets indicated in Table 12–34 can restrict NMTOKEN and its descendants.

Table 12–34   Facets applicable to NMTOKEN data type

length	A	minExclusive	totalDigits	
minLength	A	minInclusive	fractionDigits	
maxLength	A	maxInclusive	pattern	V
whiteSpace	F	maxExclusive	enumeration	A

whiteSpace is collapse, pattern is \c+

12.5.7 NMTOKENS

The data type NMTOKENS represents a list of NMTOKEN values separated by whitespace. There must be at least one NMTOKEN in the list. Table 12–35 shows some valid and invalid values of the NMTOKENS type.

Table 12–35   Values of NMTOKENS data type

Valid values	*Comment*
ABCD 123	
ABCD	one-item list
Invalid values	*Comment*
	an empty value is not valid, unless xsi:nil is used

The facets indicated in Table 12–36 can restrict NMTOKENS and its descendants.

Because NMTOKENS is a list data type, restricting an NMTOKENS value with these facets may not behave as you expect. The facets length, minLength, and maxLength apply to the number of items in the NMTOKENS list, not the length of each item. The enumeration facet applies to the whole list, not the individual items in the list. For more information, see Section 11.3.3, "Restricting list types."

Table 12–36   Facets applicable to NMTOKENS data type

length	A	minExclusive		totalDigits	
minLength	V	minInclusive		fractionDigits	
maxLength	A	maxInclusive		pattern	A
whiteSpace	F	maxExclusive		enumeration	A

whiteSpace is collapse, minLength is 1

12.5.8 NOTATION

The data type NOTATION represents a reference to a notation. A notation is a method of interpreting non-XML content. For example, if an element in an XML document contains binary graphics data in JPEG format, a notation can be declared to indicate that this is JPEG data. An attribute of type NOTATION can then be used to indicate which notation applies to the element's content. A NOTATION value must be a QName as described in Section 12.6.1, "QName."

NOTATION is the only built-in data type that cannot be the type of attributes or elements. Instead, you must define a new data type that restricts NOTATION, applying one or more enumeration facets. Each of these enumeration values must match the name of a declared notation. For more information on declaring notations and NOTATION-based data types, see Section 6.4, "Notations."

The facets indicated in Table 12–37 can restrict NOTATION and its descendants.

12.6 | Other types

12.6.1 QName

The data type QName represents an XML namespace-qualified name. The lexical representation of a QName consists of a prefix and a local part, separated by a colon, both of which are NCNames. The prefix

Table 12–37   Facets applicable to NOTATION data type

length	A	minExclusive		totalDigits	
minLength	A	minInclusive		fractionDigits	
maxLength	A	maxInclusive		pattern	A
whiteSpace	F	maxExclusive		enumeration	A

whiteSpace is collapse

and colon are optional, but if they are not present, it is assumed that either the name is namespace-qualified by other means (e.g., by a default namespace declaration), or the name is not in a namespace. QName is not based on string like the other name-related types, because it has this additional constraint that cannot be expressed with XML Schema facets. Table 12–38 shows some valid and invalid values of the QName type.

Table 12–38   Values of QName data type

Valid values	Comment
pre:myElement	valid assuming the prefix "pre" is mapped to a namespace in scope
myElement	prefix and colon are optional
Invalid values	**Comment**
:myElement	a QName must not start with a colon
pre:3rdElement	the local part must not start with a number; it must be a valid NCName
	an empty value is not valid, unless xsi:nil is used

The facets indicated in Table 12–39 can restrict QName and its descendants.

Table 12–39 Facets applicable to `QName` data type

length	A	minExclusive		totalDigits	
minLength	A	minInclusive		fractionDigits	
maxLength	A	maxInclusive		pattern	A
whiteSpace	F	maxExclusive		enumeration	A

whiteSpace is collapse

12.6.2 boolean

The data type `boolean` represents logical yes/no values. The valid values for `boolean` are `true`, `false`, `0`, and `1`. Table 12–40 shows some valid and invalid values of the `boolean` type.

Table 12–40 Values of `boolean` data type

Valid values	Comment
true	
false	
0	false
1	true
Invalid values	*Comment*
TRUE	values are case sensitive
T	the word "true" must be spelled out
	an empty value is not valid, unless `xsi:nil` is used

The facets indicated in Table 12–41 can restrict `boolean` and its descendants.

Table 12–41   Facets applicable to `boolean` data type

length		minExclusive	totalDigits	
minLength		minInclusive	fractionDigits	
maxLength		maxInclusive	pattern	A
whiteSpace	F	maxExclusive	enumeration	

`whiteSpace` is `collapse`

12.6.3 `hexBinary` *and* `base64Binary`

The data types `hexBinary` and `base64Binary` represent binary data. Their lexical representation is a sequence of binary octets. The type `hexBinary` uses hexadecimal encoding, where each binary octet is a two-character hexadecimal number. Lowercase and uppercase letters A through F are permitted. For example, `0FB8` represents the 16-bit integer 4024.

The type `base64Binary` uses base64 encoding, as described in RFC 2045. In base64 encoding, the case of the letters is significant, and some punctuation characters may be used. For more information on base64 encoding, see RFC 2045, *Multipurpose Internet Mail Extensions (MIME) Part One: Format of Internet Message Bodies*.

Table 12–42 shows some valid and invalid values of the binary types.

The facets indicated in Table 12–43 can restrict `hexBinary`, `base64Binary`, and their descendants.

The `length` facet for the binary types represents the number of binary octets (groups of 8 bits each). For example, the length of the `hexBinary` value `0FB8` is equal to 2. Since base64 characters represent 6 bits each, the length of the `base64Binary` value `0FB8` is equal to 3.

12.6.4 `anyURI`

The data type `anyURI` represents a Uniform Resource Identifier (URI). URIs are used to uniquely identify resources, and they may be absolute

Table 12–42   Values of binary data types

Valid values	Comment
0FB8	hexBinary representation of decimal 4024; base64Binary representation of decimal 20552
0fb8	hexBinary representation of decimal 4024; base64Binary representation of decimal 128712
+4	base64Binary representation of decimal 4024 (not valid for hexBinary)
	an empty value is valid

Invalid values	Comment
FB8	for hexBinary, an odd number of characters is not valid; octets come in pairs of characters

Table 12–43   Facets applicable to binary data types

length	A	minExclusive		totalDigits	
minLength	A	minInclusive		fractionDigits	
maxLength	A	maxInclusive		pattern	A
whiteSpace	F	maxExclusive		enumeration	A

whiteSpace is collapse

or relative. Absolute URIs provide the entire context for locating the resources, such as http://example.org/prod.html. Relative URIs are specified as the difference from a base URI, such as ../prod.html. It is also possible to specify a fragment identifier, using the # character, such as ../prod.html#shirt.

The three previous examples happen to be HTTP URLs (Uniform Resource Locators), but URIs also encompass URLs of other schemes (e.g., FTP, gopher, telnet), as well as URNs (Uniform Resource Names). URIs are not required to be dereferencable; that is, it is not necessary for there to be a web page at `http://example.org/prod.html` in order for this to be a valid URI reference.

URIs require that non-ASCII characters and some ASCII characters be escaped with their hexadecimal Unicode code point preceded by the % character. For example, `http://example.org/édition.html` must be represented instead as `http://example.org/%E9dition.html`, with the é escaped as `%E9`. However, the `anyURI` data type will accept unescaped non-ASCII characters.

It is valid for a URI to contain a space, but this practice is strongly discouraged. Spaces should instead be escaped using `%20`.

Table 12–44 shows some examples of valid URI references. However, the schema processor is not required to parse the contents of an `anyURI` value to determine whether it represents a valid URI, so virtually any value will be accepted.

For more information on URIs, see RFC 2396, *Uniform Resource Identifiers (URI): Generic Syntax.*

Table 12–44   Valid values of `anyURI` data type

Valid values	Comment
`http://example.org`	absolute URI (also a URL)
`mailto:priscilla@example.org`	absolute URI
`../%E9dition.html`	relative URI containing escaped non-ASCII character
`../édition.html`	relative URI containing unescaped non-ASCII character
`http://example.org/prod.html#shirt`	URI with fragment identifier
`../prod.html#shirt`	relative URI with fragment identifier
`urn:example:org`	URN

The facets indicated in Table 12–45 can restrict `anyURI` and its descendants.

Table 12–45   Facets applicable to `anyURI` data type

`length`	A	`minExclusive`		`totalDigits`	
`minLength`	A	`minInclusive`		`fractionDigits`	
`maxLength`	A	`maxInclusive`		`pattern`	A
`whiteSpace`	F	`maxExclusive`		`enumeration`	A

`whiteSpace` is `collapse`

12.7 | Type equality

When a schema processor is comparing two values, it does more than compare strings. It takes into account the data types of the values. This comes into play during validation of an instance in several places:

- validating fixed values,
- validating enumerated values,
- determining uniqueness of identity constraint fields,
- validating key references.

One of the factors used in determining the equality of two values is the relationship of their types in the derivation hierarchy. Types that are related to each other by restriction or union can have values that are equal. For example, the value 2 of type `integer` and the value 2 of type `positiveInteger` are considered equal, since `positiveInteger` is derived from `integer`. Types that are not related in the hierarchy can never have values that are equal. This means that an `integer` value will never equal a `string` value, even if they are both

2. This is true of both the built-in and user-derived types. Example 12–7 illustrates this point.[1]

Example 12–7. Equality based on type definition hierarchy

`<integer>2</integer>` does not equal `<string>2</string>`
`<integer>2</integer>` equals `<positiveInteger>2</positiveInteger>`
`<string>abc</string>` equals `<NCName>abc</NCName>`
`<string>abc</string>` does not equal `<QName>abc</QName>`
`<IDREFS>abc</IDREFS>` does not equal `<IDREF>abc</IDREF>`

Some of the built-in types have multiple lexical representations that are equivalent. For example, an `integer` may be represented as 2, 02, +2, or +00002. These values are all considered equal if they have the type `integer`, and unequal if they have the type `string`. Example 12–8 illustrates this point.

Example 12–8. Equality based on equivalent lexical representations

---

`<integer>2</integer>` equals `<integer>02</integer>`
`<integer>2</integer>` equals `<positiveInteger>02</positiveInteger>`
`<string>2</string>` does not equal `<string>02</string>`
`<boolean>true</boolean>` equals `<boolean>1</boolean>`
`<hexBinary>0fb8</hexBinary>` equals `<hexBinary>0FB8</hexBinary>`
`<time>13:20:00-05:00</time>` equals `<time>12:20:00-06:00</time>`

Another factor to take into account is whitespace normalization. Whitespace is normalized before any validation takes place. Therefore, it plays a role in determining whether two values are equal. For example,

---

1. Assume for this section that there are element types declared whose names are the same as their data type names. For example, `<element name="integer" type="integer"/>`.

the string data type has a whiteSpace facet value of preserve, while the token data type's is collapse. The value "a " that has the type string will not equal "a " that has the type token, because the leading and trailing spaces will be stripped for the token value. Example 12–9 illustrates this point.

Example 12–9. Equality based on whitespace normalization

```
<string> a </string> does not equal <token> a </token>
<string>a</string> equals <token> a </token>
<token>a</token> equals <token> a </token>
```

Complex types

Chapter

13

omplex types are used to define the content model and attributes of elements. This chapter introduces complex types. It covers the four content types (simple, element-only, mixed, and empty), and the use of element declarations, model groups, attribute declarations, and wildcards to define complex types.

13.1 | What are complex types?

Elements that have complex types have child elements or attributes. They may also have character content. Example 13–1 shows the elements `size`, `product`, `letter`, and `color` that have complex types. They have the four different content types that are described in this chapter (simple, element-only, mixed, and empty, respectively).

Attributes can never have complex types; they always have simple types. This makes sense, because attributes cannot themselves have children or attributes.

Example 13–1. Elements with complex types

```
<size system="US-DRESS">10</size>

<product>
  <number>557</number>
  <name>Short-Sleeved Linen Blouse</name>
</product>

<letter>Dear <custName>Priscilla Walmsley</custName>...</letter>

<color value="blue"/>
```

13.2 | Defining complex types

13.2.1 *Named complex types*

Complex types may be either named or anonymous. Named types can be used by multiple element and attribute declarations. They are always defined globally (i.e., their parent is always `schema` or `redefine`) and are required to have a name that is unique among the data types (both simple and complex) in the schema. The syntax to define a named complex type is shown in Table 13–1.

The `name` of a complex type must be an XML non-colonized name, which means that it must start with a letter or underscore, and may only contain letters, digits, underscores, hyphens, and periods. You cannot include a namespace prefix when defining the type; it takes its namespace from the target namespace of the schema document. All of the examples of data types in this book have the word "Type" at the end of their names, to clearly distinguish them from element-type names. However, this is not a requirement; you may in fact have a data type definition and an element declaration using the same name.

Example 13–2 shows the definition of the named complex type `ProductType`, along with an element declaration that references it.

Table 13–1   XSDL syntax: named complex type definition

Name

`complexType`

Parents

`schema`, `redefine`

Attribute name	*Type*	*Required/default*	*Description*
`id`	`ID`		unique ID
`name`	`NCName`	required	complex type name
`mixed`	`boolean`	`false`	whether the complex type allows mixed content, see Section 13.3.3
`abstract`	`boolean`	`false`	whether the type can be used in an instance, see Section 14.7.4
`block`	`"#all"` | list of (`"extension"` | `"restriction"`)	defaults to `block-Default` of `schema`	whether to block type substitution in the instance, see Section 14.7.2
`final`	`"#all"` | list of (`"extension"` | `"restriction"`)	defaults to `finalDefault` of `schema`	whether other types can be derived from this one, see Section 14.7.1

Content

`annotation?, (simpleContent | complexContent | ((group | all | choice | sequence)?, (attribute | attributeGroup)*, anyAttribute?))`

Example 13–2. Named complex type

```
<xsd:complexType name="ProductType">
  <xsd:sequence>
    <xsd:element name="number" type="ProdNumType"/>
    <xsd:element name="name" type="xsd:string"/>
    <xsd:element name="size" type="SizeType"/>
  </xsd:sequence>
</xsd:complexType>

<xsd:element name="product" type="ProductType"/>
```

13.2.2 *Anonymous complex types*

Anonymous complex types, on the other hand, must not have names. They are always defined entirely within an element declaration, and may only be used once, by that declaration. Defining a type anonymously prevents it from ever being restricted, extended, or redefined. The syntax to define an anonymous complex type is shown in Table 13–2.

Table 13–2   XSDL syntax: anonymous complex type definition

Name			
complexType			

Parents			
element			

Attribute name	*Type*	*Required/default*	*Description*
id	ID		unique ID
mixed	boolean	false	whether the complex type allows mixed content

Content
annotation?, (simpleContent | complexContent | ((group | all | choice | sequence)?, (attribute | attributeGroup)*, anyAttribute?))

Example 13–3 shows the definition of an anonymous complex type within an element declaration.

Example 13–3. Anonymous complex type

```
<xsd:element name="product">
  <xsd:complexType>
    <xsd:sequence>
      <xsd:element name="number" type="ProdNumType"/>
      <xsd:element name="name" type="xsd:string"/>
      <xsd:element name="size" type="SizeType"/>
    </xsd:sequence>
  </xsd:complexType>
</xsd:element>
```

The question of whether to use named or anonymous types is covered in Section 9.2.3, "Design hint: Should I use named or anonymous types?" in the chapter on simple types.

13.2.3 *Complex type alternatives*

There are three different branches in the content model for `complex-Type` elements, representing three different methods of creating complex types[1]:

- A single `complexContent` child, which is used to derive a complex type from another complex type. It is covered in detail in the next chapter, "Deriving complex types."
- A single `simpleContent` child, which is used to derive a complex type from a simple type. This is covered briefly in Section 13.3.1, "Simple content," of this chapter, and in more detail in the next chapter.

---

1. It is also legal for a `complexType` element to have no children at all. This results in a type that allows no attributes and no content.

■ A group (`group`, `all`, `choice`, or `sequence`) plus attributes. This is used to define a complex type without deriving it from any particular type. We will cover this method in this chapter.

13.3 | Content types

The "contents" of an element are the character data and child elements that are between its tags. The order and structure of the children of a complex type are known as its "content model." There are four types of content for complex types: simple, element-only, mixed, and empty. The content type is independent of attributes; all of these content types allow attributes. This section explains the four content types and provides an example of how each is represented in XSDL.

13.3.1 *Simple content*

Simple content allows character data only, with no children. Example 13–4 shows the element `size` that has character data (the value 10) but no child elements. Generally, the only thing that distinguishes a simple type from a complex type with simple content is that the latter may have attributes. If `size` elements could never have a `system` attribute, you could just give `size` a simple type, as described in Chapter 9, "Simple types."

Example 13–4. Instance element with simple content

```
<size system="US-DRESS">10</size>
```

The `size` element shown in Example 13–4 is an example instance for the complex type definition in Example 13–5. The character data content of the complex type `SizeType` conforms to the simple type `integer`. It extends `integer` to add the attribute `system`.

Example 13–5. Complex type with simple content

```
<xsd:complexType name="SizeType">
  <xsd:simpleContent>
    <xsd:extension base="xsd:integer">
      <xsd:attribute name="system" type="xsd:token"/>
    </xsd:extension>
  </xsd:simpleContent>
</xsd:complexType>
```

13.3.2 *Element-only content*

Element-only content allows only children, with no character data content. Example 13–6 shows an element `product` that has element-only content. It has four children: `number`, `name`, `size`, and `color`.

Example 13–6. Instance element with element-only content

```
<product>
  <number>557</number>
  <name>Short-Sleeved Linen Blouse</name>
  <size system="US-DRESS">10</size>
  <color value="blue"/>
</product>
```

Example 13–7 shows a complex type definition that might be used by the `product` element declaration.

13.3.3 *Mixed content*

Mixed content allows character data as well as child elements. This is most often used for freeform text such as letters and documents. Example 13–8 shows an element `letter` with mixed content. Note that there is character data directly contained in the `letter` element, as well as children `custName`, `prodName`, and `prodSize`.

Example 13–7. Complex type with element-only content

```
<xsd:complexType name="ProductType">
  <xsd:sequence>
    <xsd:element name="number" type="ProdNumType"/>
    <xsd:element name="name" type="xsd:string"/>
    <xsd:element name="size" type="SizeType"/>
    <xsd:element name="color" type="ColorType"/>
  </xsd:sequence>
</xsd:complexType>
```

Example 13–8. Instance element with mixed content

```
<letter>Dear <custName>Priscilla Walmsley</custName>,
Unfortunately, we are out of stock of the <prodName>Short-Sleeved
Linen Blouse</prodName> in size <prodSize>10</prodSize> that you
ordered...</letter>
```

The letter element shown in Example 13–8 is an example instance for the complex type definition in Example 13–9. To indicate that character data content is permitted, the complexType element in Example 13–9 has an attribute mixed that is set to true. The default value for mixed is false, meaning that character data content would not normally be permitted.

Example 13–9. Complex type with mixed content

```
<xsd:complexType name="LetterType" mixed="true">
  <xsd:sequence>
    <xsd:element name="custName" type="CustNameType"/>
    <xsd:element name="prodName" type="xsd:string"/>
    <xsd:element name="prodSize" type="SizeType"/>
    <!--...-->
  </xsd:sequence>
</xsd:complexType>
```

It is important to note that the character data that is directly contained in the letter element (e.g., "Dear ", "Unfortunately...") is not assigned a data type. It is completely unrestricted. Therefore, you should not use mixed content types for data that you wish to constrain in any way.

13.3.4 *Empty content*

Empty content allows neither character data nor child elements. Elements with empty content often have values in attributes. In some cases, they may not even have attributes; their presence alone is meaningful. For example, a `<br/>` element in XHTML indicates a new row, without providing any data other than its presence. Example 13–10 shows an element `color` with empty content.

Example 13–10. Instance element with empty content

```
<color value="blue"/>
```

The `color` element shown in Example 13–10 is an example instance for the complex type definition in Example 13–11. Note that there is no special attribute in the complex type definition to indicate that the content is empty. The fact that only an attribute, with no content model, is specified for the complex type is enough to indicate this.

Example 13–11. Complex type with empty content

```
<xsd:complexType name="ColorType">
  <xsd:attribute name="value" type="ColorValueType"/>
</xsd:complexType>
```

13.4 | Using element types

Element types can be included in complex type content models in three ways: as local element declarations, as references to global element declarations, and as wildcards.

13.4.1 *Local element declarations*

Complex types can contain local element declarations. This means that such an element declaration declares a name, a data type, and other properties within the complex type. The scope of that element declaration is limited to the complex type within which it appears. Local element declarations are described in detail in Section 7.1.2, "Local element declarations." All of the prior examples in this chapter have local element declarations, as evidenced by the `name` attributes of the `element` elements.

13.4.2 *Element references*

Complex types can also contain references to global element declarations. Global element declarations themselves are covered in detail in Section 7.1.1, "Global element declarations." The syntax to reference a global element declaration is shown in Table 13–3. An `element` element is used to make the reference, though it uses a `ref` attribute instead of a `name` attribute.

Example 13–12 shows the four global element declarations for child elements, with the `ProductType` definition referencing them through the `ref` attribute. Note that the `type` attribute appears in the global element declaration, while the `minOccurs` attribute is in the element reference. Occurrence constraints (`minOccurs` and `maxOccurs`) may only appear within complex type definitions, that is, in element references or local element declarations, not in global element declarations.

For a detailed discussion of local or global element declarations see Section 7.1.3, "Design hint: Should I use global or local element declarations?"

Table 13–3   XSDL syntax: element reference

Name

`element`

Parents

`all, choice, sequence`

Attribute name	Type	Required/ default	Description
`id`	`ID`		unique ID
`ref`	`QName`	required	name of the global element declaration being referenced
`minOccurs`	`nonNegativeInteger`	1	minimum number of times the element may occur
`maxOccurs`	`nonNegativeInteger | "unbounded"`	1	maximum number of times the element may occur

Content

`annotation?`

Example 13–12. Element references

```
<xsd:schema xmlns:xsd="http://www.w3.org/2001/XMLSchema">
  <xsd:element name="number" type="ProdNumType"/>
  <xsd:element name="name" type="xsd:string"/>
  <xsd:element name="size" type="SizeType"/>
  <xsd:element name="color" type="ColorType"/>

  <xsd:complexType name="ProductType">
    <xsd:sequence>
      <xsd:element ref="number"/>
      <xsd:element ref="name"/>
      <xsd:element ref="size" minOccurs="0"/>
      <xsd:element ref="color" minOccurs="0"/>
    </xsd:sequence>
  </xsd:complexType>

</xsd:schema>
```

13.4.3 *Element wildcards*

Element wildcards are used to allow flexibility as to what elements may appear in a content model. Element wildcards are represented in XSDL by an `any` element, whose syntax is shown in Table 13–4.

Table 13–4   XSDL syntax: element wildcard

Name
any

Parents
choice, sequence

Attribute name	Type	Required/ default	Description
id	ID		unique ID
minOccurs	nonNegativeInteger	1	minimum number of replacement elements that may appear
maxOccurs	nonNegativeInteger | "unbounded"	1	maximum number of replacement elements that may appear
namespace	"##any" | "##other" | (list of anyURI | "##targetNamespace" | "##local")	##any	which namespace(s) the replacement elements may be in
process-Contents	"lax" | "skip" | "strict"	strict	how strictly to validate the replacement elements

Content
annotation?

The `minOccurs` and `maxOccurs` attributes control the number of replacement elements. This number represents how many total replacement elements may appear, not how many of a particular type, or how many types. The number does not include child elements of the replacement elements.

The `namespace` attribute allows you to specify what namespaces the replacement elements may belong to. It may have the value `##any`, `##other`, or a list of values. If it is `##any`, the replacement elements can be in any namespace whatsoever, or be in no namespace.

If it is `##other`, the replacement elements can be in any namespace other than the target namespace of the schema document, but they must be in a namespace. If the schema document has no target namespace, the replacement elements can have any namespace, but they must have one. Otherwise, it can be a whitespace-separated list of values, which includes any or all of the following items:

- `##targetNamespace` to indicate that the replacement elements may be in the target namespace of the schema document,
- `##local` to indicate that the replacement elements may be in no namespace,
- specific namespaces for the replacement elements.

The namespace constraint applies only to the replacement elements. The children of each replacement element are then validated according to the type of the replacement element.

The `processContents` attribute controls how much validation takes place on the replacement elements. It may have one of three values:

- If it is `skip`, the schema processor performs no validation whatsoever, and does not attempt to find a schema document associated with the wildcard's namespace. It must, however, be well-formed XML and it must be in one of the namespaces allowed by the wildcard.
- If it is `lax`, the schema processor will validate elements for which it can find declarations and raise errors if they are invalid. It will not, however, report errors on the elements for which it does not find declarations.

- If it is strict, the schema processor will attempt to find a schema document associated with the namespace, and validate all of the elements. If it cannot find the schema document, or the elements are invalid, it will raise errors.

Suppose our product element can also contain an extended textual description that may run several paragraphs. This description is going to appear on the company's website, and we want the text to be formatted using XHTML. Example 13–13 shows an element wildcard that will allow DescriptionType to contain any elements that are part of the XHTML namespace.

Example 13–13. Complex type with element wildcard

```
<xsd:complexType name="DescriptionType" mixed="true">
  <xsd:sequence>
    <xsd:any namespace="http://www.w3.org/1999/xhtml"
             minOccurs="0" maxOccurs="unbounded"
             processContents="skip"/>
  </xsd:sequence>
</xsd:complexType>
```

Example 13–14 shows a description element which has the type DescriptionType.

Example 13–14. Instance with processContents of skip

```
<catalog xmlns:xhtml="http://www.w3.org/1999/xhtml">

  <description>
    This shirt is the <xhtml:b>best-selling</xhtml:b> shirt in
    our catalog! <xhtml:br/> Note: runs large.
  </description>
  <!--...-->
</catalog>
```

Because the `processContents` attribute is set to `skip`, it is not necessary to provide any information about where to find the schema to validate the replacement elements. It is only necessary that the elements in the instance have names that are qualified by the XHTML namespace. In our example, we accomplish this by associating the `xhtml` prefix with the XHTML namespace, and by prefixing all of the XHTML element-type names.

If we had chosen `strict` for the value of `processContents`, we would have to go further and tell the processor where to find the XHTML schema. We could do this by including the `xsi:schema-Location` attribute in the `catalog` tag, specifying a pair of values that match the namespace with its schema location, as shown in Example 13–15.

Example 13–15. Instance with `processContents` of `strict`

```
<catalog xmlns:xhtml="http://www.w3.org/1999/xhtml"
         xmlns:xsi="http://www.w3.org/2001/XMLSchema-instance"
         xsi:schemaLocation="http://www.w3.org/1999/xhtml
                             xhtml.xsd">

  <description>
    This shirt is the <xhtml:b>best-selling</xhtml:b> shirt
    in our catalog! <xhtml:br/> Note: runs large.
  </description>
  <!--...-->
</catalog>
```

13.4.4 *Duplication of element-type names*

If two element declarations or references with the same name appear anywhere in the same complex type they must have the same data type. Example 13–16 shows a complex type definition that includes two declarations for `name`. This content model represents "either `number` or `name` or both." It is valid because both `name` declarations refer to exactly the same type, `xsd:string`. See Section 13.5.6, "Deterministic content models" for a description of the deterministic content model used in this example.

Example 13–16. Legal duplication of element-type names

```
<xsd:complexType name="ProductType">
  <xsd:choice>
    <xsd:sequence>
      <xsd:element name="number" type="ProdNumType"/>
      <xsd:element name="name" type="xsd:string" minOccurs="0"/>
    </xsd:sequence>
    <xsd:element name="name" type="xsd:string"/>
  </xsd:choice>
</xsd:complexType>
```

Example 13–17, on the other hand, is illegal because the two declarations of name refer to different types.

Example 13–17. Illegal duplication of element-type names

```
<xsd:complexType name="ProductType">
  <xsd:choice>
    <xsd:sequence>
      <xsd:element name="number" type="ProdNumType"/>
      <xsd:element name="name" type="xsd:string" minOccurs="0"/>
    </xsd:sequence>
    <xsd:element name="name" type="xsd:token"/>
  </xsd:choice>
</xsd:complexType>
```

Anonymous types are never considered equal, even if they have identical content models. If either of the name declarations used an anonymous type, it would automatically be illegal.

It is the *qualified* name that is relevant here. If one of the name element-type names had been qualified, or both had been qualified with different namespace names, Example 13–17 would have been legal. This applies regardless of whether the element declarations are global or local.

Qualified element-type name and qualified data-type name are the only properties that must be identical. It is legal for the two `name` element declarations to specify different default values, annotations, or other properties.

13.5 | Using model groups

Model groups allow you to group child element declarations or references together to construct more meaningful content models. There are three kinds of model groups: `all` groups, `choice` groups, and `sequence` groups.

Every complex type (except empty content types) has exactly one model group child. This one model group child contains the element declarations or references, or other model groups that make up the content model. Element declarations are never directly contained in the `complexType` element.

13.5.1 sequence *groups*

A `sequence` group of element declarations is used to indicate the order in which the corresponding conforming elements should appear. In all of the previous examples, we used `sequence` groups. In XSDL, this is accomplished using a `sequence` element, whose syntax is shown in Table 13–5.

Example 13–18 shows a complex type definition that contains a `sequence` group. All of the children (`number`, `name`, `size`, and `color`) must appear in that order, if they appear. The fact that the `minOccurs` attribute of the `size` and `color` element declarations is set to 0 means that they are optional.

Table 13–5   XSDL syntax: sequence **group**

Name
sequence

Parents
complexType, restriction, extension, group, choice, sequence

Attribute name	Type	Required/ default	Description
id	ID		unique ID
minOccurs	nonNegativeInteger	1	minimum number of times the sequence group may occur
maxOccurs	nonNegativeInteger | "unbounded"	1	maximum number of times the sequence group may occur

Content
annotation?, (element | group | choice | sequence | any)*

Example 13–18. A sequence group

```
<xsd:complexType name="ProductType">
  <xsd:sequence>
    <xsd:element name="number" type="ProdNumType"/>
    <xsd:element name="name" type="xsd:string"/>
    <xsd:element name="size" type="SizeType" minOccurs="0"/>
    <xsd:element name="color" type="ColorType" minOccurs="0"/>
  </xsd:sequence>
</xsd:complexType>
```

Example 13–19 shows some valid instances of ProductType. They are valid because the elements that are required (i.e., do not have minOccurs set to 0) appear, and the elements that do appear are in the correct order.

Example 13–20 shows an invalid instance of ProductType. It is invalid because the elements appear in the wrong order.

Example 13–19. Valid instances of ProductType

```
<product>
  <number>557</number>
  <name>Short-Sleeved Linen Blouse</name>
  <size system="US-DRESS">10</size>
  <color value="blue"/>
</product>

<product>
  <number>557</number>
  <name>Short-Sleeved Linen Blouse</name>
</product>

<product>
  <number>557</number>
  <name>Short-Sleeved Linen Blouse</name>
  <color value="blue"/>
</product>
```

Example 13–20. Invalid instance of ProductType

```
<product>
  <number>557</number>
  <size system="US-DRESS">10</size>
  <name>Short-Sleeved Linen Blouse</name>
  <color value="blue"/>
</product>
```

13.5.1.1 Design hint: Should I care about the order of elements?

You may not be concerned about the order in which an element's children appear. However, some constraints will only work if you enforce an order. For example, it is not possible to say that a product may have one number, one name, and up to three color children, in any order. You could use an all group if you only want to allow each element once, or you could use a choice group if you do not mind there being more than one number or name. You could also use a choice group containing several sequence groups to iterate all the possible orders of the child elements, but this is rather cumbersome and becomes explosively more cumbersome as more children are added. In order to ensure that you will only have one `number` and one `name`, and allow more than one `color`, the best approach is to enforce the order and use a `sequence` group, as shown here:

```
<xsd:complexType name="ProductType">
  <xsd:sequence>
    <xsd:element name="number" type="ProdNumType"/>
    <xsd:element name="name" type="xsd:string"/>
    <xsd:element name="color" type="ColorType" maxOccurs="3"/>
  </xsd:sequence>
</xsd:complexType>
```

13.5.2 choice *groups*

A `choice` group of element declarations is used to indicate that only one of the corresponding conforming elements must appear. In XSDL, this is accomplished using a `choice` element, whose syntax is shown in Table 13–6.

Example 13–21 shows an example of a `choice` group. This means that any one of the elements (`shirt`, `hat`, or `umbrella`) must appear.

Example 13–21. A `choice` group

```
<xsd:complexType name="ItemsType">
  <xsd:choice>
    <xsd:element name="shirt" type="ShirtType"/>
    <xsd:element name="hat" type="HatType"/>
    <xsd:element name="umbrella" type="UmbrellaType"/>
  </xsd:choice>
</xsd:complexType>
```

Example 13–22 shows some valid instances of `ItemsType`. They are valid because each contains exactly one element conforming to the declarations in the `choice` group. If more than one element appeared, or no elements at all appeared, it would be invalid.

Table 13–6 XSDL syntax: `choice` group

Name
`choice`

Parents
`complexType, restriction, extension, group, choice, sequence`

Attribute name	Type	Required/ default	Description
`id`	`ID`		unique ID
`minOccurs`	`nonNegativeInteger`	`1`	minimum number of times the `choice` group may occur
`maxOccurs`	`nonNegativeInteger` `| "unbounded"`	`1`	maximum number of times the `choice` group may occur

Content
`annotation?, (element | group | choice | sequence | any)*`

Example 13–22. Valid instances of `ItemsType`

```
<items>
  <shirt>...</shirt>
</items>

<items>
  <hat>...</hat>
</items>
```

A common use case for `choice` groups is to allow any number of children to appear in any order. If, in our example above, we allowed the `choice` group to repeat itself by setting its `maxOccurs` attribute to `unbounded`, as shown in Example 13–23, that would entirely change the meaning of the group. Now it allows any of the children, any number of times, in any order.

Example 13–23. A repeating `choice` group

```
<xsd:complexType name="ItemsType">
  <xsd:choice minOccurs="0" maxOccurs="unbounded">
    <xsd:element name="shirt" type="ShirtType"/>
    <xsd:element name="umbrella" type="UmbrellaType"/>
    <xsd:element name="hat" type="HatType"/>
  </xsd:choice>
</xsd:complexType>
```

Example 13–24 shows a valid instance of the new definition of `ItemsType`.

Example 13–24. Valid instance of `ItemsType`

```
<items>
  <shirt>...</shirt>
  <hat>...</hat>
  <umbrella>...</umbrella>
  <shirt>...</shirt>
  <shirt>...</shirt>
</items>
```

In Example 13–23, we also set the `minOccurs` attribute of the `choice` group to `0`. This means that `items` would also be valid if it were completely empty.

13.5.3 *Nesting of* sequence *and* choice *groups*

In order to specify more advanced content models, `sequence` and `choice` groups can be nested within each other as many levels deep as necessary. Example 13–25 shows a slightly more complicated definition of `ProductType`. With this definition, `number` must appear first, then `name`, then any number of the properties (such as `size` and `color`) of the product, in any order. Note that the `choice` group is inside the `sequence` group, allowing you to combine the power of both kinds of model groups.

Example 13–25. Multiple nested groups

```
<xsd:complexType name="ProductType">
  <xsd:sequence>
    <xsd:element name="number" type="ProdNumType"/>
    <xsd:element name="name" type="xsd:string"/>
    <xsd:choice minOccurs="0" maxOccurs="unbounded">
      <xsd:element name="size" type="SizeType"/>
      <xsd:element name="color" type="ColorType"/>
    </xsd:choice>
  </xsd:sequence>
</xsd:complexType>
```

13.5.4 all *groups*

An all group is used to indicate that elements conforming to all of the element declarations should appear, in any order, but no more than once each. In XSDL, this is accomplished using an all element, whose syntax is shown in Table 13–7. An all group follows rules that are different from choice and sequence groups:

- It can only contain element declarations and references, not other groups. For each element it contains, maxOccurs must be 1, and minOccurs may only be 0 or 1.

- It cannot occur multiple times. For the all element itself, maxOccurs must be 1, and minOccurs may only be 0 or 1.

- It cannot appear in other model groups. An all group must be at the top level of the complex type.

Example 13–26 uses an all group to represent the same basic structure for product elements, with no specific order for the children.

Example 13–27 shows some valid instances of ProductType, according to the new definition. The name and number elements are still required, but now they may appear in any order.

As mentioned above, an all group can only appear at the top level of a complex type. Example 13–28 is illegal because the all group is inside a sequence group.

Table 13–7   XSDL syntax: `all` group

Name
`all`

Parents
`complexType, restriction, extension, group`

Attribute name	Type	Required/ default	Description
`id`	`ID`		unique ID
`minOccurs`	`"0" | "1"`	1	minimum number of times the `all` group may occur
`maxOccurs`	`"1"`	1	maximum number of times the `all` group may occur

Content
`annotation?, element*`

Example 13–26. An `all` group

```
<xsd:complexType name="ProductType">
  <xsd:all>
    <xsd:element name="number" type="ProdNumType"/>
    <xsd:element name="name" type="xsd:string"/>
    <xsd:element name="size" type="SizeType" minOccurs="0"/>
    <xsd:element name="color" type="ColorType" minOccurs="0"/>
  </xsd:all>
</xsd:complexType>
```

13.5.5 *Named model group references*

Named model groups may be referenced in complex type definitions, in order to make use of predefined content model fragments. Named model groups are described in detail in Chapter 15, "Reusable groups." Example 13–29 shows a reference to a named model group in a complex type definition.

Example 13–27. Valid instances of `ProductType` using an `all` group

```
<product>
  <color value="blue"/>
  <size system="US-DRESS">10</size>
  <number>557</number>
  <name>Short-Sleeved Linen Blouse</name>
</product>

<product>
  <name>Short-Sleeved Linen Blouse</name>
  <number>557</number>
</product>
```

Example 13–28. An illegal `all` group

```
<xsd:complexType name="ProductType">
  <xsd:sequence>
    <xsd:element name="number" type="ProdNumType"/>
    <xsd:element name="name" type="xsd:string"/>
    <xsd:all>
      <xsd:element name="size" type="SizeType" minOccurs="0"/>
      <xsd:element name="color" type="ColorType" minOccurs="0"/>
    </xsd:all>
  </xsd:sequence>
</xsd:complexType>
```

Example 13–29. Complex type with a named model group reference

```
<xsd:complexType name="ProductType">
  <xsd:sequence>
    <xsd:group ref="DescriptionGroup"/>
    <xsd:element name="number" type="ProdNumType"/>
    <xsd:element name="name" type="xsd:string"/>
  </xsd:sequence>
</xsd:complexType>
```

13.5.6 *Deterministic content models*

XML Schema, like XML 1.0, requires that content models be deterministic. A schema processor, as it makes its way through the children of an instance element, must be able to find only one branch of the content model that is applicable, without having to look ahead to the rest of the children. The classic example is shown in Example 13–30. It is intended to represent a choice among a, b, and a followed by b.

Example 13–30. Illegal non-deterministic content model

```
<xsd:complexType name="AOrBOrBothType">
  <xsd:choice>
    <xsd:element name="a" type="xsd:string"/>
    <xsd:element name="b" type="xsd:string"/>
    <xsd:sequence>
      <xsd:element name="a" type="xsd:string"/>
      <xsd:element name="b" type="xsd:string"/>
    </xsd:sequence>
  </xsd:choice>
</xsd:complexType>
```

This content model is non-deterministic because the processor, if it first encounters a child a, will not know whether it should validate it against the first declaration of a or the second declaration of a, without looking ahead to see if there is also a child b. It may seem that it should not matter which a declaration we are talking about; they both have the same type. However, they may have other different properties, such as default values, identity constraints, or annotations.

Example 13–31 represents the same desired content model, in a deterministic way. There is only one declaration of a. There are two declarations of b, but distinguishing between them does not require

Example 13–31. Deterministic content model

```
<xsd:complexType name="AOrBOrBothType">
  <xsd:choice>
    <xsd:sequence>
      <xsd:element name="a" type="xsd:string"/>
      <xsd:element name="b" type="xsd:string" minOccurs="0"/>
    </xsd:sequence>
    <xsd:element name="b" type="xsd:string"/>
  </xsd:choice>
</xsd:complexType>
```

looking ahead. If the processor encounters b as the first child, it knows to use the second declaration of b. If it encounters b after a, it uses the first declaration of b.

In this example, the conflict is between two element declarations with the same name. However, there are also more subtle conflicts, such as those between:

- two element wildcards whose valid values overlap,
- an element declaration and a wildcard for which it is a valid replacement,
- an element declaration and the head of its substitution group.

13.6 | Using attributes

Like element types, attributes can be included in complex types as local declarations, references to global declarations, and wildcards. They may also be included through attribute group references.

Within complex type definitions, attributes must appear after the content model. The local attribute declarations, attribute references, attribute group references, and attribute wildcard may appear in any order, intermixed with each other. There is no significance to the ordering of attributes in XML. There can only be one attribute wildcard in a complex type definition.

It is illegal to define a complex type that contains two attributes with the same qualified name. This is understandable, since XML forbids this. However, if two attributes have the same local name, but different namespace names, they may both appear in the same complex type.

13.6.1 *Local attribute declarations*

Complex type definitions can contain local attribute declarations. This means that the attributes are declared (that is, given a name, a type, and other properties) within the complex type. The scope of that attribute is limited to the complex type within which it appears. Local attribute declarations are described in detail in Section 8.1.3, "Local attribute declarations."

Example 13–32 shows the addition of a local attribute declaration to `ProductType`. Note that the attribute declaration appears after the `sequence` group that represents the content model.

Example 13–32. Local attribute declaration

```
<xsd:complexType name="ProductType">
  <xsd:sequence>
    <!--...-->
  </xsd:sequence>
  <xsd:attribute name="effDate" type="xsd:date"
                 default="1900-01-01"/>
</xsd:complexType>
```

13.6.2 *Attribute references*

Complex type definitions can also contain references to global attribute declarations. Global attribute declarations themselves are covered in detail in Section 8.1.2, "Global attribute declarations." The syntax used to reference a global attribute declaration is shown in Table 13–8.

The `use` attribute may be used to indicate whether the attribute is required or optional. The value `prohibited` is used only when restricting complex types. If `required` is chosen, then a default or fixed value in the global attribute declaration are ignored.

The `default` attribute may be used to add a default value, or to override the `default` attribute in the global attribute declaration. This is true for attributes only; an element reference cannot override the default value in a global element declaration.

The `fixed` attribute may be used to add a fixed value, but it cannot override or remove a fixed value specified in the global attribute declaration. Only one of `default` and `fixed` may appear; they are mutually exclusive.

Table 13–8   XSDL syntax: attribute reference

Name

`attribute`

Parents

`complexType, restriction, extension, attributeGroup`

Attribute name	Type	Required/ default	Description
`id`	`ID`		unique ID
`ref`	`QName`	required	name of the attribute being referenced
`use`	`"optional"` `| "prohibited"` `| "required"`	optional	whether the attribute is required
`default`	`string`		default value for the attribute, see Section 8.3.1
`fixed`	`string`		fixed value for the attribute, see Section 8.3.2

Content

`annotation?`

Example 13–33 shows a complex type definition with a reference to a global attribute declaration. Note that the `type` attribute is in the global attribute declaration. In this case, the `default` attribute in the attribute reference overrides the `default` attribute in the global attribute declaration.

For a detailed discussion of local or global attribute declarations see Section 8.1.4, "Design hint: Should I declare attributes globally or locally?"

Example 13–33. Attribute reference

```xsd
<xsd:schema xmlns:xsd="http://www.w3.org/2001/XMLSchema">

  <xsd:attribute name="effDate" type="xsd:date"
                 default="1900-01-01"/>

  <xsd:complexType name="ProductType">
    <xsd:sequence>
    <!--...-->
    </xsd:sequence>
    <xsd:attribute ref="effDate" default="2000-12-31"/>
  </xsd:complexType>

</xsd:schema>
```

13.6.3 *Attribute wildcards*

Attribute wildcards are used to allow flexibility as to what attributes may appear in a complex type. Attribute wildcards are represented by an `anyAttribute` element, whose syntax is shown in Table 13–9.

The `namespace` and `processContents` attributes for attribute wildcards work exactly the same way as for element wildcards, as described in Section 13.4.3, "Element wildcards." The only difference between attribute wildcards and element wildcards is that attribute wildcards cannot have `minOccurs` and `maxOccurs` specified. If an attribute wildcard is present, it is assumed that there may be zero, one, or many replacement attributes present.

Example 13–34 shows the definition of a type that may contain any attributes from any namespace other than the target namespace of the schema document.

Example 13–34. Complex type with attribute wildcard

```xsd
<xsd:complexType name="ProductType">
  <xsd:sequence>
    <!--...-->
  </xsd:sequence>
  <xsd:anyAttribute namespace="##other" processContents="lax"/>
</xsd:complexType>
```

Table 13–9   XSDL syntax: attribute wildcard

Name
anyAttribute

Parents
complexType, restriction, extension, attributeGroup

Attribute name	Type	Required/ default	Description
id	ID		unique ID
namespace	"##any" | "##other" | (list of anyURI | "##targetNamespace" | "##local")	##any	which namespace(s) the replacement attributes may be in
processContents	"lax" | "skip" | "strict"	strict	how strictly to validate the replacement attributes

Content
annotation?

13.6.4 *Attribute group references*

Attribute groups may be referenced in complex type definitions, in order to make use of predefined groups of attributes. Attribute groups are described in detail in Chapter 15, "Reusable groups." Example 13–35 shows a complex type definition that references the attribute group IdentifierGroup.

Example 13–35. Complex type with attribute group reference

```
<xsd:complexType name="ProductType">
  <xsd:sequence>
    <!--...-->
  </xsd:sequence>
  <xsd:attributeGroup ref="IdentifierGroup"/>
  <xsd:attribute name="effDate" type="xsd:date"/>
</xsd:complexType>
```

Deriving complex types

I n the previous chapter, we saw how to define new complex types that were not specifically derived from another type. This chapter covers the complexities of deriving complex types from other types, both complex and simple.

14.1 | Why derive types?

XML Schema allows you to derive a new complex type from an existing simple or complex type. While it is always possible to make a copy of an existing type and modify it to suit your needs, using type derivation has a number of advantages:

- *Subsetting.* If you want to define a more restrictive subset of a schema, the best way to do this is using restriction. Your schema processor will validate that you have in fact defined a legal subset. It also allows future modifications to the original types to be reflected in your derived types automatically.

- *Safe extensions.* If you want to add to existing schema components, XML Schema's extension mechanism ensures that you do so in a way that an application can still handle the original definition.

- *Type substitution.* Derived types can substitute for their ancestor types in instances, which is a very flexible way to support variations in content.

- *Reuse.* If several types share the same basic structure but have minor differences, it makes sense to reuse the similar parts. This makes maintenance easier and ensures consistency. Type derivation is one way to reuse content model fragments and attributes.

- Future XML technologies and applications will be much more type-aware, and will allow you to define processes on some types that may be passed down to their derived types. For example, a future stylesheet language might let you apply a specific template to "anything of type `Address` or any type derived from it."

14.2 | Restriction and extension

Complex types are derived from other types either by restriction or extension.

- *Restriction*, as the name suggests, restricts the valid contents of a type. The values for the new type are a subset of those for the base type. All values of the restricted type are also valid according to the base type.

- *Extension* allows for adding additional children and/or attributes to a type. Values of the base type are not necessarily valid for the extended type, since required elements or attributes may be added.

It is not possible to restrict and extend a complex type at the same time. However, it is legal to do this in two steps, first extending a type, and then restricting the extension.

14.3 | Simple content and complex content

A complex type always has either simple content or complex content. Simple content means that it has only character data content, with no children. Complex content encompasses the other three content types: mixed, element-only, and empty that were covered in Chapter 13, "Complex types." A complex type is derived from another complex type using either a `simpleContent` element or a `complexContent` element.

14.3.1 `simpleContent` *elements*

A `simpleContent` element is used when deriving a complex type from a simple type, or from another complex type with simple content. This can be done to add or remove attributes, or to further restrict the simple type of the character content. If a complex type has simple content, all types derived from it, directly or indirectly, must also have simple content. It is impossible to switch from simple content to complex content by deriving a type with child elements. Table 14–1 shows the syntax for a `simpleContent` element. It contains either an `extension` or a `restriction` child element. These elements are discussed in Section 14.4.1, "Simple content extensions," and Section 14.5.1, "Simple content restrictions," respectively.

14.3.2 `complexContent` *elements*

A `complexContent` element is used when deriving a complex type from another complex type which itself has complex content. This

Table 14–1   XSDL syntax: simple content definition

Name			
simpleContent			

Parents			
complexType			

Attribute name	Type	Required/default	Description
id	ID		unique ID

Content			
annotation?, (extension | restriction)			

includes mixed, element-only, and empty content types. This can be done to add or remove parts of the content model as well as attributes. Table 14–2 shows the syntax for a complexContent element. It too must contain either an extension or a restriction, but with different definitions from their counterparts in simpleContent. These

Table 14–2   XSDL syntax: complex content definition

Name			
complexContent			

Parents			
complexType			

Attribute name	Type	Required/default	Description
id	ID		unique ID
mixed	boolean	overrides mixed value of complexType	whether the complex type allows mixed content

Content			
annotation?, (extension | restriction)			

elements are discussed in Section 14.4.2, "Complex content extensions," and Section 14.5.2, "Complex content restrictions," respectively.

If `complexContent` has a `mixed` attribute, it overrides the `mixed` attribute of `complexType`. If neither is specified, the default for `mixed` is `false`.

14.4 | Complex type extensions

Complex types may be extended by adding attributes and adding to the content model. Table 14–3 shows the legal extensions for each content type.

Table 14–3   Legal extensions by content type

| | | | Simple type | BASE TYPE | | | |
| | | | | Complex type | | | |
				Simple content	Element-only	Mixed	Empty
D E R I V E D		Simple type	no	no	no	no	no
	Complex type	Simple content	yes, see Section 14.4.1	yes, see Section 14.4.1	no	no	no
		Element-only	no	no	yes, see Section 14.4.2	no	yes, see Section 14.4.4
T Y P E		Mixed	no	no	no	yes, see Section 14.4.3	yes, see Section 14.4.4
		Empty	no	no	no	no	yes, see Section 14.4.4

14.4.1 *Simple content extensions*

The only purpose of simple content extensions is to add attributes. It is not possible to extend the value space of the simple content, just as it is not possible to extend the value space of a simple type. Table 14–4 shows the syntax for an `extension` element that is the child of a `simpleContent` element.

Table 14–4   XSDL syntax: simple content extension

Name			
`extension`			

Parents			
`simpleContent`			

Attribute name	Type	Required/default	Description
`id`	ID		unique ID
`base`	QName	required	base type being extended

Content			
`annotation?, (attribute | attributeGroup)*, anyAttribute?`			

Example 14–1 shows the definition of a complex type `SizeType` that has simple content. It has a content type of `integer`, and it has been extended to add the attribute `system`. A valid instance is also shown.

14.4.2 *Complex content extensions*

Complex content extensions allow you to add to the end of the content model of the base type. You can also add attributes, but you cannot modify or remove existing attributes. Table 14–5 shows the syntax for an `extension` element that is the child of a `complexContent` element.

Example 14–1. Simple content extension

Schema:

```
<xsd:complexType name="SizeType">
  <xsd:simpleContent>
    <xsd:extension base="xsd:integer">
      <xsd:attribute name="system" type="xsd:token"/>
    </xsd:extension>
  </xsd:simpleContent>
</xsd:complexType>
```

Instance:

```
<size system="US-DRESS">10</size>
```

Table 14–5 XSDL syntax: complex content extension

Name
extension

Parents
complexContent

Attribute name	Type	Required/default	Description
id	ID		unique ID
base	QName	required	base type being extended

Content
annotation?, (group | all | choice | sequence)?, (attribute | attributeGroup)*, anyAttribute?

When defining a complex content extension, you do not need to copy the content model from the base type. The processor handles complex content extensions by appending the new content model after the base type's content model, as if they were together in a sequence group.

Example 14–2 shows a complex content extension. The complex type `ProductType` has two children: `number` and `name`. The type `ShirtType` extends `ProductType` by adding a `choice` group containing two additional children: `size` and `color`.

Example 14–2. Complex content extension

```
<xsd:complexType name="ProductType">
  <xsd:sequence>
    <xsd:element name="number" type="ProdNumType"/>
    <xsd:element name="name" type="xsd:string"/>
  </xsd:sequence>
</xsd:complexType>

<xsd:complexType name="ShirtType">
  <xsd:complexContent>
    <xsd:extension base="ProductType">
      <xsd:choice maxOccurs="unbounded">
        <xsd:element name="size" type="SizeType"/>
        <xsd:element name="color" type="ColorType"/>
      </xsd:choice>
    </xsd:extension>
  </xsd:complexContent>
</xsd:complexType>
```

The effective content model of `ShirtType` is shown in Example 14–3. It is as if there were a `sequence` group at the top level of the complex type, which contains the content model of `ProductType`, followed by the content model extensions specified in the `ShirtType` definition itself.

There is a reason for XML Schema to force the base type's content model to appear first. If the base type's content always appears first, application code written to process the base type will also work correctly on the derived type.

Extension does not work for `all` groups, since `all` groups can only appear at the top level of a complex type definition.

Example 14–3. Effective content model of `ShirtType`

```xsd
<xsd:complexType name="ShirtType">
  <xsd:sequence>
    <xsd:sequence>
      <xsd:element name="number" type="ProdNumType"/>
      <xsd:element name="name" type="xsd:string"/>
    </xsd:sequence>
    <xsd:choice maxOccurs="unbounded">
      <xsd:element name="size" type="SizeType"/>
      <xsd:element name="color" type="ColorType"/>
    </xsd:choice>
  </xsd:sequence>
</xsd:complexType>
```

14.4.2.1 Extending `choice` groups

Since extending requires the addition of an "artificial" `sequence` group, extension does not work well as a way to add elements to `choice` groups. Example 14–4 shows a type `ExpandedItemsType` that extends `ItemsType` to add new product types. Intuitively, you may think that

Example 14–4. `choice` group extension

```xsd
<xsd:complexType name="ItemsType">
  <xsd:choice maxOccurs="unbounded">
    <xsd:element ref="shirt"/>
    <xsd:element ref="hat"/>
    <xsd:element ref="umbrella"/>
  </xsd:choice>
</xsd:complexType>

<xsd:complexType name="ExpandedItemsType">
  <xsd:complexContent>
    <xsd:extension base="ItemsType">
      <xsd:choice maxOccurs="unbounded">
        <xsd:element ref="sweater"/>
        <xsd:element ref="suit"/>
      </xsd:choice>
    </xsd:extension>
  </xsd:complexContent>
</xsd:complexType>
```

the two additional element references, sweater and suit, are added to the choice group, allowing a choice between the five element declarations. In fact, the effective content model of ExpandedItemsType is a sequence group that contains two choice groups. As a result, ExpandedItemsType will require any of the shirt, hat, and umbrella elements to appear before any of the sweater or suit elements.

A better way to extend a choice group is through substitution groups. See Section 21.2.3, "Substitution groups," for more information.

14.4.3 *Mixed content extensions*

Complex types with mixed content can be extended, but the derived type must also have mixed content. The extension is treated the same way as it was for element-only complex types in the previous section. It is impossible to extend a mixed content type to result in an element-only content type. The reverse is also true; it is impossible to extend an element-only content type to result in a mixed content type.

When extending a mixed content type, you must also specify the mixed attribute for the derived type. Example 14–5 shows a mixed complex type LetterType that is extended to derive another mixed complex type, ExtendedLetterType.

14.4.4 *Empty content extensions*

Complex types with empty content can be extended to add children and/or attributes. Example 14–6 shows an empty complex type named ItemType, which is extended by ProductType to add a sequence group containing two children.

Example 14–5. Mixed content extension

```
<xsd:complexType name="LetterType" mixed="true">
  <xsd:sequence>
    <xsd:element name="custName" type="PersonNameType"/>
    <xsd:element name="prodName" type="xsd:string"/>
    <xsd:element name="prodSize" type="SizeType"/>
  </xsd:sequence>
</xsd:complexType>

<xsd:complexType name="ExtendedLetterType" mixed="true">
  <xsd:complexContent>
    <xsd:extension base="LetterType">
      <xsd:sequence>
        <xsd:element name="prodNum" type="ProdNumType"/>
      </xsd:sequence>
    </xsd:extension>
  </xsd:complexContent>
</xsd:complexType>
```

Example 14–6. Empty content extension

```
<xsd:complexType name="ItemType">
  <xsd:attribute name="routingNum" type="xsd:integer"/>
</xsd:complexType>

<xsd:complexType name="ProductType">
  <xsd:complexContent>
    <xsd:extension base="ItemType">
      <xsd:sequence>
        <xsd:element name="number" type="ProdNumType"/>
        <xsd:element name="name" type="xsd:string"/>
      </xsd:sequence>
    </xsd:extension>
  </xsd:complexContent>
</xsd:complexType>
```

14.4.5 *Attribute extensions*

When defining an extension, you may specify additional attributes in the derived type's definition. When extending complex types, attributes are always passed down from the base type to the new type. It is not necessary (or even legal) to repeat any attribute declarations from the base type or any other ancestors in the new type definition. It is not possible to modify or remove the attributes of the base type in an extension.

Example 14–7 shows the definition of ProductType, which extends ItemType. It adds two attributes: effDate and lang. It may be surprising that lang is legal, since it appears in the base type definition. This is because the new lang is in a different namespace, so it is allowed. The lang in the base type definition must be prefixed when it appears in the instance, as shown in the instance example.

Example 14–7. Attribute extension

Schema:

```
<xsd:complexType name="ItemType">
  <xsd:attribute name="id" type="xsd:ID" use="required"/>
  <xsd:attribute ref="xml:lang"/>
</xsd:complexType>

<xsd:complexType name="ProductType">
  <xsd:complexContent>
    <xsd:extension base="ItemType">
      <xsd:attribute name="effDate" type="xsd:date"/>
      <xsd:attribute name="lang" type="xsd:language"/>
    </xsd:extension>
  </xsd:complexContent>
</xsd:complexType>
```

Instance:

```
<product id="prod557"
  xml:lang="en"
  lang="en"
  effDate="2001-04-02"/>
```

14.4.6 Attribute wildcard extensions

If an attribute wildcard is specified in an extension, and there is no attribute wildcard specified in the definition of its base type or any of its ancestors, it is a straightforward matter of using the one attribute wildcard. If, however, one or more of the ancestor types have an attribute wildcard, the effective wildcard is the union of the new wildcard and all ancestor wildcards. The value for processContents is taken from the new derived type, and the union of the namespace constraints of the attribute wildcards is used. Table 14–6 shows how to take the union of the wildcard namespaces. The types are labeled "Type 1" and "Type 2" because it is irrelevant which is the base type and which is the derived type. To take the union of more than two attribute wildcards, you can take the union of two at a time, until there is only one left.

Table 14–6   Wildcard namespace unions

Type 1	*Type 2*	*Effective union namespace*
##any	any value or list of values	##any
any list of values (including ##targetNamespace and ##local)	any list of values (including ##targetNamespace and ##local)	a list of all the items that appear in at least one of the lists (the union)
##other	any list of values (including ##targetNamespace and ##local)	##other, unless the namespace of type 1 is listed in the list, then ##any
##other	##other	##other, unless the target namespaces of the two types are different, in which case it is ##any

Example 14–8 shows the definition of DerivedType that extends BaseType. Both DerivedType and BaseType have attribute wildcards specified, with different values for processContents and namespace.

Example 14–8. Attribute wildcard extension

```
<xsd:complexType name="BaseType">
  <xsd:anyAttribute processContents="lax"
                    namespace="##local
                               http://example.org/prod"/>
</xsd:complexType>

<xsd:complexType name="DerivedType">
  <xsd:complexContent>
    <xsd:extension base="BaseType">
      <xsd:anyAttribute processContents="strict"
                        namespace="##targetNamespace
                                   http://www.w3.org/1999/xhtml"/>
    </xsd:extension>
  </xsd:complexContent>
</xsd:complexType>
```

Example 14–9 shows the effective definition of `DerivedType`, after taking the union of the two attribute wildcards. Note that the value of `processContents` is taken from the derived type, and the namespace list is the union of those of the two types.

Example 14–9. Effective attribute wildcard

```
<xsd:complexType name="DerivedType">
    <xsd:anyAttribute processContents="strict"
                      namespace="##local
                                 http://example.org/prod
                                 ##targetNamespace
                                 http://www.w3.org/1999/xhtml"/>
</xsd:complexType>
```

14.5 | Complex type restrictions

Complex types may be restricted by eliminating or restricting attributes, and subsetting content models. When restriction is used, instances of the derived type will always be valid for the base type as well. Table 14–7 shows the legal restrictions for each content type.

Table 14–7   Legal restrictions by content type

| | | | | BASE TYPE | | | |
| | | | Simple type | Complex type | | | |
				Simple content	Element-only	Mixed	Empty
D E R I V E D	**Simple type**		yes, see Section 9.3.1	no	no	no	no
	Complex type	*Simple content*	no	yes, see Section 14.5.1	no	yes†, see Section 14.5.3	no
		Element-only	no	no	yes, see Section 14.5.2	yes, see Section 14.5.3	no
T Y P E		*Mixed*	no	no	no	yes, see Section 14.5.3	no
		Empty	no	no	yes†, see Section 14.5.2	yes†, see Section 14.5.3	yes, see Section 14.5.4

† If all children are optional

14.5.1 *Simple content restrictions*

The purpose of a simple content restriction is to restrict the simple content and/or attributes of a complex type. Table 14–8 shows the syntax of a `restriction` element that is the child of a `simpleContent` element. A `base` attribute or `simpleType` child must represent a complex type with simple content, not a simple type. This is because a restriction of a simple type is another simple type, not a complex type.

Table 14–8   XSDL syntax: simple content restriction

Name
restriction

Parents
simpleContent

Attribute name	Type	Required/default	Description
id	ID		unique ID
base	QName	either base attribute or simpleType child is required	base type being restricted

Content

```
annotation?, simpleType?, (enumeration | length |
maxExclusive | maxInclusive | maxLength | minExclusive |
minInclusive | minLength | pattern | fractionDigits |
totalDigits | whiteSpace)*, (attribute | attributeGroup)*,
anyAttribute?
```

In Example 14–1 we defined a complex type SizeType that had simple content, and a system attribute. Example 14–10 shows a new type, SmallSizeType, which restricts SizeType. It restricts both the content, by applying the minInclusive and maxInclusive

Example 14–10. Simple content restriction

```
<xsd:complexType name="SmallSizeType">
  <xsd:simpleContent>
    <xsd:restriction base="SizeType">
      <xsd:minInclusive value="2"/>
      <xsd:maxInclusive value="6"/>
      <xsd:attribute name="system" type="xsd:token"
                     use="required"/>
    </xsd:restriction>
  </xsd:simpleContent>
</xsd:complexType>
```

facets, and the `system` attribute, by making it required. See Section 14.5.5, "Attribute restrictions," for more information on restricting attributes.

14.5.2 *Complex content restrictions*

Complex content restrictions allow you to restrict the content model and/or attributes of a complex type. Table 14–9 shows the syntax of a `restriction` element that is the child of a `complexContent` element.

Table 14–9   XSDL syntax: complex content restriction

Name			
`restriction`			

Parents			
`complexContent`			

Attribute name	Type	Required/default	Description
`id`	`ID`		unique ID
`base`	`QName`	required	base type being restricted

Content			
`annotation?, (group | all | choice | sequence)?, (attribute | attributeGroup)*, anyAttribute?`			

When restricting complex content, it is necessary to repeat all of the content model that is desired. The full content model specified in the restriction becomes the content model of the derived type. This content model must be a restriction of the content model of the base type. This means that all instances of the new restricted type must also be valid for the base type.

Example 14–11 shows the definition of a complex type `RestrictedProductType` that restricts the complex type `ProductType` by eliminating the size and color child elements. This is legal because all instances of RestrictedProductType are also valid according to ProductType. However, if the size element declaration had a minOccurs value of 1 in ProductType, the restriction would not be legal, because values of RestrictedProductType would not be valid according to ProductType; they would be missing a required element.

Example 14–11. Complex content restriction

```xsd
<xsd:complexType name="ProductType">
  <xsd:sequence>
    <xsd:element name="number" type="ProdNumType"/>
    <xsd:element name="name" type="xsd:string"/>
    <xsd:element name="size" type="SizeType" minOccurs="0"/>
    <xsd:element name="color" type="ColorType" minOccurs="0"/>
  </xsd:sequence>
</xsd:complexType>

<xsd:complexType name="RestrictedProductType">
  <xsd:complexContent>
    <xsd:restriction base="ProductType">
      <xsd:sequence>
        <xsd:element name="number" type="ProdNumType"/>
        <xsd:element name="name" type="xsd:string"/>
      </xsd:sequence>
    </xsd:restriction>
  </xsd:complexContent>
</xsd:complexType>
```

In most cases, you can use common sense to determine what is a legal restriction. If you can think of a valid instance of the derived type that is not valid for the base type, there is a problem with your restriction. In case you want to do a more thorough analysis, the rest of this section describes the rules for legal content model restrictions.

14.5.2.1 Eliminating meaningless groups

Any meaningless groups may be eliminated. This includes:

- groups with no children,
- groups that have `minOccurs` and `maxOccurs` equal to `1`, and only have one child,
- `sequence` groups that have `minOccurs` and `maxOccurs` equal to `1` and are contained in another `sequence` group; this is illustrated in Example 14–12,
- `choice` groups that have `minOccurs` and `maxOccurs` equal to `1` and are contained in another `choice` group.

Example 14–12. Eliminating meaningless groups

Base group:

```
<xsd:sequence>
  <xsd:sequence>
    <xsd:element name="a"/>
    <xsd:element name="b"/>
  </xsd:sequence>
</xsd:sequence>
```

Legal restriction:

```
<xsd:sequence>
  <xsd:element name="a"/>
  <xsd:element name="b"/>
</xsd:sequence>
```

14.5.2.2 Restricting element declarations

When restricting a specific element declaration, several rules apply:

- The occurrence constraints in the derived element declaration must be equal or more restrictive. This is illustrated by a in Example 14–13.

- The data type in the derived element declaration must be a restriction of the data type in the base element declaration (or they must have the same data type). This is illustrated by c in Example 14–13.

- If the base element declaration specified a fixed value, the derived element declaration must specify the same fixed value. This is illustrated by b in Example 14–13.

- The identity constraints (key, keyref, unique) in the derived element declaration must be a subset of those of the base element declaration.

- The contents of the block attribute of the derived element declaration must be a subset of that of the base element declaration.

Example 14–13. Restricting element declarations

Base group:

```
<xsd:sequence>
  <xsd:element name="a" maxOccurs="3"/>
  <xsd:element name="b" fixed="bValue"/>
  <xsd:element name="c" type="xsd:string"/>
</xsd:sequence>
```

Legal restriction:

```
<xsd:sequence>
  <xsd:element name="a" maxOccurs="2"/>
  <xsd:element name="b" fixed="bValue"/>
  <xsd:element name="c" type="xsd:token"/>
</xsd:sequence>
```

Illegal restriction:

```
<xsd:sequence>
  <xsd:element name="a" maxOccurs="4"/>
  <xsd:element name="b" fixed="newValue"/>
  <xsd:element name="c" type="xsd:integer"/>
</xsd:sequence>
```

- If the base element declaration had `nillable` set to `false`, the derived element declaration cannot reverse that property.

14.5.2.3 Restricting wildcards

When replacing an element wildcard with specific element declarations or a group of element declarations, these derived declarations must yield valid replacement elements for the wildcard, in terms of their namespace and occurrence constraints. This is illustrated in Example 14–14. The illegal restriction in that example has two problems. First, b is illegal because it is in the same namespace as the other elements (while the wildcard says `##other`). Second, two replacement elements are declared, but the wildcard has a `maxOccurs` of `1`.

Example 14–14. Replacing a wildcard with element declarations

Base group:

```
<xsd:sequence>
  <xsd:element name="a"/>
  <xsd:any namespace="##other" maxOccurs="1"/>
</xsd:sequence>
```

Legal restriction:

```
<xsd:sequence>
  <xsd:element name="a"/>
  <xsd:element ref="otherns:b"/>
</xsd:sequence>
```

Illegal restriction:

```
<xsd:sequence>
  <xsd:element name="a"/>
  <xsd:element ref="b"/>
  <xsd:element name="c"/>
</xsd:sequence>
```

When replacing an element wildcard with an element wildcard, the derived wildcard's namespace constraint must be a subset of the base wildcard's namespace constraint, as described in Section 14.5.6, "Attribute wildcard restrictions." Also, the occurrence constraints must be a subset. This is illustrated in Example 14–15. The illegal restriction in that example is problematic because neither the namespace constraint nor the occurrence constraint are subsets of those of the base wildcard.

Example 14–15. Replacing a wildcard with another wildcard

Base wildcard:

```
<xsd:any namespace="urn:a:1 urn:a:2" maxOccurs="2"/>
```

Legal restriction:

```
<xsd:any namespace="urn:a:1" maxOccurs="1"/>
```

Illegal restriction:

```
<xsd:any namespace="##other" maxOccurs="3"/>
```

14.5.2.4 Restricting groups

When replacing a group with an element declaration, it must be valid for an instance of that group to just have that one element child. For example, a `choice` group that contains that element declaration, or a `sequence` group declaring all other elements optional, would work as base groups in this case. This is illustrated in Example 14–16.

When replacing a group with another group, the occurrence constraints must become more restrictive. For example, if the `maxOccurs`

Example 14–16. Replacing a group with an element declaration

Base group:

```
<xsd:sequence>
  <xsd:element name="a"/>
  <xsd:element name="b" minOccurs="0"/>
</xsd:sequence>
```

Legal restriction:

```
<xsd:element name="a"/>
```

value for a group in the base type is 5, the group in the derived type cannot have a maxOccurs that is greater than 5. This is illustrated in Example 14–17.

Example 14–17. Restricting occurrence constraints of a group

Base group:

```
<xsd:sequence minOccurs="2" maxOccurs="5">
  <xsd:element name="a"/>
  <xsd:element name="b"/>
</xsd:sequence>
```

Legal restriction:

```
<xsd:sequence minOccurs="3" maxOccurs="4">
  <xsd:element name="a"/>
  <xsd:element name="b"/>
</xsd:sequence>
```

Illegal restriction:

```
<xsd:sequence minOccurs="0" maxOccurs="6">
  <xsd:element name="a"/>
  <xsd:element name="b"/>
</xsd:sequence>
```

When replacing a group with a group of the same kind (all, choice, or sequence), the order of the children (element declarations and groups) must be preserved. This is true even for all and choice groups, when the order is not significant for validation. This is illustrated in Example 14–18.

Example 14–18. Maintaining the order of the children in an all group

Base group:

```
<xsd:all>
  <xsd:element name="a"/>
  <xsd:element name="b" minOccurs="0"/>
  <xsd:element name="c"/>
</xsd:all>
```

Legal restriction:

```
<xsd:all>
  <xsd:element name="a"/>
  <xsd:element name="c"/>
</xsd:all>
```

Illegal restriction:

```
<xsd:all>
  <xsd:element name="c"/>
  <xsd:element name="a"/>
</xsd:all>
```

When restricting an all or sequence group, if any child element declarations or groups are not included in the derived group, they must be optional in the base group. This is illustrated in Example 14–19.

When replacing a choice group with another choice group, the child element declarations of the derived group must be a subset of those in the base group. This is illustrated in Example 14–20.

Example 14–19. Restricting an `all` group

Base group:

```
<xsd:all>
  <xsd:element name="a"/>
  <xsd:element name="b" minOccurs="0"/>
  <xsd:element name="c"/>
</xsd:all>
```

Legal restriction:

```
<xsd:all>
  <xsd:element name="a"/>
  <xsd:element name="c"/>
</xsd:all>
```

Illegal restriction:

```
<xsd:all>
  <xsd:element name="a"/>
  <xsd:element name="b"/>
</xsd:all>
```

Example 14–20. Restricting a `choice` group

Base group:

```
<xsd:choice>
  <xsd:element name="a"/>
  <xsd:element name="b"/>
  <xsd:element name="c"/>
</xsd:choice>
```

Legal restriction:

```
<xsd:choice>
  <xsd:element name="a"/>
  <xsd:element name="c"/>
</xsd:choice>
```

Illegal restriction:

```
<xsd:choice>
  <xsd:element name="a"/>
  <xsd:element name="d"/>
</xsd:choice>
```

When replacing an `all` group with a `sequence` group, each element declaration in the `all` group cannot appear more than once in the `sequence` group, or appear with `maxOccurs` greater than 1. This is illustrated in Example 14–21.

Example 14–21. Replacing an `all` group with a `sequence` group

Base group:

```
<xsd:all>
  <xsd:element name="a"/>
  <xsd:element name="b" minOccurs="0"/>
  <xsd:element name="c"/>
</xsd:all>
```

Legal restriction:

```
<xsd:sequence>
  <xsd:element name="a"/>
  <xsd:element name="c"/>
</xsd:sequence>
```

Illegal restriction:

```
<xsd:sequence>
  <xsd:element name="a"/>
  <xsd:element name="b"/>
  <xsd:element name="c" minOccurs="2"/>
</xsd:sequence>
```

When replacing a choice group with a sequence group, the max-Occurs of the choice group must be enough to cover the number of elements that the sequence group will yield. This is illustrated in Example 14–22.

Example 14–22. Replacing a choice group with a sequence group

Base group:

```
<xsd:choice maxOccurs="2">
  <xsd:element name="a"/>
  <xsd:element name="b"/>
  <xsd:element name="c"/>
</xsd:choice>
```

Legal restriction:

```
<xsd:sequence>
  <xsd:element name="a"/>
  <xsd:element name="c"/>
</xsd:sequence>
```

Illegal restriction:

```
<xsd:sequence>
  <xsd:element name="a"/>
  <xsd:element name="b"/>
  <xsd:element name="c"/>
</xsd:sequence>
```

14.5.3 *Mixed content restrictions*

Complex types with mixed content may be restricted to derive other complex types with mixed content, or with element-only content. The reverse is not true: It is not possible to restrict an element-only complex type to result in a mixed complex type.

If you want the derived type to be mixed, you must specify the `mixed` attribute for the derived type, since the quality of being mixed is not inherited from the base type. Example 14–23 shows a mixed complex type `LetterType` that is restricted to derive another mixed complex type, `RestrictedLetterType`.

Example 14–23. Mixed content restriction

```
<xsd:complexType name="LetterType" mixed="true">
  <xsd:sequence>
    <xsd:element name="custName" type="PersonNameType"/>
    <xsd:element name="prodName" type="xsd:string"/>
    <xsd:element name="prodSize" type="SizeType" minOccurs="0"/>
  </xsd:sequence>
</xsd:complexType>

<xsd:complexType name="RestrictedLetterType" mixed="true">
  <xsd:complexContent>
    <xsd:restriction base="LetterType">
      <xsd:sequence>
        <xsd:element name="custName" type="PersonNameType"/>
        <xsd:element name="prodName" type="xsd:string"/>
      </xsd:sequence>
    </xsd:restriction>
  </xsd:complexContent>
</xsd:complexType>
```

It is also possible to restrict a mixed content type to derive an empty content type, or even a simple content complex type. This is only legal if all of the children in the content model of the base type are optional. Example 14–24 shows a slightly different `LetterType` definition, where the sequence group is optional. The derived type `RestrictedLetterType` will allow only character data content of type `string`, with no children. Note that this is the only case where a `restriction` element may have both a `base` attribute and a `simpleType` child.

Example 14–24. Mixed content restricted to simple content

```
<xsd:complexType name="LetterType" mixed="true">
  <xsd:sequence minOccurs="0">
    <xsd:element name="custName" type="PersonNameType"/>
    <xsd:element name="prodName" type="xsd:string"/>
    <xsd:element name="prodSize" type="SizeType"/>
  </xsd:sequence>
</xsd:complexType>

<xsd:complexType name="RestrictedLetterType" mixed="true">
  <xsd:complexContent>
    <xsd:restriction base="LetterType">
      <xsd:simpleType>
        <xsd:restriction base="xsd:string"/>
      </xsd:simpleType>
    </xsd:restriction>
  </xsd:complexContent>
</xsd:complexType>
```

14.5.4 *Empty content restrictions*

Complex types with empty content may be restricted, but the restriction applies only to the attributes. The derived type must also have empty content. Example 14–25 shows a restriction of the empty complex type `ItemType`. The only restriction is applied to the data type of the `routingNum` attribute.

Example 14–25. Empty content restriction

```
<xsd:complexType name="ItemType">
  <xsd:attribute name="routingNum" type="xsd:integer"/>
</xsd:complexType>

<xsd:complexType name="RestrictedItemType">
  <xsd:complexContent>
    <xsd:restriction base="ItemType">
      <xsd:attribute name="routingNum" type="xsd:short"/>
    </xsd:restriction>
  </xsd:complexContent>
</xsd:complexType>
```

14.5.5 *Attribute restrictions*

When defining a restriction, you may restrict or eliminate attributes of the base type. All attributes are passed down from the base type to the derived type, so the only attributes that need to appear in the derived type definition are the ones you want to restrict or remove. The legal ways to restrict an attribute are as follows:

- change the attribute's type, as long as the new type is a restriction (or a restriction of a restriction, etc.) of the original type,
- add, change or remove a default value,
- add a fixed value if none is present in the base type,
- make optional attributes required,
- make optional attributes prohibited.

It is *not* legal in a restriction to:

- change the attribute's type to one that is not a restriction of the original type,
- change or remove a fixed value,
- make required attributes optional,
- make required attributes prohibited.

Example 14–26 shows a definition of DerivedType, which legally restricts BaseType. The declarations of attributes a, b, c, d, e, f, and g represent, respectively, changing the type, adding a default, changing a default, adding a fixed value, keeping the fixed value the same, making an optional attribute required, and prohibiting an optional attribute. Instances of DerivedType can also have the attribute x, although it is not mentioned in the definition. This is because all of the attributes of BaseType are passed down to DerivedType.

Example 14–27 shows a definition of IllegalDerivedType, which illegally restricts the complex type BaseType2. Attribute h is illegal because decimal is not a restriction of integer. Attribute i is illegal because the fixed value is changed. Attribute j is illegal because the

Example 14–26. Legal restrictions of attributes

```
<xsd:complexType name="BaseType">
     <xsd:attribute name="a" type="xsd:integer"/>
     <xsd:attribute name="b" type="xsd:string"/>
     <xsd:attribute name="c" type="xsd:string" default="c"/>
     <xsd:attribute name="d" type="xsd:string"/>
     <xsd:attribute name="e" type="xsd:string" fixed="e"/>
     <xsd:attribute name="f" type="xsd:string"/>
     <xsd:attribute name="g" type="xsd:string"/>
     <xsd:attribute name="x" type="xsd:string"/>
</xsd:complexType>

<xsd:complexType name="DerivedType">
  <xsd:complexContent>
    <xsd:restriction base="BaseType">
      <xsd:attribute name="a" type="xsd:positiveInteger"/>
      <xsd:attribute name="b" type="xsd:string" default="b"/>
      <xsd:attribute name="c" type="xsd:string" default="c2"/>
      <xsd:attribute name="d" type="xsd:string" fixed="d"/>
      <xsd:attribute name="e" type="xsd:string" fixed="e"/>
      <xsd:attribute name="f" type="xsd:string" use="required"/>
      <xsd:attribute name="g" type="xsd:string" use="prohibited"/>
    </xsd:restriction>
  </xsd:complexContent>
</xsd:complexType>
```

fixed value is removed and replaced by a default value. Attribute k is illegal because a required attribute is made optional. Attribute l is illegal because a required attribute is made prohibited. Attributes pref:l and m are illegal because they do not appear in the definition of BaseType2.

14.5.6 *Attribute wildcard restrictions*

When an attribute wildcard is specified in a restriction, that wildcard becomes the effective wildcard of the type, overriding any attribute wildcards of the base type or its ancestors. However, if any ancestor has an attribute wildcard, the namespace constraint of the new wildcard must be a subset of the ancestor wildcard's namespace constraint. Table 14–10 shows the legal subsets of namespace constraints.

Example 14–27. Illegal attribute restrictions

```
<xsd:complexType name="BaseType2">
    <xsd:attribute name="h" type="xsd:integer"/>
    <xsd:attribute name="i" type="xsd:string" fixed="i"/>
    <xsd:attribute name="j" type="xsd:string" fixed="j"/>
    <xsd:attribute name="k" type="xsd:string" use="required"/>
    <xsd:attribute name="l" type="xsd:string" use="required"/>
</xsd:complexType>

<xsd:complexType name="IllegalDerivedType">
  <xsd:complexContent>
    <xsd:restriction base="BaseType2">
      <xsd:attribute name="h" type="xsd:decimal"/>
      <xsd:attribute name="i" type="xsd:string" fixed="i2"/>
      <xsd:attribute name="j" type="xsd:string" default="j"/>
      <xsd:attribute name="k" type="xsd:string"/>
      <xsd:attribute name="l" type="xsd:string" use="prohibited"/>
      <xsd:attribute ref="pref:l"/>
      <xsd:attribute name="m" type="xsd:string"/>
    </xsd:restriction>
  </xsd:complexContent>
</xsd:complexType>
```

Table 14–10 Wildcard namespace subsets

Base type	Derived type
##any	any value or list of values
any list of values (including ##targetNamespace and ##local)	any list of values that is the same or a subset of the base type's list
##other	##other (if the target namespace of the base type and the derived type are the same) or any list of values that does not include the target namespace of the base type

Example 14–28 shows a definition of DerivedType that restricts BaseType. Both DerivedType and BaseType have attribute wildcards specified, with different values for processContents and namespace.

This definition is legal because `DerivedType`'s wildcard is a subset of `BaseType`'s wildcard.

Example 14–28. Restricting an attribute wildcard

```
<xsd:complexType name="BaseType">
    <xsd:anyAttribute processContents="lax" namespace="##any"/>
</xsd:complexType>

<xsd:complexType name="DerivedType">
  <xsd:complexContent>
    <xsd:restriction base="BaseType">
      <xsd:anyAttribute processContents="strict"
                        namespace="##targetNamespace
                                   http://www.w3.org/1999/xhtml"/>
    </xsd:restriction>
  </xsd:complexContent>
</xsd:complexType>
```

It is also possible to restrict an attribute wildcard by replacing it with specific attributes that are valid according to that wildcard. This is illustrated in Example 14–29.

Example 14–29. Replacing an attribute wildcard by attributes

```
<xsd:complexType name="BaseType">
  <xsd:anyAttribute processContents="lax" namespace="##any"/>
</xsd:complexType>

<xsd:complexType name="DerivedType">
  <xsd:complexContent>
    <xsd:restriction base="BaseType">
      <xsd:attribute name="id" type="xsd:ID" use="required"/>
      <xsd:attribute name="name" type="xsd:string"/>
    </xsd:restriction>
  </xsd:complexContent>
</xsd:complexType>
```

14.6 | Type substitution

One of the elegant features of derived types is that they can substitute for their ancestor types in instances. In an instance, an element conforming to a declaration with one data type can actually have any data type that either extends or restricts it. Suppose we have a section of a purchase order that lists products of various kinds. We want repeating product elements, but we also want to allow different content models for each kind of product. For example, a shirt may have a color and a size, in addition to the normal product information.

Example 14–30 shows a definition of ShirtType that extends ProductType. It adds the additional children size and color to the end of the content model.

Example 14–30. A derived type

```
<xsd:complexType name="ProductType">
  <xsd:sequence>
    <xsd:element name="number" type="ProdNumType"/>
    <xsd:element name="name" type="xsd:string"/>
  </xsd:sequence>
</xsd:complexType>
<xsd:element name="product" type="ProductType"/>

<xsd:complexType name="ShirtType">
  <xsd:complexContent>
    <xsd:extension base="ProductType">
      <xsd:choice maxOccurs="unbounded">
        <xsd:element name="size" type="SizeType"/>
        <xsd:element name="color" type="ColorType"/>
      </xsd:choice>
    </xsd:extension>
  </xsd:complexContent>
</xsd:complexType>
```

Example 14–31 shows a valid instance of product. Instead of ProductType, it has the type ShirtType, which allows it to contain the color element. It uses the xsi:type attribute to indicate the type

Example 14–31. Substitution of `ShirtType` for `ProductType`

```
<items xmlns:xsi="http://www.w3.org/2001/XMLSchema-instance">

  <product xsi:type="ShirtType">
    <number>557</number>
    <name>Short-Sleeved Linen Blouse</name>
    <color value="blue"/>
  </product>

  <!--...-->
</items>
```

substitution. We could define an additional type for every kind of product, each with a different content model.

The `xsi:type` attribute is part of the XML Schema Instance Namespace, which must be declared in the instance. This attribute does not, however, need to be declared in the type definition for `product`; a schema processor recognizes `xsi:type` as a special attribute that may be exhibited by any element.

14.7 | Controlling type derivation and substitution

Type derivation is a powerful tool, but in some cases, you may want to control the creation or substitution of derived types. Three properties of complex types control their derivation:

- The `final` property limits the definition of derived types in schemas.
- The `block` property limits the substitution of derived types in instances.
- The `abstract` property forces the definition of derived types.

This section describes each of these three properties in detail.

14.7.1 `final`: *Preventing complex type derivation*

You may want to prevent the derivation of other complex types from your type. This is accomplished using the `final` attribute, which may have one of the following values:

- `"#all"` prevents any other types from extending or restricting your type.
- `"extension"` prevents any other types from extending your type.
- `"restriction"` prevents any other types from restricting your type.
- `"extension restriction"` and `"restriction extension"` are the values that have the same effect as `#all`.
- `" "` (an empty string) means that there are no restrictions. This value is useful for overriding the value of `finalDefault`, as described below.
- If no `final` attribute is specified, it takes its value from the `finalDefault` attribute of the `schema` element[1]. If neither `final` nor `finalDefault` are specified, there are no restrictions on derivation of that complex type.

Example 14–32 shows the definition of a complex type that cannot be restricted or extended by any other type.

14.7.2 `block`: *Blocking substitution of derived types*

As we saw in Section 14.6, "Type substitution," derived types may substitute for their ancestor types in an instance. While this is a valuable feature, there are times when you only want to allow the original type

---

1. The `finalDefault` attribute can contain the values `list` and `union` which are not applicable to complex types. If these values are present, they are ignored in this context.

Example 14–32. Preventing derivation

```
<xsd:complexType name="ProductType" final="#all">
  <xsd:sequence>
    <xsd:element name="number" type="ProdNumType"/>
    <xsd:element name="name" type="xsd:string"/>
  </xsd:sequence>
</xsd:complexType>
```

to be used. This is accomplished using the `block` attribute, which may have one of the following values:

- `"#all"` prevents any derived types from substituting for your type in instances.

- `"extension"` prevents any extensions of your type from substituting for your type in instances.

- `"restriction"` prevents any restrictions of your type from substituting for your type in instances.

- `"extension restriction"` and `"restriction extension"` are the values that have the same effect as `#all`.

- `""` (an empty string) means that there are no restrictions. This value is useful for overriding the value of `blockDefault`, as described below.

- If no `block` attribute is specified, it takes its value from the `blockDefault` attribute of the `schema` element. If neither `block` nor `blockDefault` are specified, there are no restrictions.

Example 14–33 shows a definition of `ProductType` that does not allow extensions of the type to be used in its place.

The definition of `ShirtType` in this example is completely legal. The `block` attribute does not prohibit extensions of `ProductType`, just the substitution of the extensions in place of the original type in the instance. Example 14–34 shows an illegal instance, where the element `product` is attempting to substitute `ShirtType` for

Example 14–33. Preventing substitution of derived types

```
<xsd:complexType name="ProductType" block="extension">
  <xsd:sequence>
    <xsd:element name="number" type="ProdNumType"/>
    <xsd:element name="name" type="xsd:string"/>
  </xsd:sequence>
</xsd:complexType>
<xsd:element name="product" type="ProductType"/>

<xsd:complexType name="ShirtType">
  <xsd:complexContent>
    <xsd:extension base="ProductType">
      <xsd:choice maxOccurs="unbounded">
        <xsd:element name="size" type="SizeType"/>
        <xsd:element name="color" type="ColorType"/>
      </xsd:choice>
    </xsd:extension>
  </xsd:complexContent>
</xsd:complexType>
<xsd:element name="shirt" type="ShirtType"/>
```

`ProductType`. This example would have been legal if the `block` attribute had not been used.

Example 14–34. Illegal substitution of `ShirtType`

```
<product xsi:type="ShirtType">
  <number>557</number>
  <name>Short-Sleeved Linen Blouse</name>
  <color value="blue"/>
</product>
```

14.7.3 Blocking type substitution in element declarations

You can also block type substitution for an element declaration that uses the data type, rather than the data type itself. An `element` element can also have the `block` attribute, with the same valid values as for complexType[1]. If, in Example 14–33, the `block="extension"` attribute had appeared in the `product` element declaration rather than in the `ProductType` definition, the effect would have been the same as far as the `product` instance elements are concerned. Other elements using `ProductType` would then be free to substitute derived data types.

14.7.4 `abstract`: *Forcing derivation*

Abstract complex types are types that cannot be used in instances. They exist solely as placeholders for their derived types. Example 14–35 shows our `ProductType` example as an abstract type.

Example 14–35. An abstract type

```
<xsd:complexType name="ProductType" abstract="true">
  <xsd:sequence>
    <xsd:element name="number" type="ProdNumType"/>
    <xsd:element name="name" type="xsd:string"/>
  </xsd:sequence>
</xsd:complexType>
<xsd:element name="product" type="ProductType"/>

<xsd:complexType name="ShirtType">
  <xsd:complexContent>
    <xsd:extension base="ProductType">
      <xsd:choice maxOccurs="unbounded">
        <xsd:element name="size" type="SizeType"/>
        <xsd:element name="color" type="ColorType"/>
      </xsd:choice>
    </xsd:extension>
  </xsd:complexContent>
</xsd:complexType>
<xsd:element name="shirt" type="ShirtType"/>
```

---

1. The `block` attribute of `element` may also contain the value `substitution`, as described in Chapter 16, "Substitution groups."

Note that `product` is declared to be of the type `ProductType`. This is legal, but if a `product` element appears in an instance, it must be explicitly assigned a type that is derived from `ProductType`, as shown in Example 14–36.

Example 14–36. Legal instances of `product` and `shirt`

```
<product xsi:type="ShirtType">
  <number>557</number>
  <name>Short-Sleeved Linen Blouse</name>
  <color value="blue"/>
</product>

<shirt>
  <number>557</number>
  <name>Short-Sleeved Linen Blouse</name>
  <color value="blue"/>
</shirt>
```

Example 14–37 shows two illegal `product` elements, which attempt to use the type `ProductType`.

Example 14–37. Illegal uses of the abstract `ProductType`

```
<product>
  <number>557</number>
  <name>Short-Sleeved Linen Blouse</name>
</product>

<product xsi:type="ProductType">
  <number>557</number>
  <name>Short-Sleeved Linen Blouse</name>
</product>
```

Reusable groups

X ML Schema provides the ability to define groups of element and attribute declarations that are reusable by many complex types. Named model groups are fragments of content models, and attribute groups are bundles of attributes that are commonly used together. This chapter explains how to define and reference named model groups and attribute groups.

15.1 | Why reusable groups?

Defining a group and reusing it many times has the advantages of:

- encouraging consistency across schema components,
- allowing the schema author to change the content model in only one place,
- making it obvious that certain complex types share similar children,
- in many cases, making the schema less verbose.

15.2 | Named model groups

Named model groups are reusable fragments of content models. Generally, a named model group is used to represent a part of a content model that appears in many different kinds of complex types. For example, if there are many type definitions in your schema that specify a `description`, optionally followed by a `comment`, you could define a group that represents this content model fragment. The group could then be used by many complex type definitions. Named model groups cannot contain attributes; that is the purpose of attribute groups, which are described in Section 15.3, "Attribute groups."

A note on terminology: XML Schema uses the term "model group definition" for `group` elements, and "model group" for `all`, `choice`, and `sequence` groups. In this book, `group` elements are referred to as "named model groups" to reduce confusion associated with the two similar terms.

15.2.1 *Defining named model groups*

Named model groups are represented in XSDL by a `group` element, whose syntax is shown in Table 15–1. Named model groups are required to have a `name`, and that name must be unique among all the named model groups in the schema. Named model groups are always defined globally, meaning that their parent is always `schema` or `redefine`.

Named model groups may contain any content model. However, a `group` cannot contain an `element` directly. Instead, `group` may have one and only one child, which is a model group (`choice`, `sequence`, or `all`). There is an additional constraint that this one model group child cannot have occurrence constraints (`minOccurs` and `maxOccurs`) like other model groups. If you wish to indicate that the contents of the group appear multiple times, you may put occurrence constraints on the group reference, as described in Section 15.2.2.1, "Group references."

Table 15–1   XSDL syntax: named model group definition

Name			
group			

Parents			
schema, redefine			

Attribute name	*Type*	*Required/default*	*Description*
id	ID		unique ID
name	NCName	required	name of the named model group

Content
annotation?, (all | choice | sequence)

Example 15–1 shows the definition of a named model group that contains a description optionally followed by a comment. Note that the group has one child, a sequence, which has no occurrence constraints on it.

Example 15–1. Named model group with local element declarations

```
<xsd:schema xmlns:xsd="http://www.w3.org/2001/XMLSchema">
  <xsd:group name="DescriptionGroup">
    <xsd:sequence>
      <xsd:element name="description" type="xsd:string"/>
      <xsd:element name="comment" type="xsd:string" minOccurs="0"/>
    </xsd:sequence>
  </xsd:group>
</xsd:schema>
```

In Example 15–1, the element declarations are local in the group, as evidenced by the appearance of a name attribute instead of a ref attribute. It is also possible to use global element declarations, and then reference them from the named model group, as shown in Example 15–2.

Example 15–2. Named model group with element references

```
<xsd:schema xmlns:xsd="http://www.w3.org/2001/XMLSchema">

  <xsd:element name="description" type="xsd:string"/>
  <xsd:element name="comment" type="xsd:string"/>

  <xsd:group name="DescriptionGroup">
    <xsd:sequence>
      <xsd:element ref="description"/>
      <xsd:element ref="comment" minOccurs="0"/>
    </xsd:sequence>
  </xsd:group>
</xsd:schema>
```

Note that the type attribute is now in the global element declaration, while minOccurs stays in the reference to the element declaration. This is the same syntax as that used in complex types to reference global element declarations. In fact, when a complex type references a named model group, it is as if the schema author cut and pasted the contents of the group element into the complex type definition. All local element declarations in the group become local to that complex type.

Whether to use local element declarations in the group depends on whether you want these element declarations to be local to the complex type. For a complete discussion of global vs. local element declarations, see Section 7.1.3, "Design hint: Should I use global or local element declarations?"

15.2.2 *Referencing named model groups*

Named model groups may be referenced in complex types and in other groups. Because they are named global schema components, they may be referenced not only from within the same schema document, but also from other schema documents.

15.2.2.1 Group references

The syntax to reference a named model group is shown in Table 15–2. Named model groups are referenced through the `ref` attribute, just like other global schema components.

Table 15–2 XSDL syntax: named model group reference

Name			
group			

Parents			
complexType, restriction, extension, choice, sequence			

Attribute name	*Type*	*Required/ default*	*Description*
id	ID		unique ID
ref	QName	required	name of the group being referenced
minOccurs	nonNegativeInteger	1	minimum number of times the group may appear
maxOccurs	nonNegativeInteger | "unbounded"	1	maximum number of times the group may appear

Content
annotation?

15.2.2.2 Referencing a named model group in a complex type

Example 15–3 shows the definition of the complex type `Purchase-OrderType` that references `DescriptionGroup`.

Example 15–3. Referencing a group from a complex type definition

```
<xsd:complexType name="PurchaseOrderType">
  <xsd:sequence>
    <xsd:group ref="DescriptionGroup" minOccurs="0"/>
    <xsd:element ref="items"/>
    <!--...-->
  </xsd:sequence>
</xsd:complexType>
```

Note that when referencing a group, minOccurs and maxOccurs may be specified, to indicate how many times the contents of the group may appear. If minOccurs and maxOccurs are not specified, the default for both values is 1. The value for minOccurs must be less than or equal to the value for maxOccurs. This means that if a minOccurs value is specified that is more than 1, maxOccurs must also appear, with a value greater than or equal to minOccurs.

To illustrate how XSDL handles named model group references, Example 15–4 shows a content model equivalent to Example 15–3 (assuming it was referencing DescriptionGroup from Example 15–1), if a named model group had not been used. Note that the min-Occurs="0" constraint that appeared in the group reference now appears in the sequence tag.

In Example 15–3, the group is referenced within a sequence group. Named model groups may be referenced anywhere in the content model, and multiple named group references (even to the same group) are allowed.

A named model group may also be referenced at the top level of a complexType, if the group contains the entire content model of the type. A complex type may only directly contain either one named model group (group), or one model group (all, sequence, or choice). Example 15–5 shows the definition of DescriptionType that references DescriptionGroup at the top level.

Example 15–4. Equivalent content model without a named model group reference

```
<xsd:complexType name="PurchaseOrderType">
  <xsd:sequence>
    <xsd:sequence minOccurs="0">
      <xsd:element name="description" type="xsd:string"/>
      <xsd:element name="comment" type="xsd:string" minOccurs="0"/>
    </xsd:sequence>
    <xsd:element ref="items"/>
    <!--...-->
  </xsd:sequence>
</xsd:complexType>
```

Example 15–5. Group reference at the top level of the content model

```
<xsd:complexType name="DescriptionType">
  <xsd:group ref="DescriptionGroup"/>
  <xsd:attribute ref="xml:lang"/>
</xsd:complexType>
```

15.2.2.3 Using `all` in named model groups

An `all` group may appear in named model groups, but the additional constraints on `all` groups still apply. Example 15–6 shows a legal use of an `all` group within a named model group. Remember, an `all` group may only contain element declarations or references, not other groups.

Because `all` groups can only appear at the top level of a complex type, the only way to reference a named model group that contains an `all` group is at the top level, as shown in Example 15–5.

15.2.2.4 Named model groups referencing named model groups

Named model groups may reference other named model groups. This is shown in Example 15–7, where `ProductPropertyGroup` references `DescriptionGroup`.

Example 15–6. Group with an `all` model group

```
<xsd:schema xmlns:xsd="http://www.w3.org/2001/XMLSchema">
  <xsd:group name="DescriptionGroup">
    <xsd:all>
      <xsd:element name="description" type="xsd:string"/>
      <xsd:element name="comment" type="xsd:string" minOccurs="0"/>
    </xsd:all>
  </xsd:group>
</xsd:schema>
```

Example 15–7. Group reference from a group

```
<xsd:schema xmlns:xsd="http://www.w3.org/2001/XMLSchema">
  <xsd:group name="ProductPropertyGroup">
    <xsd:sequence>
      <xsd:group ref="DescriptionGroup"/>
      <xsd:element name="number" type="ProdNumType"/>
      <xsd:element name="name" type="xsd:string"/>
    </xsd:sequence>
  </xsd:group>

  <xsd:group name="DescriptionGroup">
    <xsd:sequence>
      <xsd:element ref="description"/>
      <xsd:element ref="comment" minOccurs="0"/>
    </xsd:sequence>
  </xsd:group>
</xsd:schema>
```

The group references cannot be circular. That is, group a cannot reference itself, and group a cannot reference group b if the latter references group a or another group c which references a, etc. In addition, groups may only contain *references* to other groups, they cannot actually contain the definitions of groups, since all groups are defined globally.

15.3 | Attribute groups

Attribute groups are used to represent groups of related attributes that appear in many different complex types. For example, if the attributes id, name, and version are used in multiple complex types in your schema, it may be useful to define an attribute group that contains these three attributes, and then reference the attribute group in various complex type definitions.

15.3.1 *Defining attribute groups*

Attribute groups are represented in XSDL by an attributeGroup element, whose syntax is shown in Table 15–3. Attribute groups are required to have a name, and that name must be unique among all the attribute groups in the schema. Attribute groups are always defined globally, meaning that their parent is always schema or redefine.

Table 15–3   XSDL syntax: attribute group definition

Name
attributeGroup

Parents
schema, redefine

Attribute name	Type	Required/default	Description
id	ID		unique ID
name	NCName	required	attribute group name

Content
annotation?, (attribute | attributeGroup)*, anyAttribute?

Attribute groups may contain any number of attributes and references to other attribute groups, plus one optional attribute wildcard. An attribute group cannot contain more than one attribute with the same qualified name, nor may it contain more than one attribute of type ID.

For example, if many complex type definitions will use the attributes id and version, you could define an attribute group that contains these two attributes, as shown in Example 15–8.

Example 15–8. Attribute group with local attribute declarations

```
<xsd:schema xmlns:xsd="http://www.w3.org/2001/XMLSchema">
  <xsd:attributeGroup name="IdentifierGroup">
    <xsd:attribute name="id" type="xsd:ID" use="required"/>
    <xsd:attribute name="version" type="xsd:decimal"/>
  </xsd:attributeGroup>
</xsd:schema>
```

In Example 15–8, the attributes are declared locally in the attribute group, as evidenced by the appearance of a name attribute instead of a ref attribute. It is also possible to declare attributes globally, and then reference them from the attribute group, as shown in Example 15–9.

Example 15–9. Attribute group with attribute references

```
<xsd:schema xmlns:xsd="http://www.w3.org/2001/XMLSchema">
  <xsd:attribute name="id" type="xsd:ID"/>
  <xsd:attribute name="version" type="xsd:decimal"/>

  <xsd:attributeGroup name="IdentifierGroup">
    <xsd:attribute ref="id" use="required"/>
    <xsd:attribute ref="version"/>
  </xsd:attributeGroup>
</xsd:schema>
```

Note that the type attribute is now in the global attribute declaration, while the use attribute stays in the reference to the attribute. This is the same way complex types reference global attributes. In fact, when a complex type references an attribute group, it is as if the schema author cut and pasted the contents of the attribute group definition into the complex type definition. All attributes that are declared locally in the attribute group become local to that complex type.

Whether to declare attributes locally in the attribute group depends on whether you want the attributes to be local to the complex type. For a complete discussion of global vs. local attribute declarations, see Section 8.1.4, "Design hint: Should I declare attributes globally or locally?"

Attribute groups may reference other attribute groups, as described in the next section. Attribute groups may also contain one attribute wildcard, as shown in Example 15–10. Attribute groups are limited to one attribute wildcard because a complex type cannot contain more than one attribute wildcard. See Section 13.6.3, "Attribute wildcards," for more information.

Example 15–10. Attribute group with a wildcard

```
<xsd:schema xmlns:xsd="http://www.w3.org/2001/XMLSchema">
  <xsd:attributeGroup name="IdentifierGroup">
    <xsd:attribute name="id" type="xsd:ID" use="required"/>
    <xsd:attribute name="version" type="xsd:decimal"/>
    <xsd:anyAttribute namespace="##other"/>
  </xsd:attributeGroup>
</xsd:schema>
```

15.3.2 *Referencing attribute groups*

Attribute groups may be referenced in complex types and in other attribute groups. Because they are named global schema components, they may be referenced not only from within the same schema document, but also from other schema documents.

15.3.2.1 Attribute group references

The syntax to reference an attribute group is shown in Table 15–4. Attribute groups are referenced using the `ref` attribute, just like other global schema components.

Table 15–4   XSDL syntax: attribute group reference

Name
`attributeGroup`

Parents
`complexType, restriction, extension, attributeGroup`

Attribute name	Type	Required/default	Description
`id`	`ID`		unique ID
`ref`	`QName`	required	name of the attribute group being referenced

Content
`annotation?`

15.3.2.2 Referencing attribute groups in complex types

Example 15–11 shows the definition of the complex type `ProductType` that references the attribute group `IdentifierGroup`.

Example 15–11. Referencing an attribute group from a complex type definition

```
<xsd:complexType name="ProductType">
  <xsd:sequence>
    <!--...-->
  </xsd:sequence>
  <xsd:attributeGroup ref="IdentifierGroup"/>
  <xsd:attribute name="effDate" type="xsd:date"/>
</xsd:complexType>
```

As shown in the example, references to attribute groups must appear after the content model (a `sequence` group in this example) among the attributes. They may appear before, after, or in between attribute declarations. The order of attribute groups (and attributes) in a complex type is insignificant.

To illustrate how XML Schema handles attribute group references, Example 15–12 shows a complex type definition that is equivalent to Example 15–11 (assuming it was referencing `IdentifierGroup` from Example 15–8), if an attribute group had not been used. It is as if the schema author cut and pasted the attribute declarations from the attribute group.

Example 15–12. Equivalent complex type without an attribute group

```
<xsd:complexType name="ProductType">
  <!--...-->
  <xsd:attribute name="id" type="xsd:ID" use="required"/>
  <xsd:attribute name="version" type="xsd:decimal"/>
  <xsd:attribute name="effDate" type="xsd:date"/>
</xsd:complexType>
```

15.3.2.3 Duplicate attribute names

It is illegal to declare two attributes with the same qualified name in the same complex type. When using attribute groups, be sure that the referenced attribute group does not declare an attribute that is already declared directly in your complex type definition. Also, when referencing more than one attribute group in a complex type definition, be sure that the two attribute groups do not contain attributes with identical names.

In Example 15–13, each of the attribute groups `IdentifierGroup` and `VersionGroup` contain a declaration of `version`, and the definition of `ProductType` references both attribute groups. This results in an illegal duplication of the `version` attribute for `ProductType`.

15.3.2.4 Duplicate attribute wildcard handling

Each attribute group definition may only contain one attribute wildcard. However, it is possible for a complex type definition to reference two attribute groups, each of which contains an attribute wildcard. The complex type definition may also have a "local" wildcard, that is, an

Example 15–13. Illegal duplication of attributes

```
<xsd:schema xmlns:xsd="http://www.w3.org/2001/XMLSchema">
  <xsd:attributeGroup name="IdentifierGroup">
    <xsd:attribute name="id" type="xsd:ID" use="required"/>
    <xsd:attribute name="version" type="xsd:decimal"/>
  </xsd:attributeGroup>

  <xsd:attributeGroup name="VersionGroup">
    <xsd:attribute name="version" type="xsd:decimal"/>
  </xsd:attributeGroup>

  <xsd:complexType name="ProductType">
    <xsd:attributeGroup ref="IdentifierGroup"/>
    <xsd:attributeGroup ref="VersionGroup"/>
  </xsd:complexType>
</xsd:schema>
```

`anyAttribute` child. In such a case, the effective attribute wildcard for the complex type is the intersection of all of these wildcards.

The value of `processContents` for this "effective" wildcard is the value of `processContents` for the local wildcard, if it is present. If it is not, the schema processor takes the value of `processContents` from the first attribute wildcard among the `attributeGroup` children.

Table 15–5 shows how to take the intersection of the namespace constraints of two attribute wildcards. For more information on attribute wildcards, see Section 13.6.3, "Attribute wildcards."

15.3.2.5 Attribute groups referencing attribute groups

Definitions of attribute groups may also reference other attribute groups. This is shown in Example 15–14, where `HeaderGroup` references `IdentifierGroup`. The attribute group references cannot be circular. In addition, attribute groups may only contain *references* to other attribute groups, they cannot actually contain the definitions of attribute groups, since all attribute groups are defined globally.

Table 15–5   Wildcard namespace intersections

Type 1	Type 2	Effective
##any	any value or list of values	Type 2's value
any list of values (including ##targetNamespace and ##local)	any list of values (including ##targetNamespace and ##local)	a list of all the items that appear in both lists (the intersection)
##other	any list of values (including ##targetNamespace and ##local)	Type 2's list, excluding the target namespace of Type 1 if it is in the list
##other	##other	##other, unless the two types have different target namespaces, in which case it is illegal

Example 15–14. Attribute group referencing an attribute group

```
<xsd:schema xmlns:xsd="http://www.w3.org/2001/XMLSchema">
  <xsd:attributeGroup name="HeaderGroup">
    <xsd:attributeGroup ref="IdentifierGroup"/>
    <xsd:attribute ref="xml:lang"/>
  </xsd:attributeGroup>
</xsd:schema>
```

15.4 | Reusable groups vs. complex type derivations

There may be cases where it is unclear when to define a reusable group and when to use complex type derivation. Complex type derivation, like reusable groups, also serves the purpose of allowing reuse of content models and attributes.

For example, if there are several places in your purchase order where you allow a description that is optionally followed by a comment, you could define a named model group to represent this. You could then reuse this group in the content model of several, possibly dissimilar complex types.

However, it is also possible to represent this differently. You can define a base complex type that has the descriptive element declarations, and several complex types that extend the base type to add their additional children. Example 15–15 illustrates this approach.

Example 15–15. Reusing content model fragments through derivation

```
<xsd:complexType name="DescribedType">
  <xsd:sequence>
    <xsd:element name="description" type="xsd:string"/>
    <xsd:element name="comment" type="xsd:string" minOccurs="0"/>
  </xsd:sequence>
</xsd:complexType>

<xsd:complexType name="PurchaseOrderType">
  <xsd:complexContent>
    <xsd:extension base="DescribedType">
      <xsd:sequence>
        <xsd:element ref="items"/>
        <!--...-->
      </xsd:sequence>
    </xsd:extension>
  </xsd:complexContent>
</xsd:complexType>

<xsd:complexType name="ItemsType">
  <xsd:complexContent>
    <xsd:extension base="DescribedType">
      <xsd:sequence>
        <xsd:element ref="product" maxOccurs="unbounded"/>
        <!--...-->
      </xsd:sequence>
    </xsd:extension>
  </xsd:complexContent>
</xsd:complexType>
```

The same dilemma can apply to attributes, which can be reused both through attribute groups and through complex type extensions.

Either of these two methods is legal, but each has its advantages and disadvantages. Use a named model group if:

- The fragment you want to reuse does not appear first in some the types' content models. This is because extension adds a derived type's content model after its base type's content model as if they were in a sequence group. In the above example, if the descriptive information did not come first, it would have been impossible to use extension.

- The types are dissimilar concepts that just happen to share a small content model fragment. It may not be intuitive to derive them from the same base type.

On the other hand, use a complex type derivation if:

- The reusable content model fragments appear at the beginning of the content model.

- The data types have mostly the same content model with just a few differing element or attribute declarations.

Substitution groups

Chapter 6

S ubstitution groups are a flexible way to designate element declarations as substitutes for other element declarations in content models. You can easily designate new element declarations as substitutes, from other schema documents and even other namespaces, without changing the original content model. This chapter describes how to define and use substitution groups.

16.1 | Why substitution groups?

Substitution groups are useful for simplifying content models, making `choice` groups more flexible, and allowing more descriptive element-type names to be used, including localized names.

Suppose you have a section of a purchase order that lists products of various kinds. You could use repeating `product` elements, each having an attribute or child element to indicate what kind of a product it is. However, you may also want to allow different content models for different kinds of products. For example, shirts have a mandatory size, while umbrellas are not allowed to have a size specified. Also, you may want descriptive element-type names that indicate the kind of product. Lastly, you may want the definition to be flexible enough to accept new kinds of products without altering the original schema. This is a perfect application for substitution groups.

16.2 | The substitution group hierarchy

Each substitution group consists of a head and one or more members. Wherever the head element declaration is referenced in a content model, one of the member element declarations may be substituted in place of the head. For example, the head of your substitution group might be `product`, with the members being the different types of products such as `shirt`, `hat`, and `umbrella`. This hierarchy is depicted in Figure 16–1.

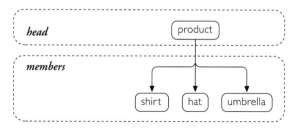

Figure 16–1   Substitution group hierarchy

This means that anywhere `product` appears in a content model, any of `product`, `shirt`, `hat`, or `umbrella` may appear in the instance. The members themselves cannot be substituted for each other. For example, if `shirt` appears in a content model, `umbrella` cannot be substituted in its place.

Substitution groups form a hierarchy. Each element declaration can only be a member of one substitution group, but there can be multiple levels of substitution, and a member of one group may be the head of another group. Other element declarations might have `shirt` as their substitution group head, as shown in Figure 16–2. In this case, `tShirt` and `blouse` may substitute for `product` (or `shirt`).

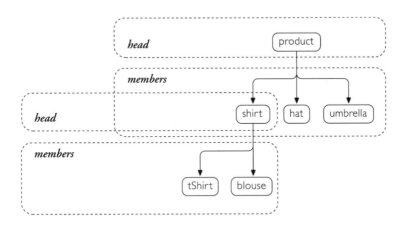

Figure 16–2 Multi-level substitution group hierarchy

16.3 | Declaring a substitution group

Example 16–1 shows the `items` element declaration whose instances may contain many `product` elements. The `product` element declaration will be the head of the substitution group, although there is nothing special about the `product` declaration to indicate this. It is significant, however, that it is a global declaration, since only a global element declaration can be the head of a substitution group.

Example 16–2 shows the three element declarations that are members of the substitution group. The `product`, `shirt`, `hat`, and `umbrella` element declarations can be used interchangeably wherever `product` appears in any content model. Each of the declarations uses the `substitutionGroup` attribute to indicate that it is substitutable for `product`. Members of a substitution group must be globally declared; it is not legal to use the `substitutionGroup` attribute in local element declarations or element references.

Example 16–1. The head of a substitution group

```xsd
<xsd:schema xmlns:xsd="http://www.w3.org/2001/XMLSchema">
  <xsd:element name="items" type="ItemsType"/>
  <xsd:complexType name="ItemsType">
    <xsd:sequence>
      <xsd:element ref="product" maxOccurs="unbounded"/>
    </xsd:sequence>
  </xsd:complexType>

  <xsd:element name="product" type="ProductType"/>
  <xsd:complexType name="ProductType">
    <xsd:sequence>
      <xsd:element ref="number"/>
      <xsd:element ref="name"/>
    </xsd:sequence>
  </xsd:complexType>
</xsd:schema>
```

Example 16–3 shows a valid instance. Because `items` can contain an unlimited number of `product` elements, any combination of `product`, `shirt`, `hat`, and `umbrella` may appear in `items`, in any order. Keep in mind that everywhere a reference to the global `product` element declaration appears in a content model, it can be replaced by these other element declarations because the substitution group is in effect. If there is a content model where you only want `product` elements to be valid, with no substitution, you can get around this by supplying a local `product` element declaration in that content model.

The `substitutionGroup` attribute takes a `QName` as its value. This means that if the head's element-type name is in a namespace (i.e., the schema document in which it is declared has a target namespace), you must prefix the element-type name you specify in the `substitution-Group` attribute. You can have an element declaration from a different namespace as the head of your substitution group, provided that the namespace of that element declaration has been imported into your schema document.

Example 16–2. Members of a substitution group

```xsd
<xsd:schema xmlns:xsd="http://www.w3.org/2001/XMLSchema">

  <xsd:element name="shirt" type="ShirtType"
          substitutionGroup="product"/>
  <xsd:complexType name="ShirtType">
    <xsd:complexContent>
      <xsd:extension base="ProductType">
        <xsd:sequence>
          <xsd:element name="size" type="ShirtSizeType"/>
          <xsd:element name="color" type="ColorType"/>
        </xsd:sequence>
      </xsd:extension>
    </xsd:complexContent>
  </xsd:complexType>

  <xsd:element name="hat" substitutionGroup="product">
    <xsd:complexType>
      <xsd:complexContent>
        <xsd:extension base="ProductType">
          <xsd:sequence>
            <xsd:element name="size" type="HatSizeType"/>
          </xsd:sequence>
        </xsd:extension>
      </xsd:complexContent>
    </xsd:complexType>
  </xsd:element>

  <xsd:element name="umbrella" substitutionGroup="product"/>

  <!--...-->
</xsd:schema>
```

16.4 | Type constraints for substitution groups

In Example 16–2, the complex types of shirt and hat are both derived from the type of product. This is a requirement; members of a substitution group must have types that are either the same as the type of the head, or derived from it by either extension or restriction. They can be directly derived from it, or derived indirectly through multiple levels of restriction or extension.

Example 16–3. Instance of `items`

```
<items>
  <product>
    <number>999</number>
    <name>Special Seasonal</name>
  </product>
  <shirt>
    <number>557</number>
    <name>Short-Sleeved Linen Blouse</name>
    <size>10</size>
    <color value="blue"/>
  </shirt>
  <hat>
    <number>563</number>
    <name>Ten-Gallon Hat</name>
    <size>L</size>
  </hat>
  <umbrella>
    <number>443</number>
    <name>Deluxe Golf Umbrella</name>
  </umbrella>
</items>
```

In our example, `shirt` is assigned a named type, `ShirtType`, which extends `ProductType`, while `hat` has an anonymous type, also an extension of `ProductType`. The third element declaration, `umbrella`, does not specify a data type. If a substitution group member is specified without a type, it automatically takes on the type of the head of its substitution group. Therefore, in this case, `umbrella` has the type `ProductType`.

This type constraint on the members of a substitution group is not as restrictive as it seems. You can make the type of the head very generic, allowing almost anything to be derived from it. In fact, you do not have to specify a data type in the head element declaration at all, which gives it the generic `anyType`. Since all types are derived (directly or indirectly) from `anyType`, the members of the substitution group in this case can have any data types, including simple types.

The example shown above uses complex types, but substitution groups may also be used for element declarations with simple types. If a member of a substitution group has a simple type, it must be a restriction of (or the same as) the simple type of the head.

Example 16–4 shows a substitution group of element declarations with simple data types. Note that the head element declaration, number, does not specify a data type, meaning that the members of the substitution group may have any data type.

Example 16–4. Substitution group with simple types

```
<xsd:schema xmlns:xsd="http://www.w3.org/2001/XMLSchema">
  <xsd:element name="number"/>
  <xsd:element name="skuNumber" type="SKUType"
               substitutionGroup="number"/>
  <xsd:element name="productID" type="ProductIDType"
               substitutionGroup="number"/>
</xsd:schema>
```

16.5 | Alternatives to substitution groups

Substitution groups are very useful, but as you may have guessed, there are other methods of achieving similar goals. This section will take a closer look at two of these methods.

16.5.1 *Reusable* choice *groups*

The behavior of substitution groups is similar to that of named choice groups. In the previous examples, we said that wherever product can appear, it can really be product, shirt, hat, or umbrella. This choice can also be represented by a named choice group that lists the relevant element declarations. Example 16–5 shows the definition of a named model group that allows a choice of product or shirt or hat or umbrella. This named model group is then referenced in the ItemsType definition.

Example 16–5. Using a choice group

```
<xsd:schema xmlns:xsd="http://www.w3.org/2001/XMLSchema">

  <xsd:element name="items" type="ItemsType"/>
  <xsd:complexType name="ItemsType">
    <xsd:group ref="ProductGroup" maxOccurs="unbounded"/>
  </xsd:complexType>

  <xsd:group name="ProductGroup">
    <xsd:choice>
      <xsd:element name="product" type="ProductType"/>
      <xsd:element name="shirt" type="ShirtType"/>
      <xsd:element name="hat" type="HatType"/>
      <xsd:element name="umbrella" type="ProductType"/>
    </xsd:choice>
  </xsd:group>

  <!--...-->
</xsd:schema>
```

It is easy to see the list of members of the "substitution group," because they are all declared within the named model group. This can be an advantage if the list of member element declarations will not change. On the other hand, if you want to be able to add element declarations to the substitution group as needed, from a variety of schema documents, using substitution groups is a much better approach. This is because named choice groups are more rigid. While you can use the redefinition mechanism to extend a named choice group, it is slightly more cumbersome and can only be done in schema documents with the same target namespace.

16.5.2 *Substituting a derived type in the instance*

Another alternative to using substitution groups is to repeat the same element-type name for all of the items (in the case `product`), and use `xsi:type` attributes to distinguish between the different types of products. Using this approach, we would not declare `shirt`, `hat`, or `umbrella` at all, just their data types, as shown in Example 16–6. Remember, it is acceptable to substitute a derived type in an instance if you specify the `xsi:type` attribute. This is described in more detail in Section 14.6, "Type substitution."

Example 16–6. Defining derived types

```
<xsd:schema xmlns:xsd="http://www.w3.org/2001/XMLSchema">
  <xsd:complexType name="ShirtType">
    <xsd:complexContent>
      <xsd:extension base="ProductType">
        <xsd:sequence>
          <xsd:element name="size" type="ShirtSizeType"/>
          <xsd:element name="color" type="ColorType"/>
        </xsd:sequence>
      </xsd:extension>
    </xsd:complexContent>
  </xsd:complexType>

  <xsd:complexType name="HatType">
    <xsd:complexContent>
      <xsd:extension base="ProductType">
        <xsd:sequence>
          <xsd:element name="size" type="HatSizeType"/>
        </xsd:sequence>
      </xsd:extension>
    </xsd:complexContent>
  </xsd:complexType>

  <xsd:complexType name="UmbrellaType">
    <xsd:complexContent>
      <xsd:extension base="ProductType"/>
    </xsd:complexContent>
  </xsd:complexType>

  <!--...-->
</xsd:schema>
```

Example 16–7 shows a valid instance for this approach. The product element is repeated many times, with the xsi:type attribute distinguishing between the different product types.

Example 16–7. Valid instance using derived types

```
<items xmlns:xsi="http://www.w3.org/2001/XMLSchema-instance">
  <product>
    <number>999</number>
    <name>Special Seasonal</name>
  </product>
  <product xsi:type="ShirtType">
    <number>557</number>
    <name>Short-Sleeved Linen Blouse</name>
    <size>10</size>
    <color value="blue"/>
  </product>
  <product xsi:type="HatType">
    <number>563</number>
    <name>Ten-Gallon Hat</name>
    <size>L</size>
  </product>
  <product xsi:type="UmbrellaType">
    <number>443</number>
    <name>Deluxe Golf Umbrella</name>
  </product>
</items>
```

The advantage of this approach is that the instance may be easier to process. A Java program or XSLT stylesheet that handles this instance can treat all product types the same based on their element-type name, but also distinguish between them using the value of xsi:type if necessary. Using substitution groups, if one wanted to retrieve all the products, it would be necessary to select them based on their position in the instance (e.g., all children of items) rather than their element-type name (product), which could be less reliable. Future versions of XSLT and XML APIs will be more type-aware, making this distinction less important.

This approach also has some disadvantages. It works fine for schema validation, but it is impossible to write a DTD that would validate this instance to the same degree. Also, it looks slightly more complicated, and requires a declaration of the XML Schema Instance Namespace, which adds an extra dependency.

16.6 | Controlling substitution groups

Substitution groups are a powerful tool, and you may want to control their use. Three attributes of element declarations control the creation and use of substitutions:

- The `final` attribute limits the declaration of substitution groups in schemas.
- The `block` attribute limits the use of substituted elements in instances.
- The `abstract` attribute forces element substitution in instances.

These three attributes only apply to global element declarations, since local element declarations can never serve as heads of substitution groups.

16.6.1 `final`: *Preventing substitution group declarations*

You may want to prevent other people from defining schemas that use your element declaration as the head of a substitution group. This is accomplished using the `final` attribute in the element declaration, which may have one of the following values:

- `"#all"` prevents any other element declaration from using your element declaration as a substitution group head.

- "extension" prevents extension in substitution group members. Element declarations that use your element declaration as its substitution group head must have data types that are either the same as, or derived by restriction from, the data type of your element declaration.

- "restriction" prevents restriction in substitution group members. Element declarations that use your element declaration as its substitution group head must have data types that are either the same as, or derived by extension from, the data type of your element declaration.

- "extension restriction" and "restriction extension" are values that have the same effect as #all.

- " " (an empty string) means that there are no restrictions. This value is useful for overriding the value of finalDefault, as described below.

- If no final attribute is specified, it takes its value from the finalDefault attribute of the schema element. If neither final nor finalDefault are specified, there are no restrictions on substitutions for that element declaration.

Example 16–8 shows four element declarations that control the use of substitution groups. With this declaration of product, the schema shown in Example 16–2 would have been illegal, since it attempts to use the product element declaration as the head of a substitution group.

Example 16–8. Using final to control substitution group declaration

```
<xsd:element name="product" type="ProductType" final="#all"/>
<xsd:element name="items" type="ItemsType" final="extension"/>
<xsd:element name="color" type="ColorType" final="restriction"/>
<xsd:element name="size" type="SizeType" final=""/>
```

16.6.2 `block`: *Blocking substitution in instances*

In the previous section, we saw how to prevent a schema from containing an element declaration that uses your element declaration as its substitution group head. There is another way to control element substitutions, this time in the instance. This is accomplished using the `block` attribute, and assigning the value `substitution` (or #all) to it[1]. Example 16–9 shows element declarations that use the `block` attribute.

Example 16–9. Using `block` to prevent substitution group use

```
<xsd:element name="product" type="ProductType" block="#all"/>
<xsd:element name="hat" type="HatType" block="substitution"/>
```

With this declaration of `product`, the schema shown in Example 16–2 would have been *legal*, but the instance in Example 16–3 would have been illegal. This is the extremely subtle difference between the `final` and `block` attributes as they relate to substitution groups.

16.6.3 `abstract`: *Forcing substitution*

An element declaration may be abstract, meaning that its sole purpose is to serve as the head of a substitution group. Abstract element declarations can never apply to instance elements. In XSDL, this is indicated by the `abstract` attribute in the element declaration. Example 16–10 shows an abstract element declaration for `product`. With this declaration, Example 16–3 would be invalid because a `product` element

---

1. The `block` attribute also accepts the values `extension` and `restriction`, which are not relevant to substitution groups. They are discussed in Section 14.7.3, "Blocking type substitution in element declarations."

appears in the instance. Instead, only shirt, hat, and umbrella would be able to appear in items.

Example 16–10. An abstract element type

```
<xsd:element name="product" type="ProductType" abstract="true"/>
```

Identity constraints

Chapter 7

I dentity constraints allow you to uniquely identify nodes in a document and ensure the integrity of references between them. This chapter explains how to define and use identity constraints.

17.1 | Identity constraint categories

There are three categories of identity constraints:

- *Uniqueness constraints* enforce that a value (or combination of values) is unique within a specified scope. For example, all product numbers must be unique within a catalog.

- *Key constraints* also enforce uniqueness, and additionally require that all values be present. For example, every product must have a number and it must be unique within a catalog.

- *Key references* enforce that a value (or combination of values) corresponds to a value represented by a key or uniqueness constraint. For example, for every product number that appears as an item in a purchase order, there must be a corresponding product number in the product description section.

17.2 | Design hint: Should I use ID/IDREF or key/keyref?

The identity constraints described in this chapter are much more powerful than the ID/IDREF feature of XML 1.0. Some of the limitations of ID and IDREF are that they:

- work only for attributes, not elements,
- are scoped to the entire document only,
- are based on one value, as opposed to multi-field keys,
- require ID or IDREF to be the data type of the attribute, precluding data validation of that attribute,
- are based on string equality, as opposed to value equality,
- require that the values be based on XML names, meaning they must start with a letter and can only contain letters, digits, and a few punctuation marks.

However, if ID/IDREF fulfills your requirements, there is no reason not to use it, particularly when converting DTDs that are already in use.

17.3 | Structure of an identity constraint

The three categories of identity constraints are similar in their definitions and associated rules. This section describes the basic structure of identity constraints. Example 17–1 shows an instance that contains product catalog information.

Example 17–1. Product catalog information

```
<catalog>
  <department number="021">
    <product>
      <number>557</number>
      <name>Short-Sleeved Linen Blouse</name>
      <price currency="USD">29.99</price>
    </product>
    <product>
      <number>563</number>
      <name>Ten-Gallon Hat</name>
      <price currency="USD">69.99</price>
    </product>
    <product>
      <number>443</number>
      <name>Deluxe Golf Umbrella</name>
      <price currency="USD">49.99</price>
    </product>
  </department>
</catalog>
```

Example 17–2 shows the definition of a uniqueness constraint that might be applied to the instance in Example 17–1.

Example 17–2. A uniqueness constraint

```
<xsd:element name="catalog" type="CatalogType">
  <xsd:unique name="prodNumKey">
    <xsd:selector xpath="*/product"/>
    <xsd:field xpath="number"/>
  </xsd:unique>
</xsd:element>
```

All three categories of identity constraints are defined entirely within an element declaration. They must be defined at the end of the element declaration, after any `simpleType` or `complexType` child.

Every identity constraint has a name, which takes on the target namespace of the schema document. The qualified name must be unique among all identity constraints of all categories within the entire schema. For example, it would be illegal to have a key constraint named `customerNumber` and a uniqueness constraint named `customer-Number` in the same schema, even if they were scoped to different elements.

There are three parts of an identity constraint definition:

1. The *scope* is an element whose declaration contains the constraint. In our example, a `catalog` element is the scope. It is perfectly valid to have two products with the same number if they are contained in two different `catalog` elements.

2. The *selector* serves to select all the nodes to which the constraint applies. In our example, the selector value is "`*/product`", which selects all the `product` grandchildren of `catalog`.

3. The one or more *fields* are the element and attribute values whose combination must be unique among the selected nodes. There can be only one instance of the field per selected node. In our example, there is one field specified: the `number` child of each `product` element.

17.4 | Uniqueness constraints

A uniqueness constraint is used to validate that the values of certain elements or attributes are unique within a particular scope. In XSDL, this is represented by a `unique` element, whose syntax is shown in Table 17–1.

In Example 17–2, we used a uniqueness constraint to ensure that all the product numbers in the catalog were unique. It is also possible to ensure uniqueness of a combination of multiple fields. In the instance shown in Example 17–3, each product may have an effective date.

It is valid for two products to have the same number, as long as they have different effective dates. In other words, we want to validate that the combinations of `number` and `effDate` are unique. Example 17–4 shows the uniqueness constraint that accomplishes this.

Table 17–1   XSDL syntax: uniqueness constraint

Name
unique

Parents
element

Attribute name	Type	Required/default	Description
id	ID		unique ID
name	NCName	required	unique name

Content
annotation?, selector, field+

Example 17–3. Product catalog information, revisited

```
<catalog>
  <department number="021">
    <product effDate="2000-02-27">
      <number>557</number>
      <name>Short-Sleeved Linen Blouse</name>
      <price currency="USD">29.99</price>
    </product>
    <product effDate="2001-04-02">
      <number>557</number>
      <name>Short-Sleeved Linen Blouse</name>
      <price currency="USD">39.99</price>
    </product>
    <product effDate="2001-04-02">
      <number>563</number>
      <name>Ten-Gallon Hat</name>
      <price currency="USD">69.99</price>
    </product>
    <product>
      <number>443</number>
      <name>Deluxe Golf Umbrella</name>
      <price currency="USD">49.99</price>
    </product>
  </department>
</catalog>
```

Example 17–4. Constraining uniqueness of two combined fields

```
<xsd:element name="catalog" type="CatalogType">
  <xsd:unique name="dateAndProdNumKey">
    <xsd:selector xpath="department/product"/>
    <xsd:field xpath="number"/>
    <xsd:field xpath="@effDate"/>
  </xsd:unique>
</xsd:element>
```

Note that this example works because both number and effDate are subordinate to the product elements. Using the instance in Example 17–3, it would be invalid to define a multi-field uniqueness constraint on the department number and the product number. If you defined the selector to select all departments, the product/number field would bring yield than one field node per selected node, which is not permitted. If you defined the selector to select all products, you would have to access an ancestor node to get the department number, which is not permitted.

You can get around this by defining two uniqueness constraints: one in the scope of catalog to ensure that all department numbers are unique within a catalog, and another in the scope of department to ensure that all product numbers are unique within a department.

17.5 | Key constraints

A key constraint is similar to a uniqueness constraint in that the combined fields in the key must be unique. Key constraints have an additional requirement that all of the field values must be present in the document. Therefore, you should not define keys on elements or attributes that are optional. In addition, the fields on which the key is defined cannot be nillable.

In XSDL, key constraints are represented by a key element, whose syntax is shown in Table 17–2. It is identical to that of the unique elements.

Table 17–2   XSDL syntax: key constraint

Name			
key			

Parents			
element			

Attribute name	Type	Required/default	Description
id	ID		unique ID
name	NCName	required	unique name

Content			
annotation?, selector, field+			

Example 17–5 changes Example 17–2 to be a key constraint instead of a uniqueness constraint. In this case, every `product` element in the instance would be required to have a `number` child, regardless of whether the complex type of `product` requires it. The values of those `number` children have to be unique within the scope of `catalog`.

Example 17–5. Defining a key on product number

```
<xsd:element name="catalog" type="CatalogType">
  <xsd:key name="prodNumKey">
    <xsd:selector xpath="*/product"/>
    <xsd:field xpath="number"/>
  </xsd:key>
</xsd:element>
```

17.6 | Key references

Key references are used to ensure that there is a match between two sets of values in an instance. They are similar to foreign keys in databases. In XSDL, key references are represented by a `keyref` element, whose syntax is shown in Table 17–3.

Table 17–3   XSDL syntax: key reference

Name			
keyref			

Parents			
element			

Attribute name	Type	Required/default	Description
id	ID		unique ID
name	NCName	required	unique name
refer	QName	required	name of the key/uniqueness constraint being referenced

Content			
annotation?, selector, field+			

The `refer` attribute is used to reference a key or uniqueness constraint by its qualified name. If the constraint is defined in a schema document with a target namespace, the `refer` attribute must reference a name that is either prefixed, or in the scope of a default namespace declaration.

Suppose we have an order for three items: two shirts and one sweater, as shown in Example 17–6. The two shirts are the same except for their color, so they both have the same product number. All the descriptive product information appears at the end of the order. We want a way to ensure that every item in the order has a corresponding product description in the document.

Example 17–6. Key references

```
<order>
  <number>123ABBCC123</number>
  <items>.
    <shirt number="557">
      <quantity>1</quantity>
      <color value="blue"/>
    </shirt>
    <shirt number="557">
      <quantity>1</quantity>
      <color value="sage"/>
    </shirt>
    <hat number="563">
      <quantity>1</quantity>
    </hat>
  </items>
  <products>
    <product>
      <number>557</number>
      <name>Short-Sleeved Linen Blouse</name>
      <price currency="USD">29.99</price>
    </product>
    <product>
      <number>563</number>
      <name>Ten-Gallon Hat</name>
      <price currency="USD">69.99</price>
    </product>
  </products>
</order>
```

Example 17–7 shows the definition of a key reference and its associated key. In this example, the number attribute of any child of items must match a number child of a product element. The meaning of the XPath syntax will be described in detail later in this chapter.

Note that the key reference field values are not required to be unique; that is not their purpose. It is valid to have duplicate shirt numbers in the items section.

As with key and uniqueness constraints, key references can be on multiple fields. There must be an equal number of fields in the key reference as there are in the key or uniqueness constraint that it

Example 17–7. Defining a key reference on product number

```
<xsd:element name="order" type="OrderType">
  <xsd:keyref name="prodNumKeyRef" refer="prodNumKey">
    <xsd:selector xpath="items/*"/>
    <xsd:field xpath="@number"/>
  </xsd:keyref>
  <xsd:key name="prodNumKey">
    <xsd:selector xpath=".//product"/>
    <xsd:field xpath="number"/>
  </xsd:key>
</xsd:element>
```

references. The fields are matched in the same order, and they must have related types.

There is an additional constraint on the scope of key references and key constraints. The `key` referenced by a `keyref` must be defined in the same element declaration, or in a declaration of one of its children. It is not possible for a `keyref` to reference a `key` that is defined in a sibling or parent element declaration. In our example, the `key` and `keyref` were both defined in the declaration of `order`. It would also have been valid if the `key` had been defined in the `products` declaration. However, it would have been invalid if the `keyref` had been defined in the `items` declaration, because `items` is a child or `order`.

17.6.1 *Key references and type equality*

When defining key references, it is important to understand XML Schema's concept of equality. When determining whether two values are equal, their data type is taken into account. Values with unrelated data types will never be considered equal. For example, a value 2 of type `string` is not equal to a value 2 of type `integer`. However, if two data types are related by restriction, such as `integer` and `positiveInteger`, they can have equal values. When you define a key reference, make sure that the types of its fields are related to the types of the fields in the referenced key or uniqueness constraint. In Example 17–7, if the `number` attribute of `shirt` were declared as an integer, and the number child of product were declared as a string, there would have been no matches. For more information on type equality, see Section 12.7, "Type equality."

17.7 | Selectors and fields

All three categories of identity constraints are specified in terms of a selector and one or more fields. This section explains selectors and fields in more detail.

17.7.1 *Selectors*

The purpose of the selector is to identify the set of nodes to which the constraint applies. The selector is relative to the scoping element. In Example 17–2, our selector was */product. This selects all the product grandchildren of catalog. There may be other grandchildren of catalog, or other product elements elsewhere in the document, but the constraint does not apply to them.

In XSDL, the selector is represented by a selector element, whose syntax is shown in Table 17–4.

17.7.2 *Fields*

Each field must identify a single node relative to each node selected by the selector. The key reference in Example 17–7 works because there can only ever be one number child per selected node. In the instance in Example 17–6, the selector selects three nodes (the three children of items), and there is only one number child per node.

You might have been tempted to define a uniqueness constraint as shown in Example 17–8. This would not work because the selector would select one node (the single department element), and there would be three product/number nodes relative to it.

Table 17–4   XSDL syntax: constraint selector

Name
selector

Parents
unique, key, keyref

Attribute name	Type	Required/default	Description
id	ID		unique ID
xpath	XPath subset	required	XPath to the selected nodes

Content
annotation?

Example 17–8. Illegal uniqueness constraint

```
<xsd:element name="catalog" type="CatalogType">
  <xsd:unique name="prodNumKey">
    <xsd:selector xpath="department"/>
    <xsd:field xpath="product/number"/>
  </xsd:unique>
</xsd:element>
```

The elements or attributes that are used as fields must have simple content, and cannot be declared nillable.

In XSDL, fields are represented by a `field` element, whose syntax is shown in Table 17–5.

17.8 | The XML Schema XPath subset

All values of the `xpath` attribute in the `selector` and `field` tags must be legal XPath expressions. However, they must also conform to a subset of XPath that is defined by XML Schema.

Table 17–5   XSDL syntax: constraint field

Name			
`field`			

Parents			
`unique, key, keyref`			

Attribute name	*Type*	*Required/default*	*Description*
`id`	`ID`		unique ID
`xpath`	XPath subset	required	XPath to the key field

Content			
`annotation?`			

XPath expressions are made up of paths, separated by vertical bars. For example, the XPath expression `department/product/name|department/product/price` uses two paths to select all the nodes that are either `name` or `price` children of `product` following the `department/product` path.

Each path may begin with the `.//` literal, which means that the matching nodes may appear anywhere in the descendants of the current scoping element. If it is not included, it is assumed that matching nodes may appear only as direct children of the scoping element.

Each path is made up of steps, separated by forward slashes. For example, the path `department/product/name` is made up of three steps: `department`, `product`, and `name`. Table 17–6 lists the types of steps that may appear in the XML Schema XPath subset.

The context node of the selector expression is the element in whose declaration the identity constraint is defined. The context node of the field expression is the result of evaluating the selector expression.

Table 17–7 shows some legal XPath expressions for selectors and fields. They assume that the scope of the identity constraint is the `catalog` element, as shown in Example 17–4.

Technically, any of the XPath expressions in Table 17–7 is legal for a field. However, since the field XPath can only identify a node that

Table 17–6   XPath subset steps

Step	Description	Example
qualified element-type name	a child element-type name, which must be prefixed if it is in a namespace	`department,` `prod:department`
period	the contents of the current element	`.`
asterisk (*)	a wildcard representing any element	`*`
prefix plus an asterisk	a wildcard representing any element in the namespace mapped to that prefix	`prod:*`
@ plus a qualified attribute name	an attribute name, which must be prefixed if the attribute name is in a namespace (legal for `field` only)	`@number,` `@prod:number`

appears once relative to the selected node, most of the expressions that contain wildcards to select multiple nodes are inappropriate for fields. The field XPath will usually consist of a single child element or a single attribute.

Table 17–8 shows some expressions that, while they are legal XPath, are not in the XML Schema XPath subset.

17.9 | Identity constraints and namespaces

Special consideration must be given to namespaces when defining identity constraints. Qualified element-type names and attribute names used in the XPath expressions must be prefixed in order to be legal. Let's take another look at our uniqueness constraint from Example 17–4. That definition assumed that the schema document had no

Table 17–7   XPath subset expressions in the scope of catalog

XPath	Nodes selected
`.`	`catalog` itself
`*`	all direct children of `catalog`
`.//*`	all elements appearing anywhere in `catalog`
`department` or `./department`	all `department` elements that are direct children of `catalog`
`./*/*`	all grandchildren of `catalog` (regardless of their or their parent's element-type name)
`.//product`	all `product` elements appearing anywhere in `catalog`
`./*/product`	all `product` elements that are grandchildren of `catalog` (regardless of their parent)
`.//product/name`	all `name` elements whose parent is `product` appearing anywhere in `catalog`
`./department/product/name`	all `name` elements whose parent is a `product`, whose parent is a `department` whose parent is `catalog`
`.//department	.//product`	all `department` elements and `product` elements appearing anywhere in `catalog`
`@effDate`	the `effDate` attribute (legal only for `field`, not `selector`)
`product/@effDate`	the `effDate` attributes of all `product` children (legal only for `field`, not `selector`)
`/prod:product/prod:*`	all grandchildren whose parent is `product`, in the namespace mapped to the `prod` prefix (see Section 17.9)

Table 17–8   Illegal XPath subset expressions

XPath(s)	Comments	Workaround
`../department` or `ancestor::department` or `parent::department`	ancestors cannot be accessed	move the constraint up one level to the parent element (this does not always work, if the fields appear at multiple levels)
`descendent::product`	the `descendent` keyword is not supported	`.//product`
`text()`	You only need to specify the element-type name; `text()` is implied	use a single period (.) if it is the current node, otherwise simply leave off the `text()`
`department//name`	all steps must contain something; double slash is not allowed except for "`.//`" at the beginning of path	`department/*/name	department/*/*/name	...` or move the constraint down one level to the `department` element
`//product`	the document root cannot be accessed	move the constraint up to the level of the root (`catalog`) element, then use `.//product`
`/catalog/product`	the document root cannot be accessed	move the constraint up to the level of the root (`catalog`) element, then use `product`

target namespace. If we add a target namespace, it looks like Example 17–9.

Example 17–9. Prefixing names in the XPath expression

```
<xsd:schema xmlns:xsd="http://www.w3.org/2001/XMLSchema"
            xmlns:prod="http://example.org/prod"
            targetNamespace="http://example.org/prod">
  <xsd:element name="catalog" type="prod:CatalogType">
    <xsd:unique name="dateAndProdNumKey">
      <xsd:selector xpath="prod:department/prod:product"/>
      <xsd:field xpath="prod:number"/>
      <xsd:field xpath="@effDate"/>
    </xsd:unique>
  </xsd:element>
  <xsd:element name="department" type="prod:DepartmentType"/>
  <xsd:element name="product" type="prod:ProductType"/>
  <xsd:element name="number" type="prod:ProdNumType"/>
  <!--...-->
</xsd:schema>
```

Each of the element-type names in the XPath is prefixed with `prod`, mapping it to the `http://example.org/prod` namespace. In our example, all element declarations (`department`, `product`, and `number`) are global, and therefore their names must be prefixed. Let's assume that the attribute `effDate` is locally declared, so its name is not prefixed in the XPath expression.

The names that must be qualified in an XPath expression are the ones that must be qualified in an instance, namely:

- all element-type names and attribute names in global declarations,
- element-type names and attribute names in local declarations whose form is `qualified`, either directly or indirectly through `elementFormDefault` or `attributeFormDefault`.

Note that the target namespace is mapped to a prefix, rather than being the default namespace. This is because XPath expressions are not affected by default namespace declarations. Unqualified names in XPath expressions are always assumed to be in no namespace.

Therefore, if you want to use identity constraints in a schema document that has a target namespace, you must map the target namespace to a prefix. Example 17–10 uses unqualified names in the XPath expressions, assuming that these names take on the default namespace. This is not the case; in fact, these elements will not be found because they will be considered to be in no namespace.

Example 17–10. Illegal attempt to apply default namespace to XPath

```
<xsd:schema xmlns:xsd="http://www.w3.org/2001/XMLSchema"
            xmlns="http://example.org/prod"
            targetNamespace="http://example.org/prod">
  <xsd:element name="catalog" type="CatalogType">
    <xsd:unique name="dateAndProdNumKey">
      <xsd:selector xpath="department/product"/>
      <xsd:field xpath="number"/>
      <xsd:field xpath="@effDate"/>
    </xsd:unique>
  </xsd:element>
  <xsd:element name="department" type="DepartmentType"/>
  <xsd:element name="product" type="ProductType"/>
  <xsd:element name="number" type="prod:ProdNumType"/>
  <!--...-->
</xsd:schema>
```

Redefining schema components

Chapter

18

R edefinition is a way to extend and modify schemas over time, while still reusing the original definitions. It involves defining a new version of a schema component, with the same name, that replaces the original definition throughout the schema. This is very useful for extending and creating a subset of an existing schema. It is also useful for performing minor modifications over time. This chapter explains redefinition in detail.

18.1 | Redefinition basics

Only certain types of schema components can be redefined, namely complex types, simple types, named model groups, and attribute groups. The new definitions must be based on the original definitions. For types, this means that the new type must restrict or extend the original type. For attribute groups and named model groups, it means that the new group must either be a subset or a superset of the original group.

Example 18–1 shows a simple redefinition where the schema document prod2.xsd redefines prod1.xsd. The simple type DressSize-Type is redefined in prod2.xsd.

Example 18–1. A simple redefinition

prod1.xsd:

```
<xsd:schema xmlns:xsd="http://www.w3.org/2001/XMLSchema">

  <xsd:simpleType name="DressSizeType">
    <xsd:restriction base="xsd:integer"/>
  </xsd:simpleType>

  <xsd:element name="size" type="DressSizeType"/>

  <xsd:element name="color" type="xsd:string"/>

</xsd:schema>
```

prod2.xsd:

```
<xsd:schema xmlns:xsd="http://www.w3.org/2001/XMLSchema"
            xmlns="http://example.org/prod"
            targetNamespace="http://example.org/prod">

  <xsd:redefine schemaLocation="prod1.xsd">
    <xsd:simpleType name="DressSizeType">
      <xsd:restriction base="DressSizeType">
        <xsd:minInclusive value="2"/>
        <xsd:maxInclusive value="16"/>
      </xsd:restriction>
    </xsd:simpleType>
  </xsd:redefine>

  <xsd:element name="newSize" type="DressSizeType"/>

</xsd:schema>
```

18.1.1 *Include plus redefine*

When a schema document is redefined, *all* of its components are included in the redefining schema document, regardless of whether they are specifically mentioned in the redefinition. In this way, the redefinition feature is similar to the include feature. In our example, the resulting schema document includes *all* of the components defined and declared in both `prod2.xsd` and `prod1.xsd`. Even though `color` is not mentioned in `prod2.xsd`, it will be included in the resulting schema document.

18.1.2 *Redefine and namespaces*

The target namespace of the redefined schema document must be the same as that of the redefining schema document, or non-existent. If the redefined schema document does not have a target namespace, all of its components will take on the target namespace of the redefining schema document. For example, since `prod1.xsd` does not have a target namespace, all of its components will take on the target namespace of `prod2.xsd`. This includes `color`, which is not specifically mentioned in the redefinition. It is not a problem that the `size` element declaration references `DressSizeType` without a prefix; the processor will correctly interpret the references between components.

18.1.3 *Pervasive impact*

Once a schema is redefined, the new definitions completely replace the original definitions, not just for components in the new redefining schema document, but also for components that reference it in the original, redefined schema document. In Example 18–1, the `size` element declaration now uses the new `DressSizeType`. If there had been data types derived from `DressSizeType` in `prod1.xsd`, they would now be derived from the new `DressSizeType`.

Redefinition of a component has a ripple effect on all the other components that depend on it. For a type, this includes all other types that are derived from it at any level. For a group, it includes all complex types that reference it, as well as the types derived from those types. While this is generally intentional and desirable, there is no guarantee that you will not break these dependent components, and schema processors are not required to warn you if you do. Specific risks associated with each kind of redefinition are described in the sections that follow.

For a comparison of redefinition, type derivation, and other methods of extending schemas see Section 21.2, "Extending schemas."

18.2 | The mechanics of redefinition

In XSDL, a `redefine` element is used to contain redefined schema components. A `redefine` element may only occur at the top level of a schema document (with `schema` as its parent), and all `redefine` children must be at the beginning of the schema document, along with the `include` and `import` elements. The syntax for a `redefine` element is shown in Table 18–1.

A schema document can contain multiple redefinitions of various other schema documents. The `schemaLocation` attribute indicates the location of the schema document to be redefined. It must reference a complete schema document with `schema` as its root element. As mentioned above, the redefined schema document must have the same target namespace as the redefining schema document, or none at all.

The `redefine` element contains the new definitions of the schema components, in any order. For every definition that appears in a `redefine` element, there must be a corresponding definition (with the same qualified name) in the redefined schema document. Only the components that need to be modified should appear in the `redefine` element. All other components of the redefined schema document will be included in the new schema as is. In fact, a `redefine` element is

Table 18–1   XSDL syntax: redefinition

Name			
redefine			

Parents			
schema			

Attribute name	Type	Required/default	Description
id	ID		unique ID
schemaLocation	anyURI	required	location of the schema document which describes the components being redefined

Content			
(annotation | attributeGroup | complexType | group | simpleType)*			

not required to have any children at all, in which case it acts exactly like an `include` element.

18.3 | Redefining simple types

When redefining a simple type, the new definition must restrict the original simple type. Example 18–2 shows how you would redefine DressSizeType to change minInclusive to be 2. The restricted DressSizeType uses itself as the base type. Redefinition is the only case where a simple type can restrict itself.

The redefinition of DressSizeType affects not only the newSize element declaration in prod2.xsd, but also the size element declaration in prod1.xsd. Because of the redefinition, size instances that conform to prod2.xsd cannot have the value 0. This illustrates the effect redefinition has on components in the original schema.

Example 18–2. Redefining a simple type

prod1.xsd:

```
<xsd:schema xmlns:xsd="http://www.w3.org/2001/XMLSchema">
  <xsd:simpleType name="DressSizeType">
    <xsd:restriction base="xsd:integer">
      <xsd:minInclusive value="0"/>
      <xsd:maxInclusive value="18"/>
    </xsd:restriction>
  </xsd:simpleType>
  <xsd:element name="size" type="DressSizeType"/>
</xsd:schema>
```

prod2.xsd:

```
<xsd:schema xmlns:xsd="http://www.w3.org/2001/XMLSchema">
  <xsd:redefine schemaLocation="prod1.xsd">
    <xsd:simpleType name="DressSizeType">
      <xsd:restriction base="DressSizeType">
        <xsd:minInclusive value="2"/>
      </xsd:restriction>
    </xsd:simpleType>
  </xsd:redefine>
  <xsd:element name="newSize" type="DressSizeType"/>
</xsd:schema>
```

When you redefine a simple type, be careful not to negatively affect other types that restrict it in the original schema. Suppose that in prod1.xsd there had been a simple type SmallDressSizeType, derived from DressSizeType, with a minInclusive value of 1. After redefinition of DressSizeType, SmallDressSizeType would be an illegal restriction, because it would be trying to extend the value space by changing minInclusive from 2 to 1.

18.4 | Redefining complex types

Complex types can also be redefined, provided that the new definition of the complex type either extends or restricts the original complex type. Example 18–3 shows how you would redefine `ProductType` to add a new element declaration and a new attribute declaration. Like a simple type, a complex type can be based on itself when it is part of a redefinition.

Example 18–3. Redefining a complex type

prod1.xsd:

```
<xsd:schema xmlns:xsd="http://www.w3.org/2001/XMLSchema">
  <xsd:complexType name="ProductType">
    <xsd:sequence>
      <xsd:element name="number" type="ProdNumType"/>
      <xsd:element name="name" type="xsd:string"/>
      <xsd:element name="size" type="SizeType"/>
    </xsd:sequence>
  </xsd:complexType>
</xsd:schema>
```

prod2.xsd:

```
<xsd:schema xmlns:xsd="http://www.w3.org/2001/XMLSchema">
  <xsd:redefine schemaLocation="prod1.xsd">
    <xsd:complexType name="ProductType">
      <xsd:complexContent>
        <xsd:extension base="ProductType">
          <xsd:sequence>
            <xsd:element name="color" type="ColorType"/>
          </xsd:sequence>
          <xsd:attribute name="effDate" type="xsd:date"/>
        </xsd:extension>
      </xsd:complexContent>
    </xsd:complexType>
  </xsd:redefine>
</xsd:schema>
```

When you redefine a complex type, be careful not to negatively affect other types that are derived from it in the original schema. Suppose that in `prod1.xsd` there had been a complex type `ShirtType` derived from `ProductType`. All changes to `ProductType` are passed down to

ShirtType, which is probably your intention. However, you can also render ShirtType illegal in a number of ways.

Some of the risks associated with redefining ProductType as an extension are:

- adding an attribute that ShirtType already has, resulting in duplicate attributes for ShirtType,
- adding an element declaration to the content model that ShirtType already has, but with a different data type. It is illegal for a complex type to contain two element declarations with the same name and different data types,
- adding element declarations to the content model that render the content model of ShirtType non-deterministic.

Some of the risks associated with redefining ProductType as a restriction are:

- restricting a content model further than ShirtType restricted it, rendering ShirtType's restriction illegal,
- restricting an attribute further than ShirtType restricted it, rendering ShirtType's restriction illegal,
- making an attribute prohibited, which is then restricted by ShirtType, resulting in an illegal attribute declaration in the definition of ShirtType.

18.5 | Redefining named model groups

When redefining named model groups, the new definition must be either a subset or a superset of the original group.

18.5.1 *Defining a subset*

Example 18–4 shows the redefinition of `DescriptionGroup` to disallow the `comment` element.

Example 18–4. Redefining a named model group as a subset

prod1.xsd:

```
<xsd:schema xmlns:xsd="http://www.w3.org/2001/XMLSchema">
  <xsd:group name="DescriptionGroup">
    <xsd:sequence>
      <xsd:element name="description" type="xsd:string"/>
      <xsd:element name="comment" type="xsd:string" minOccurs="0"/>
    </xsd:sequence>
  </xsd:group>
</xsd:schema>
```

prod2.xsd:

```
<xsd:schema xmlns:xsd="http://www.w3.org/2001/XMLSchema">
  <xsd:redefine schemaLocation="prod1.xsd">
    <xsd:group name="DescriptionGroup">
      <xsd:sequence>
        <xsd:element name="description" type="xsd:string"/>
      </xsd:sequence>
    </xsd:group>
  </xsd:redefine>
</xsd:schema>
```

Our example is legal because the `comment` elements are optional per the original definition. The exact definition of a legal subset is the same as that used for complex type restriction. In other words, if a content model is considered a legal restriction of another content model (in complex type derivation), it is also a legal subset in the redefinition of a named model group. See Section 14.5, "Complex type restrictions," for the rules of complex type restriction.

When you redefine a named model group as a subset, be careful not to negatively affect complex types that include the group. Suppose that in `prod1.xsd` there had been a complex type `ProductType` that used

DescriptionGroup in its content model, as well as another complex type ShirtType that was derived from ProductType. If ShirtType restricts the comment element declaration by changing its data type, redefining DescriptionGroup as shown in Example 18–4 will render ShirtType illegal, because comment will no longer exist.

18.5.2 *Defining a superset*

On the other hand, suppose you want to extend the definition of DescriptionGroup to include more children. Example 18–5 shows the redefinition of DescriptionGroup to add new element declarations. In this case, you are saying that you want all of the original element declarations of DescriptionGroup, followed by the new notes element declaration.

The group refers to itself the way it would refer to any other group. Redefinition is the only case where a group reference can be circular, and there are two constraints:

- The group may only reference itself once.
- maxOccurs and minOccurs of that self-reference must be 1 (or not present, in which case they default to 1).

When you redefine a named model group as a superset, be careful not to negatively affect complex types that include the group. Suppose that in prod1.xsd there had been a complex type ProductType that used DescriptionGroup in its content model. If the content model of ProductType happened to also contain a notes element declaration that had the data type token, redefining DescriptionGroup as shown in Example 18–5 will render ProductType illegal. This is because ProductType will contain two notes element declarations with different data types, which is not legal. It is also possible to render the content model of ProductType non-deterministic by altering the contents of DescriptionGroup.

Example 18–5. Redefining a named model group as a superset

prod1.xsd:

```
<xsd:schema xmlns:xsd="http://www.w3.org/2001/XMLSchema">
  <xsd:group name="DescriptionGroup">
    <xsd:sequence>
      <xsd:element name="description" type="xsd:string"/>
      <xsd:element name="comment" type="xsd:string" minOccurs="0"/>
    </xsd:sequence>
  </xsd:group>
</xsd:schema>
```

prod2.xsd:

```
<xsd:schema xmlns:xsd="http://www.w3.org/2001/XMLSchema">
  <xsd:redefine schemaLocation="prod1.xsd">
    <xsd:group name="DescriptionGroup">
      <xsd:sequence>
        <xsd:group ref="DescriptionGroup"/>
        <xsd:element name="notes" type="xsd:string"/>
      </xsd:sequence>
    </xsd:group>
  </xsd:redefine>
</xsd:schema>
```

18.6 | Redefining attribute groups

Like named model groups, attribute groups can be redefined to be a subset or superset of their original definition.

18.6.1 *Defining a subset*

Example 18–6 shows how you would redefine the IdentifierGroup as a subset. The new definition disallows the xml:lang attribute, and changes the data type of the version attribute from decimal to integer.

Example 18–6. Redefining an attribute group as a subset

prod1.xsd:

```
<xsd:schema xmlns:xsd="http://www.w3.org/2001/XMLSchema">
  <xsd:attributeGroup name="IdentifierGroup">
    <xsd:attribute name="id" type="xsd:ID" use="required"/>
    <xsd:attribute name="version" type="xsd:decimal"/>
    <xsd:attribute ref="xml:lang"/>
  </xsd:attributeGroup>
</xsd:schema>
```

prod2.xsd:

```
<xsd:schema xmlns:xsd="http://www.w3.org/2001/XMLSchema">
  <xsd:redefine schemaLocation="prod1.xsd">
    <xsd:attributeGroup name="IdentifierGroup">
      <xsd:attribute name="id" type="xsd:ID" use="required"/>
      <xsd:attribute name="version" type="xsd:integer"/>
    </xsd:attributeGroup>
  </xsd:redefine>
</xsd:schema>
```

The rules used to define a subset of an attribute group are the same as those used for attribute restriction in complex type derivation. This means that you can eliminate optional attributes, make attributes required, add a fixed value, change default values, or change data types to be more restrictive. Eliminating the xml:lang attribute in Example 18–6 is legal because it is optional (by default) in the original attribute group. Changing the type of version is legal because integer is a restriction of decimal. See Section 14.5.5, "Attribute restrictions," for more information on attribute restrictions.

Unlike complex type derivation, however, you must redeclare all attributes you want to appear in the new definition. The attribute declarations will not automatically be copied from the original definition to the new definition.

If the original definition contains an attribute wildcard, you may repeat or further restrict the wildcard. Subsetting of attribute wildcards also follows the rules used in complex type derivation. See

Section 14.5.6, "Attribute wildcard restrictions" for more information on attribute wildcard restrictions.

When you redefine an attribute group as a subset, be careful not to negatively affect complex types that include the attribute group. Suppose that in `prod1.xsd` there had been a complex type `ProductType` that contained `IdentifierGroup`, as well as another complex type `ShirtType` that was derived from `ProductType`. If `ShirtType` restricts the `xml:lang` attribute by making it required, redefining `DescriptionGroup` as shown in Example 18–6 will render `ShirtType` illegal, because the `xml:lang` attribute will no longer exist.

18.6.2 *Defining a superset*

On the other hand, suppose you want to extend the definition of `IdentifierGroup` to include more attributes. Example 18–7 shows how you would redefine `IdentifierGroup` to add attributes. You cannot alter the declarations of the attributes in the original group, only add new attributes. In this case, you are saying that you want all of the original attributes of `IdentifierGroup`, plus a new `effDate` attribute.

The attribute group refers to itself the way it would refer to any other attribute group. Redefinition is the only case where an attribute group reference can be circular.

When you redefine an attribute group as a superset, be careful not to negatively affect complex types that include the attribute group. Suppose that in `prod1.xsd` there had been a complex type `Product-Type` that used `IdentifierGroup`. If `ProductType` also happened to contain an `effDate` attribute, redefining `DescriptionGroup` as shown in Example 18–7 would render `ProductType` illegal. This is because `ProductType` will have two attributes named `effDate`, which is illegal.

Example 18–7. Redefining an attribute group as a superset

prod1.xsd:

```
<xsd:schema xmlns:xsd="http://www.w3.org/2001/XMLSchema">
  <xsd:attributeGroup name="IdentifierGroup">
    <xsd:attribute name="id" type="xsd:ID" use="required"/>
    <xsd:attribute name="version" type="xsd:decimal"/>
    <xsd:attribute ref="xml:lang"/>
  </xsd:attributeGroup>
</xsd:schema>
```

prod2.xsd:

```
<xsd:schema xmlns:xsd="http://www.w3.org/2001/XMLSchema">
  <xsd:redefine schemaLocation="prod1.xsd">
    <xsd:attributeGroup name="IdentifierGroup">
      <xsd:attributeGroup ref="IdentifierGroup"/>
      <xsd:attribute name="effDate" type="xsd:date"/>
    </xsd:attributeGroup>
  </xsd:redefine>
</xsd:schema>
```

Topics
for DTD users

Chapter 9

T his chapter provides a jump-start on XML Schema for readers who are familiar with DTDs. It provides a detailed comparison of DTD syntax with XSDL, which is useful both for understanding XML Schema and for converting existing DTDs to schemas.

19.1 | Element declarations

Table 19–1 shows examples of various DTD content models and matches them up with the various XML Schema content types. Each of these content types is explained in the rest of this section.

19.1.1 *Simple types*

Element types with (#PCDATA) content and no attributes in a DTD correspond to element declarations with simple types in schemas. Example 19–1 shows such an element declaration.

Table 19–1   Content types

Example DTD content model	*Simple type*	*Complex type*			
		Simple content	*Complex content*		
			Element-only	*Mixed*	*Empty*
(#PCDATA) with no attributes	Section 19.1.1				
(#PCDATA) with attributes		Section 19.1.2			
(a | b)*			Section 19.1.3		
(#PCDATA | a | b)*				Section 19.1.4	
EMPTY					Section 19.1.5
ANY				Section 19.1.6	

Example 19–1. Simple type

DTD:

```
<!ELEMENT price (#PCDATA)>
```

Schema:

```
<xsd:element name="price" type="xsd:decimal"/>
```

Note that the built-in type decimal is assigned to price. It is possible to assign all #PCDATA element types the built-in type string, which handles whitespace in the same way as DTD processors handle whitespace for any character data content of an element. However, it is advisable to be as specific as possible when choosing a data type for an element declaration. Chapter 12, "Built-in simple types," describes the built-in simple types in detail, and Chapter 9, "Simple types," describes how to define your own simple types.

19.1.2 *Complex types with simple content*

Element types with (#PCDATA) content that do have attributes correspond to element declarations using complex data types with simple content in schemas. Example 19–2 shows such an element declaration. It extends the simple type decimal to add the attribute currency.

Example 19–2. Simple content (with attributes)

DTD:

```
<!ELEMENT price (#PCDATA)>
<!ATTLIST price currency NMTOKEN #IMPLIED>
```

Schema:

```
<xsd:element name="price">
  <xsd:complexType>
    <xsd:simpleContent>
      <xsd:extension base="xsd:decimal">
        <xsd:attribute name="currency" type="xsd:NMTOKEN"/>
      </xsd:extension>
    </xsd:simpleContent>
  </xsd:complexType>
</xsd:element>
```

19.1.3 *Complex types with complex content*

Element types that may have children, regardless of whether they have attributes, correspond to element declarations using complex data types with complex content in schemas. Example 19–3 shows such an element declaration.

Example 19–3. Complex content

DTD:

```
<!ELEMENT product (number, name+, size?, color*)>
```

Schema:

```
<xsd:element name="product">
  <xsd:complexType>
    <xsd:sequence>
      <xsd:element ref="number"/>
      <xsd:element ref="name"  maxOccurs="unbounded"/>
      <xsd:element ref="size"  minOccurs="0"/>
      <xsd:element ref="color" minOccurs="0" maxOccurs="unbounded"/>
    </xsd:sequence>
  </xsd:complexType>
</xsd:element>
```

In Example 19–3, the content model was converted into a `sequence`. Groups, represented by parentheses in DTDs, are represented by one of the three model groups in XSDL:

- `sequence` groups require that the elements appear in order,
- `choice` groups allow a choice from among several elements,
- `all` groups require that all the elements appear 0 or 1 times, in any order.

Table 19–2 shows the mapping between DTD groups and XSDL model groups.

Table 19–2   Group compositors

DTD model	XSDL model group
(a,b,c)	sequence
(a|b|c)	choice
no equivalent	all

As shown in Example 19–3, the occurrence constraints on element types and groups are represented by the minOccurs and maxOccurs attributes in XSDL. Table 19–3 shows the mapping between occurrence constraints in DTDs and XSDL.

Table 19–3   Occurrence constraints

DTD Symbol	XSDL minOccurs *value*	XSDL maxOccurs *value*
(none)	1	1
*	0	unbounded
+	1	unbounded
?	0	1

The defaults for minOccurs and maxOccurs are both 1. XML Schema can provide more specific validation than DTDs, since any non-negative integer can be specified. For example, you can specify that the color element may appear a maximum of three times.

Groups may be nested in schemas just as they may in DTDs, as illustrated in Example 19–4. Note that minOccurs and maxOccurs may appear on groups as well as on element declarations.

Example 19–4. Nested groups

DTD:

```
<!ELEMENT el ((a | b)*, (c | d)?)>
```

Schema:

```
<xsd:element name="el">
  <xsd:complexType>
    <xsd:sequence>
      <xsd:choice minOccurs="0" maxOccurs="unbounded">
        <xsd:element ref="a"/>
        <xsd:element ref="b"/>
      </xsd:choice>
      <xsd:choice minOccurs="0" maxOccurs="1">
        <xsd:element ref="c"/>
        <xsd:element ref="d"/>
      </xsd:choice>
    </xsd:sequence>
  </xsd:complexType>
</xsd:element>
```

19.1.4 *Mixed content*

Element types which have both #PCDATA content and children are said to have mixed content.[1] In XSDL, mixed content is indicated by a mixed attribute of a complexType element, as shown in Example 19–5.

With DTDs, you are limited to the choice (|) operator with mixed content element types. In schemas, any content model can be mixed, allowing more complex validation of the children. For example, in a DTD you cannot specify that custName must appear before prodName. In XSDL, you can accomplish this using a sequence group instead of a choice group.

---

1. Technically, mixed content also refers to element types with just #PCDATA content, but this case is covered in Section 19.1.1, "Simple types," and Section 19.1.2, "Complex types with simple content."

Example 19–5. Mixed content

DTD:

```
<!ELEMENT letter (#PCDATA | custName | prodName)*>
```

Schema:

```
<xsd:element name="letter">
  <xsd:complexType mixed="true">
    <xsd:choice minOccurs="0" maxOccurs="unbounded">
      <xsd:element ref="custName"/>
      <xsd:element ref="prodName"/>
    </xsd:choice>
  </xsd:complexType>
</xsd:element>
```

19.1.5 *Empty content*

Empty content, indicated by the keyword EMPTY in DTDs, is simply indicated by an absence of a content model in XSDL. Example 19–6 shows an element declaration with empty content, containing only attribute declarations.

Example 19–6. Empty content

DTD:

```
<!ELEMENT color EMPTY>
<!ATTLIST color value NMTOKEN #IMPLIED>
```

Schema:

```
<xsd:element name="color">
  <xsd:complexType>
    <!-- no content model is specified here -->
    <xsd:attribute name="value" type="xsd:NMTOKEN"/>
  </xsd:complexType>
</xsd:element>
```

19.1.6 *Any content*

Any content, indicated by the keyword ANY in DTDs, is represented by an element wildcard any in XSDL. This is illustrated in Example 19–7.

Example 19–7. Any content

DTD:

```
<!ELEMENT anything ANY>
```

Schema:

```
<xsd:element name="anything">
  <xsd:complexType mixed="true">
    <xsd:sequence>
      <xsd:any minOccurs="0" maxOccurs="unbounded"/>
    </xsd:sequence>
  </xsd:complexType>
</xsd:element>
```

XML Schema offers much more sophisticated wildcard capabilities than DTDs. It is possible with XML Schema to put a wildcard anywhere in a content model, specify how many replacement elements may appear, restrict the namespace(s) of the replacement elements, and control how strictly they are validated. See Section 13.4.3, "Element wildcards," for more information on element wildcards.

19.2 | Attribute declarations

19.2.1 *Attribute types*

Most of the original XML 1.0 attribute types have representations in XML Schema as simple types, with the same name. Table 19–4 lists the DTD attribute types and their equivalent types in XML Schema.

Table 19–4   DTD attribute types and equivalents

DTD attribute type	XML schema equivalent
CDATA	normalizedString
NMTOKEN, NMTOKENS	NMTOKEN, NMTOKENS
ID, IDREF, IDREFS	ID, IDREF, IDREFS
ENTITY, ENTITIES	ENTITY, ENTITIES
NOTATION	simple type derived from NOTATION, see Section 19.2.3
enumerated values	simple type derivation with enumeration facets specified, see Section 19.2.2

19.2.2 *Enumerated attribute types*

In order to represent an enumerated attribute type in XSDL, it is necessary to define a new simple type and apply enumeration facets to restrict the values to the desired set. This is illustrated in Example 19–8.

Example 19–8. Representing an enumerated attribute

DTD:

```
<!ATTLIST price currency (USD | CHF) "USD">
```

Schema:

```
<xsd:attribute name="currency" default="USD">
  <xsd:simpleType>
    <xsd:restriction base="xsd:token">
      <xsd:enumeration value="USD"/>
      <xsd:enumeration value="CHF"/>
    </xsd:restriction>
  </xsd:simpleType>
</xsd:attribute>
```

The built-in type token is used as the base type for the restriction, which will result in whitespace handling identical to that of enumerated attribute types in DTDs.

19.2.3 *Notation attributes*

A NOTATION attribute type exists in XML Schema as it does in XML 1.0. However, the NOTATION data type cannot be used directly by an attribute. Instead, you must define a new simple type that restricts NOTATION, and apply enumeration facets to list the possible values for that notation. This is illustrated in Example 19–9.

Example 19–9. Representing a notation attribute

DTD:

```
<!ATTLIST picture fmt NOTATION (jpg | gif) "jpg">
```

Schema:

```
<xsd:attribute name="fmt" default="jpg">
  <xsd:simpleType>
    <xsd:restriction base="xsd:NOTATION">
      <xsd:enumeration value="jpg"/>
      <xsd:enumeration value="gif"/>
    </xsd:restriction>
  </xsd:simpleType>
</xsd:attribute>
```

19.2.4 *Default values*

Attribute default values are handled by three attributes in XSDL: the use attribute, which indicates whether the attribute being declared is required or optional, the default attribute, which specifies a default value, and the fixed attribute, which specifies a fixed value. Table 19–5 shows how the DTD attribute default values correspond to XSDL attributes.

Table 19–5   DTD default values and equivalents

DTD default value	XSDL equivalent
#REQUIRED	use="required"
#IMPLIED	use="optional"
#FIXED "x"	fixed="x"
"x"	default="x"

Example 19–10 provides some examples of attribute declarations with various types and default values.

Example 19–10. Attribute declarations

DTD:

```
<!ATTLIST product
    id ID #REQUIRED
    name CDATA #IMPLIED
    type NMTOKEN "PR"
    version NMTOKEN #FIXED "A123">
```

Schema:

```
<xsd:attribute name="id" type="xsd:ID" use="required"/>
<xsd:attribute name="name" type="xsd:normalizedString"
               use="optional"/>
<xsd:attribute name="type" type="xsd:NMTOKEN" default="PR"/>
<xsd:attribute name="version" type="xsd:NMTOKEN" fixed="A123"/>
```

19.3 | Notations

Notations are represented in a straightforward way in XSDL, as illustrated in Example 19–11. See Section 6.4, "Notations," for more information on notations in XML Schema.

Example 19–11. Notation

DTD:

```
<!NOTATION jpeg SYSTEM "JPG">
```

Schema:

```
<xsd:notation name="jpeg" system="JPG"/>
```

19.4 | Parameter entities for reuse

Internal parameter entities are often used in DTDs to reuse pieces of element or attribute declarations. Using schemas, reuse is handled by creating reusable types, named model groups, and attribute groups. This section explains how to convert internal parameter entities into XML Schema components.

19.4.1 *Reusing content models*

In DTDs, a parameter entity may be used to define a content model once and reuse it for multiple element types. Using schemas, the best way to accomplish this is to define a named complex type that is then used by multiple element declarations. This is illustrated in Example 19–12, where the AOrB content model is used by two element declarations, x and y.

A parameter entity may also be used to represent a fragment of a content model. In XML Schema, named model groups are designated for this purpose. Example 19–13 shows a content model fragment AOrB that is used as part of the entire content model in the x element declaration. See Section 15.2, "Named model groups," for more information on named model groups.

Example 19–12. Reusing entire content models

DTD:

```
<!ENTITY % AOrB "(a | b)">

<!ELEMENT x %AOrB;>
<!ELEMENT y %AOrB;>
```

Schema:

```
<xsd:complexType name="AOrBType">
  <xsd:choice>
    <xsd:element ref="a"/>
    <xsd:element ref="b"/>
  </xsd:choice>
</xsd:complexType>

<xsd:element name="x" type="AOrBType"/>
<xsd:element name="y" type="AOrBType"/>
```

19.4.2 *Reusing attributes*

In some cases, parameter entities are used in DTDs to reuse an attribute or set of attributes that are common to several element types. In XML Schema, attribute groups are used for this purpose. Example 19–14 shows the definition of an attribute group HeaderGroup containing two attributes, which is then referenced by the x element declaration.

19.5 | Parameter entities for extensibility

Parameter entities are sometimes used to make DTDs more flexible and future-proof. Empty entities are declared and placed in various parts of the DTD, most often in content models and attribute lists. This allows a parent (or internal) DTD to override the entity declaration, thus overriding the original DTD without having to completely rewrite it. Using schemas, this can be accomplished through either type derivation, substitution groups, or the redefine mechanism.

Example 19–13. Reusing fragments of content models

DTD:

```
<!ENTITY % AOrB "a | b">

<!ELEMENT x ((%AOrB;) , c)>
```

Schema:

```
<xsd:group name="AOrBGroup">
  <xsd:choice>
    <xsd:element ref="a"/>
    <xsd:element ref="b"/>
  </xsd:choice>
</xsd:group>

<xsd:element name="x">
  <xsd:complexType>
    <xsd:sequence>
      <xsd:group ref="AOrBGroup"/>
      <xsd:element ref="c"/>
    </xsd:sequence>
  </xsd:complexType>
</xsd:element>
```

19.5.1 *Extensions for* sequence *groups*

In DTDs, you can place a reference to an empty parameter entity at the end of a content model. If the extension is to be added sequentially to the end of a content model, as shown in Example 19–15, it can be accomplished using the redefinition mechanism of XML Schema.

Example 19–16 shows how these extensions would be accomplished in a new parent DTD or in a new schema. In the schema, the redefine mechanism is used to extend the complex type to add to the end of the content model. In this case, we redefined a complex type, but it is also possible to redefine a named model group, which represents a fragment of a content model. Redefinition is covered in Chapter 18, "Redefining schema components."

Example 19–14. Reusing groups of attributes

DTD:

```
<!ENTITY % HeaderGroup "id ID #REQUIRED
                variety NMTOKEN #IMPLIED">

<!ATTLIST x %HeaderGroup;>
```

Schema:

```
<xsd:attributeGroup name="HeaderGroup">
  <xsd:attribute name="id" type="xsd:ID" use="required"/>
  <xsd:attribute name="variety" type="xsd:NMTOKEN"/>
</xsd:attributeGroup>

<xsd:element name="x">
  <xsd:complexType>
    <xsd:attributeGroup ref="HeaderGroup"/>
  </xsd:complexType>
</xsd:element>
```

Example 19–15. Allowing future extensions for sequence groups

DTD:

```
<!ENTITY % ext "" >
<!ELEMENT x (a , b %ext;)>
```

Schema:

```
<xsd:complexType name="XType">
  <xsd:sequence>
    <xsd:element ref="a"/>
    <xsd:element ref="b"/>
  </xsd:sequence>
</xsd:complexType>
<xsd:element name="x" type="XType"/>
```

Example 19–16. Implementing extensions for sequence groups

DTD:

```
<!ENTITY % ext ", c, d" >
<!ENTITY % original SYSTEM "original.dtd">
%original;
```

Schema:

```
<xsd:schema xmlns:xsd="http://www.w3.org/2001/XMLSchema">
  <xsd:redefine schemaLocation="original.xsd">
    <xsd:complexType name="XType">
      <xsd:complexContent>
      <xsd:extension base="XType">
        <xsd:sequence>
          <xsd:element ref="c"/>
          <xsd:element ref="d"/>
        </xsd:sequence>
        </xsd:extension>
      </xsd:complexContent>
    </xsd:complexType>
  </xsd:redefine>
</xsd:schema>
```

19.5.2 *Extensions for* choice *groups*

On the other hand, if it is a choice group that you wish to leave open, extension will not meet your needs. This is because all extensions are added to the end of the content model as part of a sequence group. For a more detailed explanation of this, see Section 14.4.2.1, "Extending choice groups."

The best approach to extending a choice group is by using a substitution group. Substitution groups allow an element declaration to be replaced by any of a group of designated element declarations. New element declarations can be added to the substitution group at any time. The schema fragment in Example 19–17 uses a choice group that contains a reference to the ext element declaration. Because it is abstract, ext can never be used in an instance.

Example 19–17. Allowing future extensions for `choice` groups

DTD:

```
<!ENTITY % ext "" >
<!ELEMENT x (a | b %ext;)*>
```

Schema:

```
<xsd:complexType name="XType">
  <xsd:choice>
    <xsd:element ref="a"/>
    <xsd:element ref="b"/>
    <xsd:element ref="ext"/>
  </xsd:choice>
</xsd:complexType>
<xsd:element name="x" type="XType"/>
<xsd:element name="ext" abstract="true" type="xsd:string"/>
```

Example 19–18 shows how these extensions would be accomplished in a new parent DTD or in a new schema. In the schema, element declarations c and d are added to the substitution group headed by ext, allowing these element declarations to appear in the content model as part of the choice.

Example 19–18. Implementing extensions for `choice` groups

DTD:

```
<!ENTITY % ext "| c | d" >
<!ENTITY % original SYSTEM "original.dtd">
%original;
```

Schema:

```
<xsd:schema xmlns:xsd="http://www.w3.org/2001/XMLSchema">
  <xsd:include schemaLocation="original.xsd"/>
  <xsd:element name="c" substitutionGroup="ext"/>
  <xsd:element name="d" substitutionGroup="ext"/>
</xsd:schema>
```

19.5.3 *Attribute extensions*

Parameter entities may also be used in DTDs to leave attribute lists open to future additions. Using schemas, this is handled through complex type extension. Example 19–19 shows a DTD that includes an empty parameter entity in an attribute list. The corresponding schema does not have to take any special measures to leave the attribute list open.

Example 19–19. Allowing future extensions for attributes

DTD:

```
<!ENTITY % attExt "" >
<!ATTLIST x id ID #REQUIRED
        %attExt;>
```

Schema:

```
<xsd:complexType name="XType">
  <!-- content model here -->
  <xsd:attribute name="id" type="xsd:ID" use="required"/>
</xsd:complexType>
<xsd:element name="x" type="XType"/>
```

Example 19–20 shows how attribute extensions would be accomplished in a new parent DTD or in a new schema. In the schema, the redefine mechanism is used to extend the complex type to add a new attribute.

This technique can also replace the declaration of multiple ATTLISTs for a single element type that is sometimes used to extend attribute lists.

19.5.4 *Attribute group extensions*

Parameter entities may also be used in DTDs to leave groups of attributes open to future extension. Example 19–21 shows a DTD that

Example 19–20. Implementing extensions for attributes

DTD:

```
<!ENTITY % attExt "myAttr NMTOKEN #IMPLIED" >
<!ENTITY % original SYSTEM "original.dtd">
%original;
```

Schema:

```
<xsd:schema xmlns:xsd="http://www.w3.org/2001/XMLSchema">
  <xsd:redefine schemaLocation="original.xsd">
    <xsd:complexType name="XType">
      <xsd:complexContent>
        <xsd:extension base="XType">
          <xsd:attribute name="myAttr" type="xsd:NMTOKEN"/>
        </xsd:extension>
      </xsd:complexContent>
    </xsd:complexType>
  </xsd:redefine>
</xsd:schema>
```

has an empty parameter entity included in another parameter entity, `HeaderGroup`, which represents a group of attributes. The corresponding schema uses an attribute group to represent this.

Example 19–22 shows how these extensions would be accomplished in a new parent DTD or in a new schema. In the schema, the redefinition mechanism is used to extend the attribute group to add a new attribute.

19.6 | External parameter entities

External parameter entities are used to include other DTDs (or fragments of DTDs) in a parent DTD. In XSDL, this is accomplished using either `include` or `import`. An `include` can be used if both schema documents are in the same namespace (or no namespace), while `import` is used if they are in different namespaces. Example 19–23 illustrates the use of `include` to combine schema documents. See

Example 19–21. Allowing future extensions for attribute groups

DTD:

```
<!ENTITY % attExt "" >
<!ENTITY % HeaderGroup "id ID #REQUIRED
                        variety NMTOKEN #IMPLIED
                        %attExt;">
<!ATTLIST x %HeaderGroup;>
```

Schema:

```
<xsd:attributeGroup name="HeaderGroup">
  <xsd:attribute name="id" type="xsd:ID" use="required"/>
  <xsd:attribute name="variety" type="xsd:NMTOKEN"/>
</xsd:attributeGroup>

<xsd:element name="x">
  <xsd:complexType>
    <xsd:attributeGroup ref="HeaderGroup"/>
  </xsd:complexType>
</xsd:element>
```

Example 19–22. Implementing extensions for attribute groups

DTD:

```
<!ENTITY % attExt "myAttr NMTOKEN #IMPLIED" >
<!ENTITY % original SYSTEM "original.dtd">
%original;
```

Schema:

```
<xsd:schema xmlns:xsd="http://www.w3.org/2001/XMLSchema">
  <xsd:redefine schemaLocation="original.xsd">
    <xsd:attributeGroup name="HeaderGroup">
      <xsd:attributeGroup ref="HeaderGroup"/>
      <xsd:attribute name="myAttr" type="xsd:NMTOKEN"/>
    </xsd:attributeGroup>
  </xsd:redefine>
</xsd:schema>
```

Example 19–23. Including other DTDs/schema documents

DTD:

```
<!ENTITY % prodInfo SYSTEM "prod.dtd">
%prodInfo;
```

Schema:

```
<xsd:include schemaLocation="prod.xsd"/>
```

Section 4.4.1, "`include`," for more detailed information on the include mechanism.

19.7 | General entities

19.7.1 *Character and other parsed entities*

General entities are used in DTDs to represent characters or other repeated character data that appears in instances. Unfortunately, there is no direct equivalent to general entities in XML Schema. It is still possible to use an internal or external DTD to declare the entities, and use this DTD in conjunction with schemas, as explained in Section 5.7, "Using DTDs and schemas together."

19.7.2 *Unparsed entities*

Unparsed entities are used in conjunction with notations to reference external data in non-XML formats, such as graphics files. A schema-validated instance must be associated with a DTD (usually an internal DTD subset) that declares the unparsed entities. Example 19–24 shows an instance that contains unparsed entities. The entities `prod557` and `prod563` are declared in an internal DTD subset, while the schema is used to validate the structure of the document only. The notation `jpeg` is declared in the DTD, not the schema, so that the entity declarations can reference it.

Example 19–24. Unparsed entity

Schema:

```
<xsd:element name="product">
  <xsd:complexType>
    <xsd:attribute name="number" type="ProdNumType"/>
    <xsd:attribute name="picture" type="xsd:ENTITY"/>
  </xsd:complexType>
</xsd:element>
```

Instance:

```
<!DOCTYPE catalog [
<!NOTATION jpeg SYSTEM "JPG">
<!ENTITY prod557 SYSTEM "prod557.jpg" NDATA jpeg>
<!ENTITY prod563 SYSTEM "prod563.jpg" NDATA jpeg>
]>

<catalog>
  <product number="557" picture="prod557"/>
  <product number="563" picture="prod563"/>
</catalog>
```

19.8 | Comments

DTDs often use comments to further explain the declarations they contain. Schema documents, as XML, can also contain comments. However, XML Schema also offers an annotation facility that is designed to provide more structured, usable documentation of schema components. Example 19–25 shows a DTD fragment that has a comment describing a section (CUSTOMER INFORMATION), and two element declarations with element-specific comments appearing before each one.

Example 19–25. Comments

DTD:

```
<!-- ******************** -->
<!-- CUSTOMER INFORMATION -->
<!-- ******************** -->

<!-- billing address -->
<!ELEMENT billTo (%AddressType;)>
<!-- shipping address -->
<!ELEMENT shipTo (%AddressType;)>
```

Schema:

```
<xsd:schema xmlns:xsd="http://www.w3.org/2001/XMLSchema"
            xmlns:doc="http://example.org/doc">

  <xsd:annotation>
    <xsd:documentation>
      <doc:section>CUSTOMER INFORMATION</doc:section>
    </xsd:documentation>
  </xsd:annotation>

  <xsd:element name="billTo" type="AddressType">
    <xsd:annotation>
      <xsd:documentation>
        <doc:description>billing address</doc:description>
      </xsd:documentation>
    </xsd:annotation>
  </xsd:element>

  <xsd:element name="shipTo" type="AddressType">
    <xsd:annotation>
      <xsd:documentation>
        <doc:description>shipping address</doc:description>
      </xsd:documentation>
    </xsd:annotation>
  </xsd:element>
</xsd:schema>
```

The corresponding schema places each of these comments within an `annotation` element. The first `annotation` element, which describes the section, appears as a direct child of the `schema`. The element-specific annotations, on the other hand, are defined entirely within the element declarations to which they apply. In all three cases, documentation elements are used, which are designed for human-readable information. The schema is considerably more verbose than the DTD, but the descriptive information is much better structured. Chapter 6, "Schema documentation and extension" covers schema documentation in detail.

19.9 | Using DTDs and schemas together

There is nothing to prevent an instance from being validated against both a DTD and a schema. In fact, if you wish to use general entities, you must continue to use DTDs alongside schemas. Generally, it is recommended to only put entity declarations in the DTD, but there may be cases where you want to also include element declarations in the DTD. For more information on validating instances against both DTDs and schemas, see Section 5.7, "Using DTDs and schemas together."

Naming
considerations

Chapter 20

T his chapter provides detailed recommendations for choosing and managing names for XML element types and attributes, as well as for other XML Schema components. It discusses naming guidelines, the use of qualified and unqualified names, and structuring of a namespace.

20.1 | Naming guidelines

Consistency in naming can be as important as the names themselves. Consistent names are easier to understand, remember, and maintain. This section provides guidelines for defining an XML naming standard to ensure the quality and consistency of names.

These guidelines apply primarily to the names that will appear in an instance, namely element-type, attribute, and notation names. However, much of this section is also applicable to the names used within the schema, such as data type, group, and identity constraint names.

20.1.1 *Rules for valid XML names*

Names in XML must start with a letter or underscore (_), and can contain only letters, digits, underscores (_), colons (:), hyphens (-), and periods (.). Colons should be reserved for use with namespace prefixes. In addition, an XML name cannot start with the letters xml in either upper or lower case.

Names in XML are always case sensitive, so accountNumber and AccountNumber are two different element-type names.

Because schema components have XML names, these name restrictions apply not only to the element-type and attribute names that appear in instances, but also to the names of the data types, named model groups, attribute groups, identity constraints, and notations you define in your schemas.

20.1.2 *Separators*

If a name is made up of several terms, such as "account number," you should decide on a standard way to separate the terms. It can be done through capitalization (e.g., accountNumber), or through punctuation (e.g., account-number).

Some programming languages, database management systems, and other technologies do not allow hyphens or other punctuation in the names they use. Therefore, if you want to directly match your element-type names, for example, with variable names or database column names, you should use capitalization to separate terms.

If you choose to use capitalization, the next question is whether to use mixed case (e.g., AccountNumber) or camel case (e.g., account-Number)? In some programming languages, it is a convention to use mixed case for class names, and camel case for instance variables. In XML, this maps roughly to using mixed case for data type names, and camel case for element-type names. This is the convention used in this book.

Regardless of which approach you choose, the most important thing is to be consistent.

20.1.3 *Name length*

There is no technical limit to the length of an XML name. However, the ideal length of a name is somewhere between four and twelve characters. Excessively long element-type names, such as `Hazardous-MaterialsHandlingFeeDomestic`, can, if used frequently, add dramatically to the size of the instance. They are also difficult to type, hard to distinguish from other long element-type names, and not very readable. On the other hand, very short element-type names, such as `b`, can be too cryptic for people who are not familiar with the vocabulary.

20.1.4 *Standard terms and abbreviations*

In order to encourage consistency, it is helpful to choose a standard set of terms that will be used in your names. Table 20–1 shows a sample list of standard terms. This term list is used in the examples in this book. Synonyms are included in the list to prevent new terms from being created that have the same meaning as other terms.

These consistent terms are then combined to form element-type and attribute names. For example, "product number" might become `productNumber`.

In some cases, the name will be too long if all of the terms are concatenated together. Therefore, it is useful to have a standard abbreviation associated with each term. Instead of `productNumber`, `prodNumber` may be more manageable because it is shorter.

20.1.5 *Use of subject terms*

In some contexts, using an element-type name such as `prodNumber` may be redundant. In Example 20–1, it is obvious from the context that the number is a product number.

Table 20–1   Terms

Term	Abbreviation	Synonyms
color	color	
currency	curr	
customer	cust	client, purchaser, account holder
date	date	
description	desc	
effective	eff	begin, start
identifier	id	
name	name	
number	num	code
order	ord	purchase order
price	price	cost
product	prod	item
size	size	

Example 20–1. Repetition of terms

```
<product>
  <prodNumber>557</prodNumber>
  <prodName>Short-Sleeved Linen Blouse</prodName>
  <prodSize sizeSystem="US-DRESS">10</prodSize>
</product>
```

In this case, it may be clearer to leave off the `prod` term on the child elements, as shown in Example 20–2.

There may be other cases where the subject is not so obvious. In Example 20–3, there are two names: a customer name and a product name. If we took out the terms `cust` and `prod`, we would not be able to distinguish between the two names. In this case, it should be left as shown.

Example 20–2. No repetition of terms

```
<product>
  <number>557</number>
  <name>Short-Sleeved Linen Blouse</name>
  <size system="US-DRESS">10</size>
</product>
```

Example 20–3. Less clear context

```
<letter>Dear <custName>Priscilla Walmsley</custName>,
Unfortunately, we are out of stock of the
<prodName>Short-Sleeved Linen Blouse</prodName> in size
<prodSize>10</prodSize> that you ordered...</letter>
```

When creating element-type and attribute names, it is helpful to list two names: one to be used when the subject is obvious, and one to be used in other contexts. This is illustrated in Table 20–2.

Table 20–2   Element-type or attribute names

Logical name	Subject	Name inside subject context	Name outside subject context
customer name	customer	name	custName
product name	product	name	prodName
customer number	customer	number	custNum
product number	product	number	prodNum
order number	order	number	ordNum
product size	product	size	prodSize
product color	product	color	prodColor

20.2 | Qualified vs. unqualified names

Many instances include elements from more than one namespace. This can potentially result in instances with a large number of different prefixes, one for each namespace. However, when an element declaration is local — that is, when it isn't at the top level of a schema document — you have the choice of using either qualified or unqualified element-type names in instances. Let's explore the two alternatives.

20.2.1 *Qualified local names*

Example 20–4 shows an instance where all element-type names are qualified. Every element-type name has a prefix that maps it to either the product namespace or the order namespace.

Example 20–4. Qualified local names

```
<ord:order xmlns:ord="http://example.org/ord"
           xmlns:prod="http://example.org/prod">
  <ord:number>123ABBCC123</ord:number>
  <ord:items>
    <prod:product>
      <prod:number>557</prod:number>
    </prod:product>
  </ord:items>
</ord:order>
```

This instance is very explicit about which namespace each element is in. There will be no confusion about whether a particular number element is in the order namespace, or in the product namespace. However, the application or person that generates this instance must be aware which element types are in the order namespace, and which are in the product namespace.

20.2.2 *Unqualified local names*

Example 20–5, on the other hand, shows an instance where only the root element-type name, order, is qualified. The other element-type names have no prefix, and since there is no default namespace provided, this means that they are not in any namespace.

Example 20–5. Unqualified local names

```
<ord:order xmlns:ord="http://example.org/ord">
  <number>123ABBCC123</number>
  <items>
    <product>
      <number>557</number>
    </product>
  </items>
</ord:order>
```

This instance has the advantage of looking slightly less complicated, and not requiring the instance author to care about what namespace each element type belongs in. In fact, the instance author does not even need to know of the existence of the product namespace.

20.2.3 *Using* elementFormDefault

Let's look at the schemas that would describe these two instances. Example 20–6 shows the schema for the instance in Example 20–4, which has qualified element-type names. It is made up of two schema documents: ord.xsd, which defines components in the order namespace, and prod.xsd, which defines components in the product namespace.

Both schema documents have elementFormDefault set to qualified. As a result, elements conforming to local declarations must use qualified element-type names in the instance. In this example, the declaration for order is global and the declarations for product, items, and number are local.

Example 20–6. Schema for qualified local element-type names

ord.xsd:

```
<xsd:schema xmlns:xsd="http://www.w3.org/2001/XMLSchema"
            xmlns:prod="http://example.org/prod"
            xmlns="http://example.org/ord"
            targetNamespace="http://example.org/ord"
            elementFormDefault="qualified">
  <xsd:import schemaLocation="prod.xsd"
              namespace="http://example.org/prod"/>
  <xsd:element name="order" type="OrderType"/>
  <xsd:complexType name="OrderType">
    <xsd:sequence>
      <xsd:element name="number" type="OrderNumType"/>
      <xsd:element name="items" type="prod:ItemsType"/>
    </xsd:sequence>
  </xsd:complexType>
</xsd:schema>
```

prod.xsd:

```
<xsd:schema xmlns:xsd="http://www.w3.org/2001/XMLSchema"
            xmlns="http://example.org/prod"
            targetNamespace="http://example.org/prod"
            elementFormDefault="qualified">
  <xsd:complexType name="ItemsType">
    <xsd:sequence maxOccurs="unbounded">
      <xsd:element name="product" type="ProductType"/>
    </xsd:sequence>
  </xsd:complexType>
  <xsd:complexType name="ProductType">
    <xsd:sequence>
      <xsd:element name="number" type="ProdNumType"/>
    </xsd:sequence>
  </xsd:complexType>
</xsd:schema>
```

To create a schema for the instance in Example 20–5, which has unqualified names, you can simply change the value of element-FormDefault in both schema documents to unqualified. Since the default value is unqualified, you could alternatively simply omit the attribute. In this case, elements conforming to global declarations still must use qualified element-type names, hence the use of `ord:order` in the instance.

20.2.4 *Form and global element declarations*

An important thing to notice is that the choice between qualified and unqualified names applies only to local element declarations. All elements conforming to global declarations must have qualified element-type names in the instance; there is no way to override this. In our example, all of the element declarations except `order` are local. If the `product` declaration had been global, the conforming elements would have to use qualified element-type names, regardless of the value of `elementFormDefault`.

This can cause confusion if you choose to use unqualified local element-type names, and you want to mix global and local element declarations. Not only would an instance author be required to know what namespace each element type is in, but he or she would also need to know whether the corresponding element declaration is global or local in the schema.

This can be avoided by making all element declarations local, except for the declaration for the root elements. However, you may not have this choice if you import element declarations from namespaces that are not under your control. Also, if you plan to use substitution groups, the participating element declarations must be global.

20.2.5 *Default namespaces and unqualified names*

Default namespaces do not mix well with unqualified element-type names. The instance in Example 20–7 declares the order namespace as the default namespace. However, this will not work with a schema document where `elementFormDefault` is set to `unqualified`, because it will be looking for the element types `items`, `product`, and `number` to be in the orders namespace, which they are not; they are not in any namespace.

Example 20–7. Invalid mixing of unqualified names and default namespace

```
<order xmlns="http://example.org/ord">
  <number>123ABBCC123</number>
  <items>
    <product>
      <number>557</number>
    </product>
  </items>
</order>
```

20.2.6 *Design hint: Should I use qualified or unqualified local names?*

Whether to use qualified or unqualified local element-type names is a matter of style. The advantages of using qualified local element-type names are:

- You can tell by looking at the document which namespace a name is in. If you can see that a b element is in the XHTML namespace, you can more quickly understand its meaning.

- There is no ambiguity to a person or application what namespace an element belongs in. In our example, there was a number element in each of the namespaces. In most cases, you can determine from its position in the instance whether it is an order number or a product number, but not always.

- Certain applications or processors, for example an XHTML processor, might be expecting the element-type names to be qualified with the appropriate namespace.

- You can mix global and local element declarations without affecting the instance author. You may be forced to make some element declarations global because you are using substitution groups, or because you are importing a schema document over which you have no control. If you use unqualified local names, the instance author has to understand which element declarations are global and which are local.

The advantages of using unqualified local element-type names are:

- The instance author does not have to be aware of which namespace each element-type name is in. If a large number of namespaces are used in the instance, this can simplify creation of instances.

- The lack of prefixes and namespace declarations makes the instance look less cluttered.

In general, it is best to use qualified element-type names, for the reasons stated above. If consistent prefixes are used, they just become part of the name, and users get used to using `prod:number` rather than just `number`. Most XML editors assist instance authors in choosing the right element-type names, prefixed or not.

20.2.7 *Qualified vs. unqualified attribute names*

XML Schema also allows you to choose qualified or unqualified forms for locally declared attribute names. Since default namespace declarations do not apply to attributes, this is essentially a question of whether you want the attribute names to be prefixed or unprefixed.

Example 20–8 shows a schema that declares several attributes, along with a valid instance. In the instance, the `global` attribute's name is qualified (prefixed) because it is globally declared. The attributes `unqual` and `qual` both have a `form` attribute specified, and their names appear in the instance as designated. The `unspec` attribute's name is unqualified (unprefixed) because that is the default when neither `form` nor `attributeFormDefault` are present.

Qualified attribute names should only be used for attributes that apply to a variety of elements in a variety of namespaces, such as `xml:lang` or `xsi:type`. For locally declared attributes, whose scope is only the type definition in which they appear, prefixes add extra text without any additional meaning.

Example 20–8. Qualified and unqualified attribute names

Schema:

```
<xsd:schema xmlns:xsd="http://www.w3.org/2001/XMLSchema"
            xmlns="http://example.org/prod"
            targetNamespace="http://example.org/prod">
  <xsd:attribute name="global" type="xsd:string"/>
  <xsd:element name="size" type="SizeType"/>
  <xsd:complexType name="SizeType">
    <xsd:attribute ref="global"/>
    <xsd:attribute name="unqual" form="unqualified"/>
    <xsd:attribute name="qual" form="qualified"/>
    <xsd:attribute name="unspec"/>
  </xsd:complexType>
</xsd:schema>
```

Valid instance:

```
<prod:size prod:global="x" unqual="x" prod:qual="x" unspec="x"/>
```

The best way to handle qualification of attribute names is to ignore the `form` and `attributeFormDefault` attributes completely. Then, globally declared attributes will have qualified names, and locally declared attributes will have unqualified names, which makes sense. For more information on global vs. local attribute declarations, see Section 8.1.4, "Design hint: Should I declare attributes globally or locally?"

20.3 | Structuring namespaces

Consider a project that involves orders for retail products. An order will contain information from several different domains. It will contain general information that applies to the order itself, such as order number and date. It may also contain customer information, such as customer name, number, and address. Finally, it may contain product information, such as product number, name, description, and size. Is it best to use the same namespace for all of them, or break them up into separate namespaces? There are three approaches:

1. *Same namespace*: use the same namespace for all of the schema documents.

2. *Different namespaces*: use multiple namespaces, perhaps a different one for each schema document.

3. *Chameleon namespaces*: use a namespace for the parent schema document, but no namespaces for the included schema documents.

20.3.1 *Same namespace*

It is possible to give all the schema documents the same target namespace and use the `include` function to assemble the multiple schema documents into one schema that has a consistent namespace. This is depicted in Figure 20–1.

Example 20–9 shows our three schema documents using this approach. They all have the same target namespace, and `ord.xsd` includes the other two schema documents.

Example 20–10 shows an instance that conforms to the schema. Since there is only one namespace for all of the elements, a default namespace declaration is used.

The advantages of this approach are that it is uncomplicated and the instance is not cluttered by prefixes. The disadvantage is that you cannot have multiple global components with the same name in the same namespace, so you will have to be careful of name collisions.

This approach assumes that you have control over all the schema documents. If you are using elements from a namespace over which you have no control, such as the XHTML namespace, you should use the approach described in the next section.

This approach is best within a particular application where you have control over all the schema documents involved.

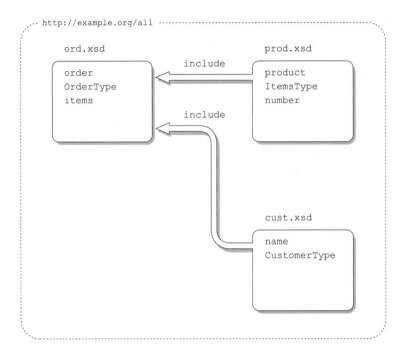

Figure 20–1 Same namespace

Example 20–9. Same namespace in a schema

ord.xsd:

```
<xsd:schema xmlns:xsd="http://www.w3.org/2001/XMLSchema"
            xmlns="http://example.org/all"
            targetNamespace="http://example.org/all"
            elementFormDefault="qualified">
  <xsd:include schemaLocation="prod.xsd"/>
  <xsd:include schemaLocation="cust.xsd"/>
  <xsd:element name="order" type="OrderType"/>
  <xsd:complexType name="OrderType">
    <xsd:sequence>
      <xsd:element name="customer" type="CustomerType"/>
      <xsd:element name="items" type="ItemsType"/>
    </xsd:sequence>
  </xsd:complexType>
  <!--...-->
</xsd:schema>
```

prod.xsd:

```
<xsd:schema xmlns:xsd="http://www.w3.org/2001/XMLSchema"
            xmlns="http://example.org/all"
            targetNamespace="http://example.org/all"
            elementFormDefault="qualified">
  <xsd:complexType name="ItemsType">
    <xsd:sequence maxOccurs="unbounded">
      <xsd:element name="product" type="ProductType"/>
    </xsd:sequence>
  </xsd:complexType>
  <xsd:complexType name="ProductType">
    <xsd:sequence>
      <xsd:element name="number" type="ProdNumType"/>
    </xsd:sequence>
  </xsd:complexType>
</xsd:schema>
```

cust.xsd:

```
<xsd:schema xmlns:xsd="http://www.w3.org/2001/XMLSchema"
            xmlns="http://example.org/all"
            targetNamespace="http://example.org/all"
            elementFormDefault="qualified">
  <xsd:complexType name="CustomerType">
    <xsd:sequence>
      <xsd:element name="name" type="CustNameType"/>
    </xsd:sequence>
  </xsd:complexType>
  <xsd:simpleType name="CustNameType">
    <xsd:restriction base="xsd:string"/>
  </xsd:simpleType>
</xsd:schema>
```

20.3.2 *Different namespaces*

It is also possible to give each schema document a different target namespace and use the `import` function (or other method) to amass the multiple schema documents into the same schema. This is depicted in Figure 20–2.

Example 20–10. Same namespace in an instance

```
<order xmlns="http://example.org/all"
       xmlns:xsi="http://www.w3.org/2001/XMLSchema-instance"
       xsi:schemaLocation="http://example.org/all ord.xsd">
  <customer>
    <name>Priscilla Walmsley</name>
  </customer>
  <items>
    <product>
      <number>557</number>
    </product>
  </items>
</order>
```

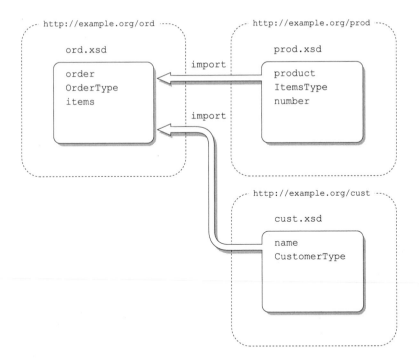

Figure 20–2   Different namespaces

Example 20–11 shows our three schema documents using this approach. They all have different target namespaces, and `ord.xsd` imports the other two schema documents.

Example 20–11. Different namespaces in a schema

ord.xsd:

```
<xsd:schema xmlns:xsd="http://www.w3.org/2001/XMLSchema"
            xmlns:prod="http://example.org/prod"
            xmlns:cust="http://example.org/cust"
            xmlns="http://example.org/ord"
            targetNamespace="http://example.org/ord"
            elementFormDefault="qualified">
  <xsd:import schemaLocation="prod.xsd"
              namespace="http://example.org/prod"/>
  <xsd:import schemaLocation="cust.xsd"
              namespace="http://example.org/cust"/>
  <xsd:element name="order" type="OrderType"/>
  <xsd:complexType name="OrderType">
    <xsd:sequence>
      <xsd:element name="customer" type="cust:CustomerType"/>
      <xsd:element name="items" type="prod:ItemsType"/>
    </xsd:sequence>
  </xsd:complexType>
</xsd:schema>
```

prod.xsd:

```
<xsd:schema xmlns:xsd="http://www.w3.org/2001/XMLSchema"
            xmlns="http://example.org/prod"
            targetNamespace="http://example.org/prod"
            elementFormDefault="qualified">
  <xsd:complexType name="ItemsType">
    <xsd:sequence maxOccurs="unbounded">
      <xsd:element name="product" type="ProductType"/>
    </xsd:sequence>
  </xsd:complexType>
  <xsd:complexType name="ProductType">
    <xsd:sequence>
      <xsd:element name="number" type="ProdNumType"/>
    </xsd:sequence>
  </xsd:complexType>
</xsd:schema>
```

cust.xsd:

```
<xsd:schema xmlns:xsd="http://www.w3.org/2001/XMLSchema"
            xmlns="http://example.org/cust"
            targetNamespace="http://example.org/cust"
            elementFormDefault="qualified">
  <xsd:complexType name="CustomerType">
    <xsd:sequence>
      <xsd:element name="name" type="CustNameType"/>
    </xsd:sequence>
  </xsd:complexType>
  <xsd:simpleType name="CustNameType">
    <xsd:restriction base="xsd:string"/>
  </xsd:simpleType>
</xsd:schema>
```

Example 20–12 shows an instance that conforms to this schema. You are required to declare all three namespaces in the instance, and to prefix the element-type names appropriately. However, since ord.xsd imports the other two schema documents, you are not required to specify xsi:schemaLocation pairs for all three schema documents, just the "main" one.

Example 20–12. Different namespaces in an instance

```
<order xmlns="http://example.org/ord"
       xmlns:prod="http://example.org/prod"
       xmlns:cust="http://example.org/cust"
       xmlns:xsi="http://www.w3.org/2001/XMLSchema-instance"
       xsi:schemaLocation="http://example.org/ord ord.xsd">
  <customer>
    <cust:name>Priscilla Walmsley</cust:name>
  </customer>
  <items>
    <prod:product>
      <prod:number>557</prod:number>
    </prod:product>
  </items>
</order>
```

To slightly simplify this instance, different default namespace declarations could appear at different levels of the document, resulting in the instance shown in Example 20–13. It could be simplified even further by the use of unqualified local element-type names, as discussed in Section 7.5, "Qualified vs. unqualified forms."

Example 20–13. Different namespaces in an instance, with default namespaces

```
<order xmlns="http://example.org/ord"
       xmlns:xsi="http://www.w3.org/2001/XMLSchema-instance"
       xsi:schemaLocation="http://example.org/ord ord.xsd">
  <customer>
    <name xmlns="http://example.org/cust">Priscilla Walmsley</name>
  </customer>
  <items>
    <product xmlns="http://example.org/prod">
      <number>557</number>
    </product>
  </items>
</order>
```

This is an obvious approach when you are using namespaces over which you have no control, for example, if you want to include XHTML elements in your product description. There is no point trying to copy all the XHTML element declarations into a new namespace. This would create maintenance problems and would not be very clear to users. In addition, applications that process XHTML may require that the elements be in the XHTML namespace.

The advantage to this approach is that the source and context of an element are very clear. In addition, it allows different groups to be responsible for different namespaces. Finally, you can be less concerned about name collisions, because the names must only be unique within a namespace.

The disadvantage of this approach is that you cannot use the `rede-fine` feature on these components, since they are in a different namespace. Also, instances become more complex, requiring prefixing with multiple different namespaces.

20.3.3 *Chameleon namespaces*

The third possibility is to specify a target namespace only for the "main" schema document, not the included schema documents. The included components then take on the target namespace of the including document. In our example, all of the definitions and declarations in both `prod.xsd` and `cust.xsd` would take on the `http://example.org/ord` namespace once they are included in `ord.xsd`. This is depicted in Figure 20–3.

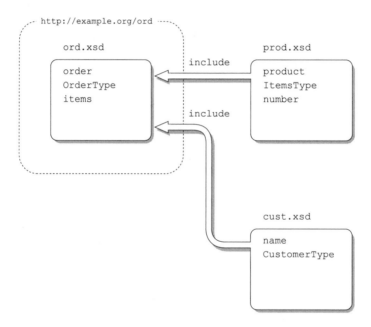

Figure 20–3   Chameleon namespaces

Example 20–14 shows our three schema documents using this approach. Neither `prod.xsd` nor `cust.xsd` have a target namespace, while `ord.xsd` does. `ord.xsd` includes the other two schema documents, and changes their namespace as a result.

The instance in this case would look identical to that of the same namespace approach shown in Example 20–10, since all the elements would be in the same namespace.

The advantage of this approach is the flexibility. Components can be included in multiple namespaces, and redefined whenever desired.

The disadvantage is that the risk of name collisions is even more serious. If the non-namespace schema documents grow over time, the risk increases that there will be name collisions with the schema documents that include them. If they were in their own namespace, unexpected collisions would be far less likely.

Example 20–14. Chameleon namespaces in a schema

ord.xsd:

```
<xsd:schema xmlns:xsd="http://www.w3.org/2001/XMLSchema"
            xmlns="http://example.org/ord"
            targetNamespace="http://example.org/ord"
            elementFormDefault="qualified">
  <xsd:include schemaLocation="prod.xsd"/>
  <xsd:include schemaLocation="cust.xsd"/>
  <xsd:element name="order" type="OrderType"/>
  <xsd:complexType name="OrderType">
    <xsd:sequence>
      <xsd:element name="number" type="xsd:string"/>
      <xsd:element name="items" type="ItemsType"/>
    </xsd:sequence>
  </xsd:complexType>
  <!--...-->
</xsd:schema>
```

prod.xsd:

```
<xsd:schema xmlns:xsd="http://www.w3.org/2001/XMLSchema"
            elementFormDefault="qualified">
  <xsd:complexType name="ItemsType">
    <xsd:sequence maxOccurs="unbounded">
      <xsd:element name="product" type="ProductType"/>
    </xsd:sequence>
  </xsd:complexType>
  <xsd:complexType name="ProductType">
    <xsd:sequence>
      <xsd:element name="number" type="ProdNumType"/>
    </xsd:sequence>
  </xsd:complexType>
</xsd:schema>
```

cust.xsd:

```
<xsd:schema xmlns:xsd="http://www.w3.org/2001/XMLSchema"
            elementFormDefault="qualified">
  <xsd:complexType name="CustomerType">
    <xsd:sequence>
      <xsd:element name="name" type="CustNameType"/>
    </xsd:sequence>
  </xsd:complexType>
  <xsd:simpleType name="CustNameType">
    <xsd:restriction base="xsd:string"/>
  </xsd:simpleType>
</xsd:schema>
```

Another disadvantage is that the chameleon components lack an identity. Namespaces can be well-defined containers that provide a recognizable context as well as specific semantics, documentation, and application code.

20.4 | Multiple languages

Often, XML documents are shared between groups of people who speak different languages. It is useful to be able to express an XML document in more than one language, especially when it is going to be viewed or edited by a human being rather than an application.

XML Schema does not provide any built-in mechanisms intended for language independence of schemas or instances. However, it is possible to use substitution groups for the translation of element-type names into multiple languages.

Example 20–15 shows some element declarations with English-language element-type names. Example 20–16 shows a schema that contains substitute element declarations with French names for some of the element declarations in the original schema.

Example 20–15. English-language element-type names

```
<xsd:schema xmlns:xsd="http://www.w3.org/2001/XMLSchema">
  <xsd:complexType name="ProductType">
    <xsd:sequence>
      <xsd:element ref="number"/>
      <xsd:element name="name" type="xsd:string"/>
      <xsd:element ref="size"/>
    </xsd:sequence>
  </xsd:complexType>
  <xsd:complexType name="SizeType">
    <xsd:simpleContent>
      <xsd:extension base="xsd:integer">
        <xsd:attribute name="system" type="SizeSystemType"/>
      </xsd:extension>
    </xsd:simpleContent>
  </xsd:complexType>
  <xsd:element name="product" type="ProductType"/>
  <xsd:element name="number" type="ProdNumType"/>
  <xsd:element name="size" type="SizeType"/>
</xsd:schema>
```

Example 20–16. Using substitution groups for localization

```
<xsd:schema xmlns:xsd="http://www.w3.org/2001/XMLSchema">
  <xsd:element name="produit" substitutionGroup="product"/>
  <xsd:element name="numéro" substitutionGroup="number"/>
  <xsd:element name="taille" substitutionGroup="size"/>
</xsd:schema>
```

Example 20–17 shows a valid instance with translated element-type names.

Example 20–17. Localized instance

```
<produit>
  <numéro>557</numéro>
  <name>Short-Sleeved Linen Blouse</name>
  <taille system="US-DRESS">10</taille>
</produit>
```

However, using substitution groups for localization has some significant weaknesses:

- It only works for element-type names. Since there are no substitution groups for attributes, the attribute names would still have to be in the original language.

- All the element declarations have to be global. In our example, it is not possible to declare a substitute for `name`, because its declaration is local.

- The application processing the instance has to be schema-aware and take the extra step of checking the head of the substitution group.

- The element-type names have been translated, but the data is still in English.

- An XML editor working with the schema shown in Example 20–16 will still show the instance author all of the options (e.g., both `number` and `numéro`).

A better approach would be to translate the document, and the names used in the schema, using XSLT. A stylesheet can be created to transform them in either direction, as long as a one-to-one mapping can be defined between the element-type and attribute names of both languages. This way, a user can edit the document in an XML editor and see only the names in their native language.

Extensibility
and reuse

464

S ometimes we forget that the "X" in XML is for "eXtensible." One of the beauties of XML is that additional elements and attributes can appear in an instance without affecting the core information. Specialized requirements for particular applications, industries, or organizations can be addressed using extensions.

However, in order to make XML extensible, you need to leave avenues open to do that. If you write schemas and applications that require very strict validation of an instance, the major benefit of XML is not realized! This chapter provides detailed recommendations for developing schemas that will be reusable and extensible in the future. It also provides guidelines for extending existing schemas.

21.1 | Reuse

First, let's talk about reusing schema components exactly as they are. Later in this chapter, we will look at extending and restricting existing schema components. The benefits of reuse are numerous:

- It reduces development time, because schema developers are not reinventing the wheel. In addition, developers of stylesheets and program code to process instances can reuse their code, saving their time too.

- It reduces maintenance time, because changes only need to be made in one place. Again, this applies not just to schemas, but also to applications.

- It results in better-designed schemas with fewer errors. Two heads are better than one, and reused components tend to be designed more carefully and reviewed more closely.

- It reduces the learning curve on schemas, because the reused components only need to be learned once. In addition, it encourages consistency, which also reduces learning curves.

When you are creating a schema, you should attempt to reuse components that have already been developed, either within your organization, by standards bodies, or by technology vendors. In addition, you should attempt to reuse as much within your schema as possible.

You do not have to reuse everything from a schema document that you import or include. If it was properly modularized, you should not have to include many components that you do not want to reuse. Components that can be reused include:

- named types, both simple and complex,
- named model groups and attribute groups,
- global element and attribute declarations,
- notations.

You should also consider the reusability of your components as you define them. To increase the reusability of your components:

- Use named types, because anonymous types cannot be reused.
- Use named model groups for fragments of content models that could be reused by multiple unrelated types.
- Name your data types and element types using general names. For example, if you are defining an address type for customers, call it `AddressType` rather than `CustomerAddressType`.
- Think about a broader applicability of your type. For example, when defining an address type, consider adding a `country` element declaration, even if you will only be using domestic addresses.
- Modularize your schemas into smaller documents, so that others who will reuse your components will not have to include or import them all.

21.2 | Extending schemas

In some cases, you want to reuse existing schema components, but you have specific extensions you need to add to make them useful to you. Creating a completely new schema that copies the original definitions is tempting because it is easy and flexible. You do not have to worry about basing the new definitions on the original ones. However, there are some important drawbacks.

- Your new instances could be completely incompatible with the original ones.
- You will have duplicate definitions of the same components, assuming that you do not plan to redefine every component in the original schema. This makes maintenance more difficult and discourages consistency.

- You do not have a record of the differences between the two definitions.

This section identifies several ways in which XML Schema allows extension. It describes both how to make your schemas extensible, and how to extend others' schemas. The various extension mechanisms are summarized in Table 21–1.

Table 21–1   Comparison of extension mechanisms

	Wildcards	*Type derivation*	*Substitution groups*	*Type redefinition*	*Named model group redefinition*
Is an extended instance valid against original definition?	yes	no	no	no	no
Does it require use of `xsi:type` in instance?	no	yes	no	no	no
Can it define extended types in a different namespace?	yes	yes	yes	no	no
Must element extensions appear at the end of a content model?	no	yes	no	yes	no

21.2.1 *Wildcards*

Wildcards are the most straightforward way to define extensible types. They can be used to allow additional element and attribute declarations in your complex types. Of the methods of extension discussed in this chapter, this is the only one that allows an instance with extensions to validate against the original schema. All the other methods require definition of a new schema for the extensions.

Example 21–1 shows a complex type definition that contains both an element wildcard (the `any` element) and an attribute wildcard (the `anyAttribute` element). For a complete discussion of element and attribute wildcards, see Section 13.4.3, "Element wildcards," and Section 13.6.3, "Attribute wildcards," respectively.

Example 21–1. Original type using wildcards

```
<xsd:complexType name="ProductType">
  <xsd:sequence>
    <xsd:element name="number" type="ProdNumType"/>
    <xsd:element name="name" type="xsd:string"/>
    <xsd:element name="size" type="SizeType" minOccurs="0"/>
    <xsd:any minOccurs="0" maxOccurs="unbounded"
            namespace="##other" processContents="lax"/>
  </xsd:sequence>
  <xsd:anyAttribute namespace="##other" processContents="skip"/>
</xsd:complexType>
```

There are several things to note about the definition of Product-Type:

- The namespace constraint is set to `##other`. This will avoid erroneous content from being validated, such as a product element that contains two `color` elements. It also avoids non-deterministic content models. If the namespace constraint were set to `##any`, and the processor encountered a `size` element, it would be impossible for it to tell whether it was the `size` element that was explicitly declared, or one that was replacing the wildcard.
- The value of `processContents` is `lax`. This allows the instance author to provide hints as to where to find the declarations for the additional elements or attributes. If they do not provide hints, or the particular processor ignores the hints, it is not a problem; no errors will be raised. However, if the declarations can be found, they will be validated.

- The values of `minOccurs` and `maxOccurs` are 0 and unbounded, respectively. This allows zero, one or many replacement elements to appear. The values of these two attributes default to 1, which is generally not the intention of the schema author.

- The wildcard appears at the end of the complex type definition. This allows replacement elements only after the defined content model. This is similar to the way extension works. You are permitted to put wildcards anywhere in the content model, but it might make processing the instance more difficult. With a wildcard at the end, the application can process what it is expecting and ignore the rest.

Suppose some additional features have been added to the ordering process, such as a points system to reward regular customers, and a gift wrap capability. The instance shown in Example 21–2 takes advantage of the wildcards in the `ProductType` definition to add an `spc:giftWrap` element declaration to the end of the content model, as well as an `spc:points` attribute declaration.

Example 21–2. Instance with extensions

```
<order xmlns="http://example.org/ord"
       xmlns:spc="http://example.org/spc">
  <product spc:points="100">
    <number>557</number>
    <name>Short-Sleeved Linen Blouse</name>
    <size>10</size>
    <spc:giftWrap>ADULT BDAY</spc:giftWrap>
  </product>
</order>
```

Because `processContents` was set to `lax`, the instance shown would be valid according to the original schema, without specifying any declarations for the new attribute and element. If you want to validate the new attribute and element, you can create a schema that contains their declarations, as shown in Example 21–3.

Example 21–3. Schema for extensions

```
<xsd:schema xmlns:xsd="http://www.w3.org/2001/XMLSchema"
            xmlns="http://example.org/spc"
            targetNamespace="http://example.org/spc">
  <xsd:element name="giftWrap" type="GiftWrapType"/>
  <xsd:attribute name="points" type="xsd:nonNegativeInteger"/>
</xsd:schema>
```

Note that the element and attribute declarations are global. This is necessary so that the processor can find the declarations.

Another approach for "extending" complex types with wildcards is actually to restrict them. You could define a complex type that restricts ProductType and includes the declarations of giftWrap and points. For more information, see Section 14.5.2.3, "Restricting wildcards."

The advantage of using wildcards to make types extensible is that this is very flexible, because the instance author is not required to have a schema that declares the replacement elements and attributes. However, in some cases this flexibility may be a little too forgiving, and it can obscure real errors.

21.2.2 *Type derivation*

Deriving new types from the existing types is another possibility. You can create a new schema whose types extend the original types. You would then have to indicate the new types in the instance, using the xsi:type attribute. Unlike the wildcard approach, instances that contain extensions would not be valid according to the original schema. If you want to use the extended instance as a replacement for the original instance, you should first check to make sure that your application can handle the new extended instance.

This approach is appropriate when you want to extend a schema over which you have no control. Example 21–4 shows a complex type that you might want to extend.

Example 21–4. Original type

```
<xsd:complexType name="ProductType">
  <xsd:sequence>
    <xsd:element name="number" type="ProdNumType"/>
    <xsd:element name="name" type="xsd:string"/>
    <xsd:element name="size" type="SizeType" minOccurs="0"/>
  </xsd:sequence>
</xsd:complexType>
```

There are several things to note about the definition of Product-Type:

- It is a named complex type. Anonymous complex types cannot be extended.

- There are no block or final attributes to prohibit type derivation or substitution.

- A sequence group is used. Extension does not work well for all or choice groups.

Example 21–5 shows an extension of the original ProductType. For more information on complex content extension, see Section 14.4.2, "Complex content extensions"

The instance shown in Example 21–6 conforms to the extended type definition, but not the base type definition. It is identical to the instance using wildcards shown in Example 21–2, except that the xsi:type attribute appears in the product tag. For more information on type substitution, see Section 14.6, "Type substitution."

Example 21–5. Extended type

```
<xsd:complexType name="ExtendedProductType">
  <xsd:complexContent>
    <xsd:extension base="ProductType">
      <xsd:sequence>
        <xsd:element ref="spc:giftWrap" minOccurs="0"/>
      </xsd:sequence>
      <xsd:attribute ref="spc:points"/>
    </xsd:extension>
  </xsd:complexContent>
</xsd:complexType>
```

Example 21–6. Instance using extended type

```
<order xmlns="http://example.org/ord"
       xmlns:spc="http://example.org/spc"
       xmlns:xsi="http://www.w3.org/2001/XMLSchema-instance">
  <product spc:points="100" xsi:type="ExtendedProductType">
    <number>557</number>
    <name>Short-Sleeved Linen Blouse</name>
    <size>10</size>
    <spc:giftWrap>ADULT BDAY</spc:giftWrap>
  </product>
</order>
```

21.2.3 *Substitution groups*

As we saw in Section 14.4.2.1, "Extending `choice` groups," extending a content model which contains a `choice` group can have unexpected results. Example 14–4 shows a type `ExpandedItemsType` that extends `ItemsType` to add new product types. Intuitively, you may think that the two additional element declarations, `sweater` and `suit`, are added to the `choice` element, allowing a choice between the five element types. In fact, the effective content model of `ExpandedItemsType` is a `sequence` group that contains two `choice` groups. As a result, `ExpandedItemsType` will require any of the `shirt`, `hat`, and `umbrella` elements to appear before any of the `sweater` or `suit` elements.

Example 21–7. choice group extension

```xsd
<xsd:complexType name="ItemsType">
  <xsd:choice maxOccurs="unbounded">
    <xsd:element ref="shirt"/>
    <xsd:element ref="hat"/>
    <xsd:element ref="umbrella"/>
  </xsd:choice>
</xsd:complexType>

<xsd:complexType name="ExpandedItemsType">
  <xsd:complexContent>
    <xsd:extension base="ItemsType">
      <xsd:choice maxOccurs="unbounded">
        <xsd:element ref="sweater"/>
        <xsd:element ref="suit"/>
      </xsd:choice>
    </xsd:extension>
  </xsd:complexContent>
</xsd:complexType>
```

Substitution groups are a better way to extend choice groups. If you add another element declaration, otherProduct, to the choice group in ItemsType, it can serve as the head of a substitution group. This makes extending the choice much easier. The element declarations for sweater and suit can be supplied in another schema document, even in another namespace.

In Example 21–8, the otherProduct element declaration is added to act as the head of the substitution group. It would also have been legal to simply make umbrella the head of the substitution group, but this would be less intuitive and would prevent you from ever allowing umbrella without also allowing sweater and shirt in its place.

Example 21–9 shows the two element declarations to be substitutable for otherProduct.

Example 21–10 shows a valid instance. As you can see, the child elements can appear in any order. In this case, they are all in the same namespace. It is also possible for substitution element declarations to be in different namespaces.

Example 21–8. Original data type with an abstract element declaration

```
<xsd:complexType name="ItemsType">
  <xsd:choice maxOccurs="unbounded">
    <xsd:element ref="shirt"/>
    <xsd:element ref="hat"/>
    <xsd:element ref="umbrella"/>
    <xsd:element ref="otherProduct"/>
  </xsd:choice>
</xsd:complexType>

<xsd:element name="otherProduct" type="ProductType"
             abstract="true"/>
```

Example 21–9. Extension using substitution groups

```
<xsd:element name="sweater" substitutionGroup="otherProduct"/>
<xsd:element name="suit" substitutionGroup="otherProduct"/>
```

Example 21–10. Instance using extension via substitution groups

```
<items>
  <shirt>...</shirt>
  <sweater>...</sweater>
  <shirt>...</shirt>
  <suit>...</suit>
</items>
```

It would have also been valid to put an element wildcard in the `choice` group. However, the substitution group approach is more controlled, because you can specifically designate the substitutable element declarations.

21.2.4 *Type redefinition*

Redefinition, unlike derivation, does not require the use of the `xsi:type` attribute in instances. The redefined components have the same name as they had in the original definition. However, redefinition can only be done within the same namespace, so it is not appropriate for altering schemas over which you have no control. In addition, redefinition has some risks associated with it, as detailed in Chapter 18, "Redefining schema components."

The original type might look exactly like the one shown in Example 21–4, with similar constraints. It must be named, and it should use a sequence group. Example 21–11 shows a redefinition of Product-Type to add a new element declaration and attribute declaration. It is similar to the definition of the derived type shown in Example 21–5, with two important differences:

1. It is defined entirely within the redefine element.
2. The extended type and the original type have the same name.

For more information on type redefinition, see Section 18.4, "Redefining complex types."

Again, a valid instance would look like Example 21–2.

Example 21–11. Redefined type

```
<xsd:schema xmlns:xsd="http://www.w3.org/2001/XMLSchema"
            xmlns:spc="http://example.org/spc"
            xmlns="http://example.org/ord"
            targetNamespace="http://example.org/ord">
  <xsd:import namespace="http://example.org/spc"/>
  <xsd:redefine schemaLocation="original.xsd">
    <xsd:complexType name="ProductType">
      <xsd:complexContent>
        <xsd:extension base="ProductType">
          <xsd:sequence>
            <xsd:element ref="spc:giftWrap" minOccurs="0"/>
          </xsd:sequence>
          <xsd:attribute ref="spc:points"/>
        </xsd:extension>
      </xsd:complexContent>
    </xsd:complexType>
  </xsd:redefine>
</xsd:schema>
```

Although a redefinition of the type must take place in the same namespace, the extended element and attribute declarations are not required to be in that namespace. In our example, they are not.

21.2.5 *Named model group redefinition*

Another alternative is to define content models in named model groups, and redefine the groups. This is not as rigid as redefinition of types because the extensions do not have to be at the end of the content models.

Example 21–12 shows the original `ProductType` definition, this time using a named model group and an attribute group. The entire content model of the type is contained in the group `Product-PropertyGroup`.

Example 21–12. Original type

```
<xsd:complexType name="ProductType">
  <xsd:group ref="ProductPropertyGroup"/>
  <xsd:attributeGroup ref="ExtensionGroup"/>
</xsd:complexType>

<xsd:group name="ProductPropertyGroup">
  <xsd:sequence>
    <xsd:element name="number" type="ProdNumType"/>
    <xsd:element name="name" type="xsd:string"/>
    <xsd:element name="size" type="SizeType" minOccurs="0"/>
  </xsd:sequence>
</xsd:group>

<xsd:attributeGroup name="ExtensionGroup"/>
```

Example 21–13 shows a redefinition of the named model group and attribute group. Redefining the groups affects all the complex types that reference those groups.

A valid instance would look like the one shown in Example 21–14. In this case, `giftWrap` appears as the first child of `product`.

Example 21–13. Redefined named model group and attribute group

```
<xsd:schema xmlns:xsd="http://www.w3.org/2001/XMLSchema"
            xmlns:spc="http://example.org/spc"
            xmlns="http://example.org/ord"
            targetNamespace="http://example.org/ord">
  <xsd:import namespace="http://example.org/spc"/>
  <xsd:redefine schemaLocation="original.xsd">
    <xsd:group name="ProductPropertyGroup">
      <xsd:sequence>
        <xsd:element ref="spc:giftWrap"/>
        <xsd:group ref="ProductPropertyGroup"/>
      </xsd:sequence>
    </xsd:group>
    <xsd:attributeGroup name="ExtensionGroup">
      <xsd:attributeGroup ref="ExtensionGroup"/>
      <xsd:attribute ref="spc:points"/>
    </xsd:attributeGroup>
  </xsd:redefine>
</xsd:schema>
```

Example 21–14. Instance using redefined named model group and attribute group

```
<order xmlns="http://example.org/ord"
       xmlns:spc="http://example.org/spc">
  <product spc:points="100">
    <spc:giftWrap>ADULT BDAY</spc:giftWrap>
    <number>557</number>
    <name>Short-Sleeved Linen Blouse</name>
    <size>10</size>
  </product>
</order>
```

21.3 | Versioning of schemas

As business and technical requirements change over time, you will need to define new versions of your schemas. Defining new versions is a special case of extension and restriction. You may be both adding and removing components, with the intention of replacing the older version.

In many cases, you will want to maintain some compatibility among the versions. You might want to allow instances to be validated against either schema, or be processed by an application that supports either version. This is especially true if your instances persist for a period. If your instances are short-lived messages between applications, version compatibility is less of an issue. However, you should still try to be as consistent as possible to reduce learning curves and the changes required to the applications that process the instances.

When you create a new version that is intended to replace a previous one, you should create a completely new schema rather than attempt to extend or restrict the existing one. Otherwise, as time goes on, and additional versions are created, the definitions could become unnecessarily complicated and difficult to process. If you are not using the restriction and extension mechanisms of XML Schema, though, you need to take extra care to make the new definitions compatible with the old ones.

21.3.1 *Schema compatibility*

Ideally, you can have backward compatibility of the schemas for both versions. That is, all instances that conform to the previous version of the schema are also valid according to the new version. This is possible if you are only adding optional new components, and/or reducing restrictiveness. To accomplish this, the previous version must be a subset of the new version. You can:

- Add declarations for optional elements to content models, in both complex types and named model groups.
- Add optional attributes. If appropriate, consider giving them default values so that they are automatically added to instances of the previous version.
- Make required elements and attributes optional.

- Make occurrence constraints less restrictive. For example, allow more than one `color` element where only one was allowed before.

- Turn specific element declarations into `choice` groups. For example, where `color` was allowed, now it can be `color` or `size` or `weight`. Similarly, you can declare new substitution groups. For example, where the content model allowed `color`, now `size` and `weight` are valid substitutes.

- Make simple types less restrictive, by making bounds facets and length facets less restrictive, adding enumeration values, or making patterns less restrictive.

In the new version, if you have to make structural changes, remove any element declarations, change the order of element declarations, or make content models more restrictive, you will not be able to retain backwards compatibility across schema versions.

21.3.2 *Application compatibility*

Whether or not you can achieve schema compatibility, it is also worthwhile to try to achieve application compatibility. Well-designed applications that were written to process the previous version should be able to process instances of the new version without crashing. Section 21.4, "Designing applications to support change," describes some techniques for writing flexible applications.

Likewise, applications that process the new version can be made to support both versions. If the new version only contains optional additions, the application can use the same logic for both versions of instances. Alternatively, the application can check the version number (as described in Section 21.3.4, "Using version numbers") and process each version differently.

21.3.3 *Conversion capability*

If neither schema compatibility nor application compatibility can be achieved, you should provide a clear upgrade path from the old version to the new version. A good way to do this is by providing a stylesheet to upgrade instances, which can even be done automatically by the application. If required components are added or removed when creating the new version, you should clearly document how to handle their absence when converting between versions.

21.3.4 *Using version numbers*

When creating new versions of your schemas, you should assign a version number to the new schema. There are several possible places to indicate the version number of a schema:

- *In the schema document.* The `version` attribute of `schema` is an arbitrary string that represents the version of the schema document. It is strictly for documentation; the processor does not use it.

- *In the schema location.* The file name or URL of the schema document can contain the version number. For example, the new version may have a file name of `ord_1_1.xsd`. Changing the URL allows other schema documents that may include or import your schema document to continue to use the previous version until they can upgrade.

- *In the instance.* It may be worthwhile to have instances identify the schema version to which they conform. This will allow an application to process it accordingly. For example, in XSLT, the `stylesheet` element has a required attribute named `version`. This is a signal to processors that the stylesheet instance conforms to, for example, version 1.0 of XSLT.

- *In the namespace name.* When you change a namespace name, it is as if you are completely renaming the components in that namespace. This can cause problems because instances of the old version will never be compatible with the new version, both for schema validation and application processing. Also, you may want to have one resource directory that describes both versions; this is more logical when there is only one namespace.

21.4 | Designing applications to support change

Applications should be as flexible as possible when processing XML documents. If designed correctly, applications that work for one schema should work for any well-designed extension or restriction of that schema. Ideally, they can also work for previous versions of that schema.

It is impossible to predict how people will modify or extend a schema over time, but two simple practices can help handle changes more gracefully:

- *Ignore irrelevant elements or attributes.* The application should process the elements and attributes it is expecting, without generating errors if additional elements or attributes appear. This is especially true if they are in a different namespace. The application should treat every content model as if it has both attribute and element wildcards, even if it does not.

- *Avoid overdependence on the document structure.* Minimize the amount of structural checking you do in the application code. If you are using a SAX parser, process the element you are interested in by name, but do not necessarily keep track of its parent or grandparent. In XSLT, consider using expressions such as `.//product/number` instead of `./catalog/product/number`. This will allow the expression to still be valid even if a `department` element is added between `catalog` and `product`.

Table of XSDL keywords

Appendix A

A.1 | XSDL element types

Table A–1 XSDL element types

Name	Section	Role	Possible parents	Attributes	Content model
`all`	13.5.4	all group	`complexType,` `restriction,` `extension,` `group`	`id,` `minOccurs,` `maxOccurs`	`annotation?,` `element*`
`annota-tion`	6.1.1	annota-tion	all XSDL element types except `annotation,` `appinfo,` **and** `documenta-tion`	`id`	`(appinfo |` `documenta-tion)*`

Table A–1 XSDL element types

Name	Section	Role	Possible parents	Attributes	Content model
any	13.4.3	element wildcard	choice, sequence	id, minOccurs, maxOccurs, namespace, process-Contents	annotation?
any-Attribute	13.6.3	attribute wildcard	attribute-Group, complexType, extension, restriction	id, namespace, process-Contents	annotation?
appinfo	6.1.3	application information	annotation	source	ANY
attribute	8.1.2	global attribute declaration	schema	id, **name**, type, default, fixed	annotation?, simpleType?
attribute	8.1.3	local attribute declaration	attribute-Group, complexType, extension, restriction	id, **name**, type, form, use, default, fixed	annotation?, simpleType?
attribute	13.6.2	attribute reference	attribute-Group, complexType, extension, restriction	id, **ref**, use, default, fixed	annotation?
attribute-Group	15.3.1	attribute group definition	redefine, schema	id, **name**	annotation?, (attribute | attribute-Group)*, anyAttribute?

Table A–1   XSDL element types

Name	Section	Role	Possible parents	Attributes	Content model
attribute-Group	15.3.2.1	attribute group reference	attribute-Group, complexType, extension, restriction	id, **ref**	annotation?
choice	13.5.2	choice group	choice, complexType, extension, group, restriction, sequence	id, minOccurs, maxOccurs	annotation?, (element | group | choice | sequence | any)*
complex-Content	14.3.2	complex content	complexType	id, mixed	annotation?, (restriction | extension)
complex-Type	13.2.1	named complex type definition	redefine, schema	id, **name**, mixed, abstract, block, final	annotation?, (simple-Content | complex-Content | ((group | all | choice | sequence)?, (attribute | attribute-Group)*, any-Attribute?))

Table A–1   XSDL element types

Name	Section	Role	Possible parents	Attributes	Content model
complex-Type	13.2.2	anony-mous complex type defi-nition	element	id, mixed	annotation?, (simple-Content | complex-Content | ((group | all | choice | sequence)?, (attribute | attribute-Group)*, any-Attribute?))
documenta-tion	6.1.2	documen-tation	annotation	source, xml:lang	ANY
element	7.1.1	global element declara-tion	schema	id, **name**, type, default, fixed, nillable, abstract, substitu-tionGroup, block, final	annotation?, (simpleType | complex-Type)?, (key | keyref | unique)*
element	7.1.2	local element declara-tion	all, choice, sequence	id, **name**, form, type, minOccurs, maxOccurs, default, fixed, nillable, block	annotation?, (simpleType | complex-Type)?, (key | keyref | unique)*
element	13.4.2	element reference	all, choice, sequence	id, **ref**, minOccurs, maxOccurs	annotation?

Table A–1   XSDL element types

Name	Section	Role	Possible parents	Attributes	Content model
enumera-tion	9.4.4, 11.3.3.2	facet	restriction	id, **value**	annotation?
extension	14.4.1	simple content extension	simple-Content	id, **base**	annotation?, (attribute | attribute-Group)*, any-Attribute?
extension	14.4.2	complex content extension	complex-Content	id, **base**	annotation?, (group | all | choice | sequence)?, (attribute | attribute-Group)*, any-Attribute?
field	17.7.2	constraint field	key, keyref, unique	id, **xpath**	annotation?
fraction-Digits	9.4.3	facet	restriction	id, **value**, fixed	annotation?
group	15.2.1	named model group definition	redefine, schema	id, **name**	annotation?, (all | choice | sequence)
group	15.2.2.1	named model group ref-erence	choice, com-plexType, extension, restriction, sequence	id, **ref**, minOccurs, maxOccurs	annotation?
import	4.4.3	import	schema	id, namespace, schema-Location	annotation?

Table A–1   XSDL element types

Name	*Section*	*Role*	*Possible parents*	*Attributes*	*Content model*
include	4.4.1	include	schema	id, **schema-Location**	annotation?
key	17.5	key constraint	element	id, **name**	annotation?, selector, field+
keyref	17.6	key reference	element	id, **name**, **refer**	annotation?, selector, field+
length	9.4.2, 11.3.3.1	facet	restriction	id, **value**, fixed	annotation?
list	11.3.1	list type	simpleType	id, itemType	annotation?, simpleType?
max-Exclusive	9.4.1	facet	restriction	id, **value**, fixed	annotation?
max-Inclusive	9.4.1	facet	restriction	id, **value**, fixed	annotation?
maxLength	9.4.2, 11.3.3.1	facet	restriction	id, **value**, fixed	annotation?
min-Exclusive	9.4.1	facet	restriction	id, **value**, fixed	annotation?
min-Inclusive	9.4.1	facet	restriction	id, **value**, fixed	annotation?
minLength	9.4.2, 11.3.3.1	facet	restriction	id, **value**, fixed	annotation?
notation	6.4.1	notation	schema	id, **name**, **public**, system	annotation?
pattern	9.4.5, 11.3.3.3	facet	restriction	id, **value**	annotation?

Table A–1   XSDL element types

Name	Section	Role	Possible parents	Attributes	Content model
redefine	18.2	redefini-tion	schema	id, **schema-Location**	(annotation | attribute-Group | com-plexType | group | sim-pleType)*
restric-tion	9.3.1	simple type restric-tion	simpleType	id, base	annotation?, simpleType?, (minExclusive | minInclu-sive | max-Exclusive | maxInclusive | length | minLength | maxLength | totalDigits | fraction-Digits | enumeration | pattern | whiteSpace)*
restric-tion	11.3.3	list type restric-tion	simpleType	id, base	annotation?, simpleType?, (length | maxLength | minLength | pattern | enumeration)*
restric-tion	11.2.2	union type restric-tion	simpleType	id, base	annotation?, simpleType?, (enumeration | pattern)*

Table A–1   XSDL element types

Name	Section	Role	Possible parents	Attributes	Content model
restric-tion	14.5.1	simple content restric-tion	simple-Content	id, base	annotation?, simpleType?, (enumeration | length | maxExclusive | max-Inclusive | maxLength | minExclusive | min-Inclusive | minLength | pattern | totalDigits | fraction-Digits | white-Space)*, (attribute | attribute-Group)*, any-Attribute?
restric-tion	14.5.2	complex content restric-tion	complex-Content	id, **base**	annotation?, (group | all | choice | sequence)?, (attribute | attribute-Group)*, any-Attribute?

Table A–1   XSDL element types

Name	Section	Role	Possible parents	Attributes	Content model
schema	4.2.1	schema document	root of the document	id, version, target-Namespace, attribute-Form-Default, element-Form-Default, block-Default, final-Default	(include | import | redefine | annotation)*, ((attribute | attribute-Group | complexType | element | group | notation | simpleType), annotation*)*
selector	17.7.1	constraint selector	key, keyref, unique	id, **xpath**	annotation?
sequence	13.5.1	sequence group	choice, complexType, extension, group, restriction, sequence	id, minOccurs, maxOccurs	annotation?, (element | group | choice | sequence | any)*
simple-Content	14.3.1	simple content	complexType	id	annotation?, (restriction | extension)
simple-Type	9.2.1	named simple type definition	redefine, schema	id, **name**, final	annotation?, (restriction | list | union)
simple-Type	9.2.2	anonymous simple type definition	attribute, element, list, restriction, union	id	annotation?, (restriction | list | union)

Table A–1 XSDL element types

Name	Section	Role	Possible parents	Attributes	Content model
total-Digits	9.4.3	facet	restriction	id, **value**, fixed	annotation?
union	11.2.1	union type	simpleType	id, member-Types	annotation?, simpleType*
unique	17.4	uniqueness constraint	element	id, **name**	annotation?, selector, field+
white-Space	9.4.6	facet	restriction	id, **value**, fixed	annotation?

A.2 | XSDL attributes

Table A–2 XSDL attributes

Attribute	Section	Description	Element types	Valid values	Default value
abstract	14.7.4, 16.6.3	whether a data type or element type can be used in an instance	complexType, element	boolean	false
attribute-Form-Default	8.4	whether local attributes should be qualified in instances	schema	"qualified" | "unqualified"	unqualified
base	various	base type of the derivation	extension, restriction	QName	

Table A–2   XSDL attributes

Attribute	Section	Description	Element types	Valid values	Default value
block	14.7.2	whether to block type substitution in the instance	complexType	"#all", or list of ("exten-sion" | "restric-tion")	defaults to block-Default of schema
block	14.7.3, 16.6.2	whether data type and/or element sub-stitutions should be blocked from the instance	element	"#all", or list of ("exten-sion" | "restric-tion" | "sub-stitution")	defaults to block-Default of schema
block-Default	14.7.2, 14.7.3, 16.6.2	whether the use of derived types in instances should be blocked	schema	"#all", or list of ("exten-sion" | "restric-tion" | "sub-stitution")	
default	7.3.1, 8.3.1	default value for the element type or attribute	attribute, element	string	
element-Form-Default	7.5	whether local element-type names should be qualified in instances	schema	"qualified" | "unquali-fied"	unquali-fied
final	14.7.1	whether other types can be derived from this one	complexType	"#all", or list of ("exten-sion" | "restric-tion")	defaults to final-Default of schema

Table A–2   XSDL attributes

Attribute	Section	Description	Element types	Valid values	Default value
final	16.6.1	whether the element declaration can be the head of a substitution group	element	"#all", or list of ("extension" | "restriction")	defaults to final-Default of schema
final	9.5	whether other types can be derived from this one	simpleType	"#all", or list of ("restriction" | "list" | "union")	defaults to final-Default of schema
final-Default	14.7.1, 16.6.1, 9.5	whether type derivation should be disallowed	schema	"#all", or list of ("extension" | "restriction" | "list" | "union")	
fixed	7.3.2, 8.3.2	fixed value for the element type or attribute	attribute, element	string	
fixed	9.3.4	whether the facet is fixed and therefore cannot be restricted further	fractionDigits, length, maxExclusive, maxInclusive, maxLength, minExclusive, minInclusive, minLength, totalDigits, whiteSpace	boolean	false

Table A–2   XSDL attributes

Attribute	Section	Description	Element types	Valid values	Default value
form	7.5, 8.4	whether the element-type or attribute name must be qualified in the instance	attribute, element	"qualified" | "unqualified"	defaults to attributeForm-Default or element-Form-Default of schema
id		unique ID	all XSDL element types except appinfo and choice	ID	
itemType	11.3.1	the simple type of each item in the list	list	QName	
lang[†]	6.1.2	natural language	schema, documentation	language	
maxOccurs	13.5	maximum number of times the group may appear	all	"1"	1
maxOccurs	13.4, 13.5	maximum number of times the element type or group may appear	any, choice, element, group, sequence	non-Negative-Integer | "unbounded"	1

Table A–2   XSDL attributes

Attribute	Section	Description	Element types	Valid values	Default value
member-Types	11.2.1	member types that make up the union type	union		
minOccurs	13.5	minimum number of times the group may appear	all	"0" | "1"	1
minOccurs	13.4, 13.5	minimum number of times the element type or group may appear	any, choice, element, group, sequence	non-Negative-Integer	1
mixed	13.3.3, 14.3.2	whether the complex type allows mixed content	complex-Content, complexType	boolean	false for complex-Type, no default for complex-Content
name	various	name of the schema component	attribute, attribute-Group, com-plexType, element, group, key, keyref, notation, simpleType, unique	NCName	

Table A–2   XSDL attributes

Attribute	Section	Description	Element types	Valid values	Default value
namespace	13.4.3, 13.6.3	which namespace(s) the replacement elements/ attributes may belong to	any, any-Attribute	"##any" or "##other" or list of (anyURI | "##target-Namespace" | "##local")	##any
namespace	4.4.3	namespace to be imported	import	anyURI	
nil[††]	7.4	whether the element's value is nil	any instance element	boolean	false
nillable	7.4	whether elements can exhibit the xsi:nil attribute	element	boolean	false
noName-space-Schema-Location[††]	5.4.2	location of the schema in instances with no namespaces	any instance element	anyURI	
process-Contents	13.4.3, 13.6.3	how strictly to validate the replacement element types or attributes	any, any-Attribute	("lax" | "skip" | "strict")	strict
public	6.4.1	public ID of a notation	notation	public identifier	

Table A–2   XSDL attributes

Attribute	Section	Description	Element types	Valid values	Default value
ref	various	name of the schema component being referenced	attribute, attribute-Group, element, group	QName	
refer	17.6	name of the key being referenced	keyref	QName	
schema-Location	4.4	location of the schema which describes included or imported components	import, include, redefine	anyURI	
schema-Location††	5.4.1	list of locations of the schemas that correspond to namespaces in an instance	any instance element	list of anyURI	
source	6.1.2, 6.1.3	source of further documentation	appinfo, documentation	anyURI	
substitutionGroup	16.3	head of the substitution group to which the element declaration belongs	element	QName	

Table A–2 XSDL attributes

Attribute	Section	Description	Element types	Valid values	Default value
system	6.4.1	system ID of a notation	notation	anyURI	
target-Namespace	3.3.1	namespace to which all global schema components belong	schema	anyURI	
type	7.2, 8.2	data type of the attribute or element type	attribute, element	QName	
type††	14.6	data type of the element type, used in type substitution and union types	any instance element	QName	
use	13.6	whether an attribute is required or optional	attribute	optional | prohibited | required	optional
value	9.4.4, 9.4.1	value of the facet	enumeration, maxExclusive, maxInclusive, minExclusive, minInclusive	various, depending on the base type	
value	9.4.3, 9.4.2	value of the facet	fraction-Digits, length, maxLength, minLength	non-Negative-Integer	

Table A–2   XSDL attributes

Attribute	Section	Description	Element types	Valid values	Default value
`value`	9.4.5	value of the facet	`pattern`	regular expression	
`value`	9.4.3	value of the facet	`totalDigits`	`positive-Integer`	
`value`	9.4.6	value of the facet	`whiteSpace`	`"collapse" | "replace" | "preserve"`	
`version`	21.3.4	version number of the schema	`schema`	`token`	
`xpath`	17.8	XPath to the selected nodes or key field	`field`, `selector`	XPath subset	

[†] Namespace is `http://www.w3.org/XML/1998/namespace`, mapped to the prefix `xml`.

[††] Namespace is `http://www.w3.org/2001/XMLSchema-instance`, often mapped to the prefix `xsi`.

Built-in
simple types

Appendix

B

B.1 | Built-in simple types

Table B–1 Built-in simple types

Name	Description or range	Examples
String and name types		
string	character string	This is a string!
normalized-String	character string with "replace" whitespace processing	This is a normalized-String!
token	character string with "collapse" whitespace processing	This is a token!
Name	valid XML name	size
NCName	non-colonized (unprefixed) name	size
language	natural language identifier	en-GB, en-US, fr

Table B–1 Built-in simple types

Name	Description or range	Examples
Numeric types		
float	single-precision 32-bit floating-point number	-INF, -3E2, -0, 0, 24.3e-3, 12, 15.2, INF, NaN
double	double-precision 64-bit floating-point number	-INF, -3E2, -0, 0, 24.3e-3, 12, 15.2, INF, NaN
decimal	any decimal number	-3, +3.5, +.5, 3, 3., 003.0, 3.0000
integer	any integer	-3, 0, +3, 05, 4268
long	-9223372036854775808 to 9223372036854775807	-9223372036854775808, +3, 9223372036854775807
int	-2147483648 to 2147483647	-2147483648, +3, 2147483647
short	-32768 to 32767	-32768, +3, 32767
byte	-128 to 127	-128, +3, 127
positive-Integer	1,2,...	1, +426822752
nonPositive-Integer	...-2,-1,0	-426822752, -1, 0
negative-Integer	...-2,-1	-426822752, -1
nonNegative-Integer	0,1,2,...	0, +1, 426822752
unsignedLong	0 to 18446744073709551615	0, 18446744073709551615
unsignedInt	0 to 4294967295	0, 4294967295
unsignedShort	0 to 65535	0, 65535
unsignedByte	0 to 255	0, 255

Table B–1   Built-in simple types

Name	Description or range	Examples
Date and time types		
date	date, CCYY-MM-DD	1968-04-02
time	time, hh:mm:ss.sss	13:20:00.000, 13:20:00Z, 13:20:00-05:00
dateTime	date and time, CCYY-MM-DDThh:mm:ss.sss	1968-04-02T13:20:00, 1968-04-02T13:20:00.000-05:00
gYear	specific year, CCYY	1968
gYearMonth	specific year and month, CCYY-MM	1968-04
gMonth	recurring month of the year, --MM	--04
gMonthDay	recurring day of the year, --MM-DD	--04-02
gDay	recurring day of the month, ---DD	---02
duration	length of time, PnYnMnDTnHnMnS	P2Y6M5DT12H35M30.5S, P2Y
Legacy types		
ID	unique identifier	
IDREF	reference to a unique identifier	
IDREFS	list of IDREF	
ENTITY	unparsed entity reference	
ENTITIES	list of ENTITY	
NMTOKEN	single token (no whitespace)	small
NMTOKENS	list of NMTOKEN	small medium large

Table B–1   Built-in simple types

Name	Description or range	Examples
NOTATION	notation reference	

Other types		
QName	qualified name (may be prefixed or unprefixed)	clo:size, size
boolean	logical	true, false, 0, 1
hexBinary	binary with hex encoding	0FB8, 0fb8
base64Binary	binary with base64 encoding	0FB8, 0fR8, +4
anyURI	URI reference (absolute or relative)	http://example.org, ../prod.html#shirt, urn:example:org

Table B–2   Applicability of facets to built-in simple types

Name	length	minLength	maxLength	minExclusive	minInclusive	maxInclusive	maxExclusive	totalDigits	fractionDigits	whiteSpace	pattern	enumeration
String and name types												
string	A	A	A							V	A	A
normalizedString	A	A	A							V	A	A
token	A	A	A							V	A	A
Name	A	A	A							V	V	A
NCName	A	A	A							V	V	A
language	A	A	A							V	V	A
Numeric types												
float				A	A	A	A			F	A	A

Table B–2   Applicability of facets to built-in simple types

Name	length	minLength	maxLength	minExclusive	minInclusive	maxInclusive	maxExclusive	totalDigits	fractionDigits	whiteSpace	pattern	enumeration
double				A	A	A	A			F	A	A
decimal				A	A	A	A	A	A	F	A	A
integer				A	A	A	A	A	F	F	A	A
long				A	V	V	A	A	F	F	A	A
int				A	V	V	A	A	F	F	A	A
short				A	V	V	A	A	F	F	A	A
byte				A	V	V	A	A	F	F	A	A
positiveInteger				A	A	A	A	A	F	F	A	A
nonPositiveInteger				A	A	V	A	A	F	F	A	A
negativeInteger				A	A	V	A	A	F	F	A	A
nonNegativeInteger				A	V	A	A	A	F	F	A	A
unsignedLong				A	V	V	A	A	F	F	A	A
unsignedInt				A	V	V	A	A	F	F	A	A
unsignedShort				A	V	V	A	A	F	F	A	A
unsignedByte				A	V	V	A	A	F	F	A	A
Date and time types												
date				A	A	A	A			F	A	A
time				A	A	A	A			F	A	A
dateTime				A	A	A	A			F	A	A
gYear				A	A	A	A			F	A	A
gYearMonth				A	A	A	A			F	A	A
gMonth				A	A	A	A			F	A	A
gMonthDay				A	A	A	A			F	A	A

Table B–2   Applicability of facets to built-in simple types

Name	length	minLength	maxLength	minExclusive	minInclusive	maxInclusive	maxExclusive	totalDigits	fractionDigits	whiteSpace	pattern	enumeration
gDay				A	A	A	A			F	A	A
duration				A	A	A	A			F	A	A
Legacy types												
ID	A	A	A							F	V	A
IDREF	A	A	A							F	V	A
IDREFS	A	V	A							F	A	A
ENTITY	A	A	A							F	V	A
ENTITIES	A	V	A							F	A	A
NMTOKEN	A	A	A							V	V	A
NMTOKENS	A	V	A							F	A	A
NOTATION	A	A	A							F	A	A
Other types												
QName	A	A	A							F	A	A
boolean										F	A	
hexBinary	A	A	A							F	A	A
base64Binary	A	A	A							F	A	A
anyURI	A	A	A							F	A	A
Other varieties												
List types	A	A	A							F	A	A
Union types											A	A

A — Facet is applicable to this type.
V — Facet has a value for this type, but it is not fixed.
F — Facet has a fixed value for this type, so it cannot be overridden.

Index

▌ *Symbols*

▌ C

F

G

H

I

#PCDATA, element content specifier
      (DTDs), 413–415, 418
Pd, category escape, 189
Pe, category escape, 189
percent sign *see* %
period *see* .
Perl, programming language, 181
Pf, category escape, 189
Pi, category escape, 189
plus sign *see* +
Po, category escape, 189
positive sign *see* +
positive zero *see* 0, numeric value
positiveInteger, built-in data type,
      24, 235, 262–263, 506
   facets applicable to, 509
prefixed names *see* names, prefixed
prefixes, 28, 48, 53, 227, 444
   in attribute names, 147
   in XPath expressions, 390–391, 393
   mapping to the target namespace, 29,
      53
   mapping to the XML Schema
      Namespace, 51
preserve, value of facet whiteSpace,
      131, 176–177, 224, 263
processContents, attribute, 278–279,
      296–297, 313, 332–333, 469, 499
programming languages, variable names
      in, 440
prohibited, value of attribute use, 294
Ps, category escape, 189
public, attribute, 112, 114, 499
punctuation, in category escapes, 189

▌ Q

QName, built-in data type, 24, 256, 263,
      508
   facets applicable to, 258, 510
   length of values in, 169
qualified, value of attribute form, 61,
      64, 124, 138, 146, 152, 393, 445,
      494–495, 497
qualified names, 42, 256, 508
   advantages of, 448
   in XPath expressions, 390
   local part of, 42, 227

of attributes *see* attribute names,
      qualified
of data types, 282
of element types *see* element-type
      names, qualified
of identity constraints, 379
uniqueness of, 62, 379
quantifiers *see* regular expressions,
      quantifiers in
question mark *see* ?
", entity reference (quote), 185
quote *see* "

▌ R

\r, single-character escape, 185, 187
RDDL (Resource Directory Description
      Language), 84
redefine, element type, 69, 98, 106,
      344, 351, 398, 400–409, 457, 491
   location of, in a schema, 400
ref, attribute, 145, 276–277, 295, 345,
      347, 354, 500
refer, attribute, 384, 500
regular expressions, 24, 173, 181–199
   atoms in, 183–199
   branches in, 181–182
   character class escapes in *see* character
      class escapes
   character class expressions in *see*
      character class expressions
   characters in, 183–184, 188
   combining characters and ranges in,
      196
   nested, 198
   pieces in, 181–182
   quantifiers in, 183, 186, 198–199
RELAX NG, schema language, 11–13
   validation by, 11
replace, value of facet whiteSpace,
      176–177, 224
replacement elements *see* elements,
      replacement
#REQUIRED, attribute value specifier
      (DTDs), 423
required, value of attribute use, 294
Resource Directory Description Language
      see RDDL

Y

Z